SPIRITUAL HOMECOMING

For Rabbi Shapiro,
For your warm welcome
and gentle receptiveness to
my inquiries about Judaism ..
thanks.

— Armando Quiros

D1617256

Order additional books from:
Armando Quiros
718 N Voluntario St
SB, CA 93103 (805) 963-0309

Spiritual Homecoming

A Catholic Priest's
Journey to Judaism

Armando Quiros M.A., J.C.L

2001
FITHIAN PRESS
SANTA BARBARA, CALIFORNIA

Published by Fithian Press
A division of Daniel and Daniel, Publishers, Inc.
Post Office Box 1525
Santa Barbara, CA 93102
www.danielpublishing.com

LIBRARY OF CONGRESS CATALOGING-IN-PUBLICATION DATA
Quiros, Armando, (date)
    Spiritual homecoming : a Catholic priest's journey to Judaism / by
Armando Quiros.
    p.   cm.
    ISBN 1-56474-356-X (pbk. : alk. paper)
    1. Quiros, Armando, (date).   2. Jewish converts from Christianity—
United States—Biography.   3. Jews—United States—Biography.
    4. Catholic ex-priests—United States—Biography.   I. Title.
    BM755.Q85 A3 2001
    296.7'14'092—dc21   00-009927

*In tribute to the millions of innocent Jews,
the* kedoshim, *who perished in the Holocaust,
to the survivors of that villainy,
and to their progeny,
all of whom bear the burden and the privilege
of helping the world remember.*

Contents

Introduction 11

Part I: Childhood 15

Part II: First Tentative Steps of a
　　　Thirteen-year Journey 37

Part III: Early Ministries 73

Part IV: The Stirrings of Freedom 96

Part V: Psychological Awakening 124

Part VI: Berkeley and Beyond:
　　　Steps Toward Freedom 157

Part VII: Life as a Layman 188

Part VIII: Suddenly—Jews and Judaism . . . 206

Epilogue 245

SPIRITUAL HOMECOMING

Introduction

I FIRST BEGAN to think about writing a book when my wife, Ruth, introduced me to the concept of a Jewish ethical will. For some reason the notion fascinated me but receded into the background just a hair's breadth out of my awareness. Like any other unfinished gestalt, it periodically pressed me for attention until my attraction became a wish and the wish a decision. My reading revealed that a Jewish ethical will admitted of wide variation in purpose and format. I chose to author a book-sized document about my spiritual journey. I would describe this long trek through all of its stages, carrying the reader from the strict Catholic upbringing of my childhood through the long years of priestly preparation and ministry to my ultimate embrace of Judaism.

The Jewish ethical will is usually an instrument, drafted by parents for their progeny, which sets out the moral and spiritual values that guided their lives. I had no children of my own. I embraced the celibate state at age eighteen and lived as a faithful member of a religious community for the next thirty years. Despite this fact, the idea of writing for my relatives still intrigued me. I had three brothers and they each had families. Except for sporadic brief contacts, I had spent most of my life away from them. There was much about me that they did not know. My story would be primarily for them. It was especially important to me that they know my religious values and the persons and events that formed me spiritually along the way. Secondarily, it would be for the large number of men and women who had come into my life and knew me fairly intimately. Some of these friends in particular were encouraging me to write my story; others insisted that I do so.

By nature and training I have always been aware of the spiritual dimension of life. I believe it was not coincidence but synchronicity that throughout the years time and circumstance abundantly provided me the opportunity to follow this inclination. Even in the earlier years of my life when a solicitous ecclesiastical authority strove to moderate this pursuit of mine, my beliefs and practice at some level remained untrammeled. In fact, they continued to evolve and prosper deep within me.

The goal of my ethical will can be expressed in negative and positive terms. Negatively, my purpose in writing it is not to prove anything, not to denounce any institution or its members, not to flout old authorities, not to flaunt new freedoms, not to admonish, not to guide or advise others about their own spiritual path.

Positively, my goal is the clear and honest description of my life-long spiritual journey, which is based on the conviction that openness to voices from within and without my world breaks me open to new possibilities of oneness with human beings. Because of this orientation I can honestly say that my present religious beliefs represent the most carefully considered, deliberately chosen religious stance of my life.

Like any other ethical will, therefore, this document is intensely personal. I place it in your hands because I trust that you will hold it compassionately, listen to it empathically, and accept it as my unique story. If it connects strongly with your own at any particular point, I trust that you will let it speak to you and that you will listen to what your heart says in response.

Some of the early theological material in my narrative may be difficult for you to decipher. In some instances you may even marvel at how tenaciously I embraced these tenets and tried to live them literally. I urge you to stay with me at these times so that you may understand the screen of beliefs through which I was peering at the world.

I accept that not every Catholic took the doctrinal beliefs of the Church as literally as did I. I am not sure whether my gullibility was a matter of temperament, of learning, or of both. But I do know the mammoth effort it took to spring me loose from years of what had become a lethal Church embrace.

I also know that despite the sometimes disgraceful Vatican efforts to rein in brilliant Catholic minds, some heroic souls have, particularly in the last three decades since the Second Vatican Ecumenical Council, written articles and books that see the Church in new and exciting ways, that try to engage other world religions in the kind of dialogue in which each learns from the other. I use the word "heroic" advisedly to allude to the kind of suffering these men and women have endured in their attempts to be true to their considerable insights.

I awoke to the depth and sweep of Christian anti-Semitism very late in life. Once I did, I went deeply into the literature that recorded and analyzed this scandal of scandals. Most of these books were written by Christians—Catholic and non-Catholic alike. All of them made it clear to me that the seeds of this insane hatred still lie buried in Christian soil. As long as this is so there is a continuing threat of further outbreaks of persecution. I will be saying more about this complex and sensitive matter late in the text.

Because of this insight, however late, I struggled with how much of the history of Catholic anti-Semitism to include in this book. I found that anything substantial interrupted the flow of the journey. I then considered including an epilogue about this topic. I could conclude with a *faux* encyclical letter by Pope John Paul II on anti-Semitism (penned by me), in which he would acknowledge that Jesus was a Jew faithful to his tradition and would invite Christians to explore Judaism through the study of Jewish texts and dialogue with Jews themselves. But I was soon convinced by friends that this aspect of my story could be another book altogether.

I decided to include in the text itself bracketed, italicized allusions to historical events related to the theme of anti-Semitism. Their only relation to the events described in the text is chronological. That slim connection of the two worlds is in itself striking. I want this juxtaposition to indicate that in most instances, until late in life, I had little or no awareness of the sometimes dramatically impactful world events that were decidedly my business to know but from which I was shielded.

Last, I want to thank a number of people who were of great help to me in writing this book. First and foremost is my loving wife, Ruth Ann Glater, Ph.D., who was my inspiration, my light— and a tough editor. I am also grateful to her illustrious cousin, Dr. Benjamin J. Cohen for his encouragement and valuable critique; to Dr. David Richo for his constant friendship and guidance over the years; and to Dr. Max Lan who taught me so much.

Part I
Childhood

I CAME INTO THIS WORLD on October 28, 1925, in Phoenix, the capital of Arizona, a city of about 35,000 people at that time. I was the fourth child born to José and Aurelia Quiros. The first child had been a girl, born dead. This first failed attempt at beginning their family had been a severe blow to my parents, who were intent on having children suitably spaced out by the use of rhythm, the only method blessed by the Catholic Church for limiting the size of family. Because the troubled pregnancy and birth also gravely threatened my mother's life, my father unilaterally decided that they would risk no more pregnancies; he couldn't bear the thought of losing the woman he loved so much.

This one-sided, momentous decision created serious tension between the two of them because my mother refused to let go of her dream of a family. She was a person of strong, faith-based conviction and could effectively express wishes of substance; her calling to bear and rear children was one of these. She won the day. A year later she successfully bore a son whom they named Joseph Henry after our father.

Three years later she bore another son who would bear the name Henry and three years after that I was born. Since the projected date of my birth was October 4, the feast day of Saint Francis of Assisi, they had decided to name me Francis, and although I postponed my birth for three and a half weeks, they persisted in this decision. Within a week of first seeing the light of day, I was baptized with this name into the Catholic Church by Father Novatus Benzing, the Franciscan Pastor of Saint Mary's Catholic Church. I remember him as a German immigrant with a booming voice who was by the time of my arrival already a central figure in our family.

My upbringing was strict, very religious. My father had at one time contemplated becoming a Franciscan priest; he got as far as the train heading for the seminary in Santa Barbara, California, before he turned back. His attraction to a priestly life in the Franciscan Order was understandable.

When his mother, widowed early in life in Sonora, Mexico, had brought her two young sons, José and Luis, to Phoenix, she took up residence in a Franciscan parish, Saint Mary's. Here her work was attending to the altar cloths, laundering, starching, and ironing them weekly. She felt strongly that this work was in the direct service of God. Some of the immaculate, white linens even came into direct contact with the Body of His Son, Jesus, present on the altar table and in the golden chalice under the appearances of bread and wine.

This loving labor brought her into familiar contact with the parish staff and it was therefore not unusual for the priests to visit our home. They always came dressed in their religious garb, a full-length, brown woolen tunic bound at the waist with a woolen cord, one strand of which bore three knots representing the vows of poverty, chastity and obedience. Around their shoulders they wore a capuche or hood of the same brown woolen material. Simple sandals cradled their feet, which were bare most of the year.

Their odd dress and other-worldliness awed me. So did Father Novatus' deep, bass voice and his expansive style, which over-whelmed the tiny space of our poor house on North Seventh Street.

Everyone deferred to him. While he was among us, I was con-stantly on the alert for the unexpected. Once, as he was about to leave, he jokingly said to my parents that he wished he could take me back to the monastery with him. Then with a laugh he ges-tured toward me as if to snatch me up. With a frightened cry I fled to the back bedroom. The priest's amused laughter at my plight did nothing to allay my fear, and it took my mother's comforting to reassure me that I was in no peril of being kidnapped.

There were numerous religious images throughout our home, three the most prominent by their size and significance. First was the crucifix in the living room, a large cross with the white body of Jesus nailed to it through his hands and his feet. A lance had opened his chest near his heart and blood streamed from it. His head drooped but his eyes still looked lovingly at us through his pain. Our sins had done this to him. My sins. My disobedience, my stubbornness, my selfishness.

A second, more comforting image stood atop the chiffonier in my parents' bedroom. It was a statue of the Sacred Heart of Jesus. There he presided over the household, clad in a long white tunic with a bright red shawl around his right shoulder. "This is the intensity of my love for you," he seemed to say, his right hand pointing toward his chest where the familiar gaping wound received on Calvary bled profusely.

The third icon was a statue of the modest Mary, Mother of Jesus, who watched over us protectively from a table in the small dining area. She wore a white, floor-length gown and a pale blue veil, arms close to her sides and palms turned outward in invitation. We invoked her name in one of the Church's most common prayers, the Hail Mary.

Occasionally, especially in May, the whole family would gather in the living room, there to kneel facing her and repeat the rosary's Our Fathers and Hail Marys like a mantra to commemorate certain "mysteries" or events in the life of Jesus.

Such a sustained silence and seriousness was difficult for us children to maintain. The slightest miscue, such as starting a response too early, would trigger a restless giggling in us and evoke a scowl from Mother. But even her deep-brown, expressive eyes were no match for the mounting silliness, once it began. This kind of severe piety was difficult for three young boys to understand.

Two months after my fifth birthday, my brothers and I were told to walk to our maternal grandmother's house and stay there until summoned. While we were there Mother gave birth to a fourth boy at home. Within a week he was baptized Carlos. "Remember, call him 'Carlos'," said mother intently, "not 'Charlie.' That sounds Chinese."

On Sundays my excitement would center around the arrival of

the newspaper, the *Arizona Republic*, and the multi-colored section at its core, the funnies, which would track the latest antics of the Katzenjammer Kids or Mutt and Jeff. In my pre-school days the problem was to get Joe or Henry to stop whatever they were doing and read these aloud to me. After all, there was breakfast to get, a kitchen to clean up, beds to be made, and church-going clothes to don. After Mass was the best time to prevail upon someone to accommodate me. This always took persuasion, sometimes even begging, which I despised for the one-down position it put me in. I hated the dependency. I resolved to learn to read enough to get through the funnies by myself. This, of course, also took some begging for help, but every lesson learned led me out of the Egypt of illiteracy and made it worthwhile. By the time I started first grade at St. Mary's Grammar School I could read.

I was two months shy of my sixth birthday when my mother took me to school to register with Sister Esperanza, a member of the Ohio-based Congregation of the Precious Blood. This nun was a short, loving German woman who had taught my mother in first grade. It was she who handled my intake, in the course of which it emerged that I could already read a bit. The nun tested me with simple words on the blackboard; I read them with ease.

Throughout this experience I was fixed on my first close-up contact with yet another person in strange garb: an all-black, floor-length dress; a starched white linen cloth wrapping her head so tightly that not a single hair could be seen (except, of course, for the eyebrows and eyelashes and a few wispy hairs on her chin and upper lip); a stiff black veil covering her head; a heavy silver crucifix hanging at her breast; a red cord around her waist with three knots tied into one length of it; and severe black shoes.

This pre-school visit was very helpful because I was having a desperately painful time leaving home for the first time and entering this strange environment. Upon leaving the school I clung to my mother's arm.

Once school got started, I quickly got past the fright of leaving the cocoon of home. I was captivated by the challenge of learning, especially reading. Almost from the beginning I was the male standard bearer against the girls in spelling bees.

It was because of my advanced reading abilities that, later in the year, I was asked to help Freddie, a cousin of mine with a special problem: he was hearing impaired—"deaf," we used to say. He was getting very little from the nun's teaching because on the one hand he could not hear well and on the other she could not understand the simple sounds he uttered. I could. So Sister Esperanza asked me to go out on a little balcony adjoining the classroom and teach him some of the elements of reading.

Because we had grown up together I was accustomed to his distorted words and could easily decode them. He was quite bright but could only pronounce words as he heard them, a dim approximation of what others had actually said.

At any rate, I undertook this task of helping him and we were doing quite well until my mother discovered what I had been asked to do and intervened. She didn't question my ability to help him but she wanted me to be in the classroom learning and not out of the classroom teaching. In my heart, though, I wanted to help him. He needed me.

In July 1932 a particularly virulent wave of anti-Semitism raged from the Rhine to the Vistula, from the Baltic to the Aegean Sea, perhaps the worst since the end of World War I.

Two months into second grade I turned seven, a critical moment for Catholics because we arrived at what was considered the age of "the use of reason." Later in the year we were prepared for our first Confession and first Holy Communion. I learned that this meant that I was now capable not only of offending God, but of offending God gravely, or mortally.

"Mortal" was the preferred word because its root carried the meaning of "death" and referred to the spiritual death inflicted by mortal sin and, if one were physically to die unrepentant, a death that would last forever and ever. Furthermore, this spiritual death would be a continuing existence in a world of flames, not in the fire of Purgatory, that place of cleansing preparation for an innocent entry into Heaven, but a fire relentless in its punitive aspect.

This was a difficult concept for young minds to catch. To stress the enormity of this notion before our first Confession and first Holy Communion, Sister Wilbrodia presented us with the following analogy to help us understand the radical endlessness of eternity which we might face should we sin.

"Imagine, children, the Sahara Desert, that vast stretch of sand in Egypt. Who can ever grasp the enormity of miles and miles and miles of nothing but sand? Who could ever count the seemingly infinite number of grains of sand deposited there? Now further imagine that every thousand years a bird flies over the desert, swoops down, plucks one grain of sand with his beak and flies away with it. Well, when that bird finishes plucking every last grain of sand from the floor of that desert, eternity would just be beginning!"

Children's "Oohs" and "Ahs" filled the room. I could relate because I had already suffered small burns on the kitchen stove and a bad burn from the pot-bellied stove in the living room when once I stood too close on a bitterly cold morning. These burns, for all their being brief and minor, were very painful—no match for the pain of eternal flames should I sin.

On the other hand, the Catholic experience was not presented as time spent teetering on the edge of a precipice where a mortal fall was easy and expected. No, most of the time each of us stood well away from this edge. The moral theologians of Mother Church had, with useful clarity, provided us with exact catechetical descriptions of mortally sinful behaviors.

Thus we could, with moderate effort, prepare ourselves to avoid committing them. A mortal sin, we learned, required three conditions: a serious or grave matter, our awareness of that gravity, and the full consent of our will to the act. It was with this comforting mindset that I began instructions to prepare for my first Confession when all my repented sins would be washed away, and for my first Holy Communion, when Jesus Christ, the very Son of God—Body, Blood, Soul, and Divinity—would be placed on my tongue.

I had thought it easy to walk a safe path and to walk well away from what could kill the spiritual life of my immortal soul. My faults to date had been the use of bad language or taking God's name in vain, anger, pouting, selfishness, disobedience (a useful and capacious category)—venial sins all—that is, technically pardonable through some good work or a heartfelt prayer, even

without going to Confession and having them sacramentally
pardoned.

Despite this alternate route to forgiveness, we were cautioned, it was still preferable to submit even these sins to the
priest, who by his ordination, could forgive sin because he participated in "the power of the keys" (a reference to Jesus' transmis-
sion of the power to forgive to the first Pope, Saint Peter, to the
Apostles and his successors).

For the examination of conscience we were provided with ex-
amples of sins, possible ways to violate the Ten Commandments,
most of which were fortunately beyond my embryonic capacity
for sin. That is, for the most part. I was surely not likely to deny
God's existence or to worship false gods. I might take God's name
in vain. But I could not conceive of missing Mass on Sunday or a
Holy Day of Obligation (there were eight of them, the most no-
table being Christmas).

The most common pitfall would clearly be disobedience and
therefore failing to honor father and mother. I could not imagine
taking another's life, even though I sometimes got very angry at
my brothers when teased. I would not steal, certainly nothing of
substance—a candy bar perhaps—but surely nothing greater. This
would not constitute grave matter and would not subject me to
the possibility of hell fire, even were I to die unrepentant.

I could and did lie, most of the time to deny some peccadillo.
But for me this was a poor and perilous strategy because my
shamed demeanor quickly gave me away and only doubled my sin.
As for lust and adultery, I could scarcely understand what these
meant, though I did register the nun's discomfort when she spoke
about committing these acts, the Sixth Commandment, and lust-
ing after them, the Ninth.

The code words for sexual thoughts and actions were "impure" and "impurity." Soon in my preparation I was stunned to
discover that my sense of spiritual safety was nothing but blind-
ness, for I had been impure all along; in fact, for as long as I could
remember. My days of blissful ignorance about the seriousness of
touching my private parts were suddenly, unexpectedly, at an end.

I now found myself looking back in moral judgment upon the
brief span of years I had been in the world, scanning my behavior

in disbelief through the lenses of moral categories, purity and impurity, sanctifying grace (the very life of God within) and mortal
sin, that is, condemning-to-hell sin, condemning-to-burning-
forever sin, an unbearable searing pain until, as Sister Wilbrodia
had described eternity, the grains of sand of a million Saharas
were plucked away by a bird totally unaware of my need for it to
hurry up.

I was struck dumb. I had thought I was safe, but not only was
I standing on the crumbling rim of a precipice looming over a pit
of ruthless, relentless fire, I was at that very moment falling
through the air to a painful death below. I needed to repent and be
restored to the state of sanctifying grace. Immediately.

"Children," I heard the strangely garbed, perfect presence ad-
monishing, her narrowing eyes fixed on us intently, "if you should
ever commit a mortal sin, which our merciful Father forbid, you
must have that sin removed or forgiven through the Sacrament of
Confession. It is not enough, as in the case of venial sins, to pray
for forgiveness; on the contrary we must confess it to the priest
with at least imperfect contrition."

Contrition, we had learned, was either perfect or imperfect.
Contrition was perfect when we were sorry for having offended a
loving Father. This lofty love of the Other could forgive sin without confession only if the sacrament were unavailable to us. Perfect
contrition was ideal when combined with confession but imperfect
contrition would suffice. Contrition was imperfect when we were
sorry merely out of fear of losing heaven and/or going to hell.

This distinction proved anguishing for me, for now I would
have to tell the priest—I, a mere seven-year-old—that I had not
only been thinking impure thoughts and enjoying them, but that
when bathing I had touched myself impurely with a pleasure that
confused but delighted me. Who could believe this youthful de-
pravity? Who would not recoil in disgust at someone so young already immersed in such unthinkably sinful activity? And, since the
enormity of sexual sins was so extravagant, why had I not known
of their immoral nature?

This meant that not only was I a sinner, but I had not even a
shred of the moral sophistication that others must have enjoyed in
abundance.

Well, the numbing, depressing truth was that I could not possibly take this risk, this step of awesome self-disclosure. I was too stupefied, not to say too young, to figure this all out. I just knew that I had come to an impasse. Somehow I must be mistaken; I would have to continue to live as I had been living. Some day when I was older I would find a way out. After all, no one had seemed to notice my tainted nature. On the contrary, everyone who knew me seemed excited about the impending first Confession and first Holy Communion. I was to wear a white shirt, white pants, white shoes, carry a white prayerbook with gilt edges and would look angelic. God help me.

My classmates and I were well rehearsed for Confession. We had been walked through it by an expert so that nothing unexpected would happen. We were allowed to see the three cubicles that comprised the confessional—the central one for the priest and the other two for the penitents. We were to enter the confessional, kneel down and wait.

For the actual sacrament, one day we were marched over to the church in the afternoon, then told to kneel down and await our turn. When my turn came to enter the confessional I was breathless. I went in and stared straight ahead, rehearsing in my mind what I would say when the priest would open the little sliding door. Then I heard the whir of the slider and could see a white cloth with the priest's silhouette behind it and could hear him whisper a Latin prayer that I was told to expect.

After a brief silence to make sure he was finished I intoned the formula I had memorized: "Bless me, Father, for I have sinned. In the name of the Father, the Son and the Holy Ghost. I was disobedient three times. I was angry twice. That's all (a sacrilegious lie!). For these sins and all the sins of my past life I am heartily sorry."

He apparently sensed nothing of my anxiety, or perhaps imputed any tentativeness to the newness of the experience. At any rate, he muttered a few pious platitudes, gave me three Hail Marys to say, spoke the words that were to wash away my sins and dismissed me with, "Go in peace." The sliding door whispered as it closed. For a brief momen I knelt there, surprised by how empty my first Confession felt. None of this highly touted experience had the solid feel of a mother's scolding eyes or healing touch. None of the ritual came close to eating supper with my loving brothers and parents. I returned to my pew to complete my penance.

On the following Sunday we made our first Holy Communion. Our youth and seeming innocence touched our families and friends. For most it seemed a day of pure rejoicing.

In Germany on January 30, 1933, Adolf Hitler was named Chancellor. The Enabling Act of March 23, 1933 gave dictatorial powers to Hitler. Jews were the principal target of Nazi hatred. The party blamed Jews for Germany's economic depression and the country's defeat in World War I.

The primary language of my parents was Spanish. Both learned to read and write English but at a very early age each had been forced to leave elementary school to help with the housework and to work at whatever they could do to augment the family income. In our home my parents preferred to speak Spanish to one another and both Spanish and English to the first two children. By the time I was born, however, they were speaking less and less Spanish to my younger brother and me. If it had not been for my monolingual paternal grandmother, Guadalupe, who lived with us, I would have learned very little Spanish.

My parents went to Mass at Immaculate Heart of Mary Church near the corner of Washington and Twelfth Streets where all services were in Spanish. The parish was staffed by priests and brothers from Spain who belonged to a religious congregation called Claretians, after their Spanish founder, Saint Anthony Claret. The culture there was quite different from that of Saint Mary's, where I began to go after starting school. The Spanish hymnology was more sentimental and lively, the relationships among the communicants more animated. But I didn't like the Claretian priests. They fancied themselves better than the Mexican parishioners whom they served. My parents were careful not to discuss this in our presence but our home was small, their voices loud, and we kids could hear confirmation of our sense of the priests' snobbishness.

Before I started school, my parents were more likely to take us to "their" Church for Mass and other services. My earliest memories are of extreme boredom. This was true particularly during the Rosary, when the priest would mercilessly drone on in a monotone, racing through Hail Mary after Hail Mary, the congregants responding antiphonally in an equally drab, flat way their Holy Mary.

Once I discovered that by making a loose fist I could approximate a kind of pseudo-telescope and peer all around the Church for my amusement. I did this quietly and with sweet innocence, never imagining that this could be disruptive. Periodically my mother would glare at me and I would cease and desist, only to resume after a discreet interval. Already foreshadowing the canon lawyer that I would one day become, I reasoned that unless told explicitly what behavior to stop I could justifiably return to my distraction. Only when my mother glared and spoke, "Put your hand down and stop that!" did I fold my hands, suck my lower lip and go inside myself, there to contemplate the injustices of the Church World.

My mother and father both loved to sing in the parish choir under the direction of a friend, Mamie Romo. At rehearsals she would call the choristers "boys and girls" much to their merriment. The language of the Mass was Latin, which they pronounced easily but with a distinct Spanish accent.

Once I began school, I much preferred to go to my church, Saint Mary's—my turf. The children with whom I attended were my friends. The nuns and priests, especially at a distance, were somewhat comforting and they were in charge; things were kept in order. Sermons were in my primary English language as were the prayers and the hymns. For all that, however, some of the parish staff and the administrative personnel were from Germany and their vocal prayers and their voicing of the hymns sounded a guttural German. For a long time I thought, therefore, that in our Tuesday devotions to Saint Anthony we were praying: "De seezo bay, de fedders bray," when in reality I later learned the words were: "The seas obey, the fetters break."

The most traumatic event of my young school life sprang from my inability to relate to the other-worldliness of the nuns.

Their odd dress that revealed almost no skin at all save for hands and face (did they have bodies?), their utterly private life in the convent across the street, the total lack of evidence that they participated in normal human functions like eating, drinking, going to the bathroom and sleeping kept me on red alert. I would imagine that since they were not quite normal they could easily read minds, especially mine. Thus they needed only to scowl and I would be transfixed. It was no wonder that I did my homework faithfully. Some classmates, willing to risk transgression, received a resounding slap with a ruler across the knuckles for their cheekiness. Not I.

Furthermore, the nuns had strange names. In second grade our teacher was Sister Willbrodia. In third, Sister Francetta. Despite their exotic names, both of these teachers were easy to be with. I was studious and did very well.

In fourth grade our teacher was the feared Sister Isabel, quick to anger and quick of tongue. On several occasions she thoroughly humiliated me. It never occurred to me to measure her behavior against the norm of "love thy neighbor" which applied to the rest of us.

For example, I was a picky eater, unwilling to try certain disgusting foods, like milk. My parents were understandably concerned that I was not getting enough calcium to build my young growing bones. They were always on the lookout for some way past my food biases. My fascination with the then-popular radio show, "Little Orphan Annie," seemed to offer such an opportunity.

When the show enticed its young listeners to send for a Little Orphan Annie Ovaltine Mug and I showed some interest, my parents hastened to encourage me to do so. The mug availed little, for I substituted water for milk in the preparation of the Ovaltine.

I did the same thing with another food, *pinole*, which was roasted wheat ground to a fine powder that was meant to be mixed with milk and sugar and drunk for breakfast or a between-meal snack. Once again I would be consistent, using water instead of milk. Even milk shakes and malts were unacceptable.

As a result of these dietary peculiarities my mother had a difficult time preparing lunches for me. One day Sister Isabel, apparently concerned because of my low weight, opened my lunch bag and in public extracted its contents. Judging it too meager, Sister Isabel announced to the class, "Frankie's parents are poor and can't afford anything more than the little bit he brings to school. I would ask those of you who have brought extra to share some with this child."

I was stunned. I could feel myself separating from my body. Off to one side, I looked back at myself, rigid with shame, as classmates charitably volunteered sandwich-halves made with mayonnaise (another disgusting food!). The split between my inner and outer reality was heightened as I found myself thanking everyone for what "out there" seemed kindness despite my inner shame for not speaking up, not defending my poor mother, and not addressing the real reasons for my "inadequate" lunch. Besides, I wasn't aware that my family was poor, although we certainly were. Worse still, the split and the agony were aggravated as I heard the nun demanding that I eat the damn food in her presence. Anger, a sin!

I must say, on the positive side, that I learned a great deal from these nuns. There were standards and discipline and homework. Sometimes, particularly on the first Friday of each month, most of us attended Mass before beginning our school day. The belief was that there were special graces available to those who manifested their love of the first Fridays. In truth there were huge doughnuts with chocolate icing and mugs of hot chocolate in the school cafeteria for those who had sacrificed and gone without breakfast in order to receive Communion. In those days a strict fast from everything, even water, was required for communicants. I was careful on those mornings when brushing my teeth not to swallow any toothpaste-tainted saliva; this might spoil my fast and deprive me of Communion and a doughnut.

We were taught the importance of feast days. Especially at Christmas were we reminded not to stress gift-giving; the chief focus was to celebrate God's love in sending His only Son to live and die for us. At home mother would prepare an elaborate creche on top of the upright piano in the living room (although we were poor, music was an important part of our family life).

She began her beloved task by waxing bleached muslin, pressing sand into the material to simulate stone, then carefully shaping it into mountains and a cave. Lo and behold, we had a landscape! A small red light from behind would create a warm glow throughout the entire space. Then she would lovingly place small statues of Joseph and Mary gazing down at the Christ Child lying in the crib. An ox reclined nearby, a donkey stood respectfully, and several sheep, some with their babies nuzzling them, nibbled at straw strewn on the cave floor. I was always enchanted with the scene. It was holy to me. Gifts within the family were minimal, but this mattered little, caught up as I was in the warmth, the pageantry, the ritual, and the music.

Mother had once arranged for Joe to take piano lessons. Though he had a light touch and could have done something more with music, his interest didn't hold. Now it was apparently my turn. She signed me up to take piano lessons from a guitarist named Juan Cárdenas. I went as far as he could take me and then switched to a Jewish woman, Mrs. Aronson, an inspiring pianist and teacher.

To pay for these lessons, my mother did the Aronson family wash over a two-year period. This extra work, laid on the shoulders of my already busy mother, forced me to take the lessons seriously. If she believed in me to this extent, the least I could do was to practice faithfully, even scales and arpeggios. Whenever I needed her help with a difficult rhythm, she would sit patiently beside me and tap out the timing.

Lent, forty days long, was the period of preparation for Easter, the most important feast of the year. It marked the miraculous event of Jesus rising from the dead after three days. We were taught that without the resurrection His death would mean nothing. During the weeks preceding this feast we were to prepare our hearts by depriving ourselves of something we loved, like candy. This discipline was imposed to fine-tune our spiritual senses, to discipline our disorderly desires, and atone for our sins.

For me as a child, the most deadly moral failure centered around sex. Since sex was declared to be of such a spiritually lethal magnitude, all of this focus was very painful. After all, I was trying to blur the sharp edges of the distinction between mortal and venial sin in an attempt to ignore the stark reality that I was most probably not in the state of sanctifying grace.

In fact I was living a terrible lie which threatened my eternal salvation. As further evidence of my perversity, despite all the spiritual risk involved, I continued to be fascinated with sex. I wanted to know more and more about it. I couldn't outright ask for books about this forbidden matter. Indeed I couldn't even hint at any interest in it. Then one day, when I was about eleven years old, I stumbled on a safe way to educate myself.

My discovery was this: there were sexual reading materials in our house! Nobody knew of these, least of all my parents. The discovery of this treasure trove was a great thrill. Like historical inventors I had read of, I, too, had a "eureka" experience. Understand, there were very few books in our home; we couldn't afford them. Nor could we house them for we lived in a very small quarters—a two-bedroom home of about 1,000 square feet. My father was fond of reading westerns, so I read all these plus the daily newspaper. But there was a dictionary, a quite substantial one, and it was a storehouse of sexual information. I could already read well; all I needed was a formula and persistence.

My pursuit started with the word "intercourse." I cannot remember who spoke this word in my presence or on what occasion. However, having once heard it, I went immediately to the dictionary. I tried to look as casual as I could. Somehow I imagined that my parents or my brothers would note my excitement and ask me what I was up to. I needed to tame my anticipation and move slowly.

I opened the volume and tracked down the word. There, buried in a paragraph of other meanings, was this: "Physical sexual contact between individuals that involves the genitalia of at least one person." After savoring this for a suitable moment, I realized, "Aha! I'm on to something." If I continued to look up words unfamiliar to me, I would find other new words whose definitions I could look up *ad infinitum.*

So I flipped back the pages to the word "genitalia." The definition said: "The organs of the reproductive system; esp: the external genital organs of the reproductive system." Under this word I encountered the word "sexual," then "sexual intercourse," then "penetration of the vagina by the penis." And on and on.

When the trail seemed to end, I just leafed through the

dictionary until once again I came across a word with some sort of relationship to sex, however distant, and tracked it until once again I found a rich vein of ore. This was an excellent educational exercise. The dictionary and I became fast friends, and my dexterity and speed in its use grew far beyond my years. My gifts in spelling were also sharpened the longer I engaged in this titillating hunt.

Sadly, there was no one with whom to share my glee. I could trust no one with my talent. Who knew where the secret might end? And worst of all, I daily faced the problem of the morality of this exercise. I was clearly taking delight in what I was doing; that is, what I was doing was pleasuring me, both physically and mentally, something forbidden to me under "the pain of serious sin." Would I therefore be doomed to the eternal flames of hell if I died unrepentant?

I tried every which way to give myself the benefit of the doubt. I would theorize: this is an educative process, after all, and education is good. But if that were so, why could I not share this with my family, with my teacher, with my priest? I ruminated about this a long time and never once confessed it. Indeed, I was terrified of confessing it. Thus, my unrepentant state convinced me that I was truly a lost soul. Since I had no intention of ever confessing my sin, was I doomed to eternal hellfire?

Of the first three children in my family, the second, Henry, was the most involved in assisting at Mass—"serving," we used to call it; the one assisting the priest was a "server." This sometimes required that Henry rise very early in the morning since the first daily Mass of the day was at six o'clock. He was committed to his task and punctual; this endeared him to those in charge.

On the other hand, I had been a sickly child, unfit for this duty. This did not offend me in the least; I was inordinately fond of sleeping and would often seek excuses to sleep in. For example, I was prone to earaches. On these occasions my mother would dip cotton balls in hot oil and gingerly insert these into my ear for temporary relief.

At times I would exploit my illness, pleading with my mother to let me stay home from school. This stratagem did not escape my older brothers' notice; they would tease me about my convenient

Monday morning earaches, which occurred only upon awakening. Mother would often yield to my entreaties, but since I was home "sick," I would have to stay in bed all day and be treated with the cotton ball therapy.

Sometimes it was worth it, sometimes not. As a result, I got a very late start at serving Mass and was only a tentative rookie when my older brothers and my classmates were seasoned veterans. Once, while handling the thurible or incense pot at a Benediction service, I grew frightened at the mechanics of lifting the lid and presenting the thurible to the priest and spilled incense all over the marble floor. I will never forget how much my awkwardness embarrassed me.

In 1937 Pope Pius XI published "Mit Brennender Sorge," "With Burning Dismay," denouncing Nazism in general but mainly condemning Hitler for his failure to observe his concordat with the Vatican. In 1938 Pope Pius XI gave the Jesuit Father John LaFarge a mission to be carried out in utmost secrecy. The priest was to write an encyclical letter for the Pope condemning the racial policies of Nazi Germany. He was given the assistance of several Jesuits. One of these, Father Gustave Desbuquois of France, was the author of an encyclopedia article defending a "permissible anti-Semitism." In December Fr. LaFarge delivered the text to one of his Jesuit collaborators in Rome. Its suggested title was "Humani Generis Unitas," "The Unity of the Human Race." The encyclical letter never saw the light of day.

When I was in the eighth grade, a young priest came to the parish, Father Brian Lyons. Tall, with sparkling eyes, a frequent, mischievous smile on his lips, he mesmerized me in the classroom and on the playgrounds. There seemed to be some special chemistry between us; I expected him momentarily to utter a message that would touch me deeply and change my life. This made me so uncomfortable that I would instinctively withdraw from his presence for some time to avoid further interaction between us.

But he was patient. One day, halfway into my eighth grade year, throwing all caution to the winds, despite the familiar presentiment in my bones, I went up to him and made small talk. The crowd around him had thinned by the time he turned to me personally. This was the moment I had been fearing. Quietly and matter of factly, he asked me to step into the monastery grounds with him for a little talk.

This invitation took my breath away; I had never been inside the monastery, the "enclosure," closed to lay males most of the time and to women at all times. I heard him asking,

"Have you ever thought of becoming a priest?"

I thought for a moment. I had indeed as a little child "thought" about achieving this lofty position, though no one in the family had ever directly pointed me in that direction. I had, as a very young child, in response to relatives' questions about what I wanted to be when I grew up, offered, "A priest." This was usually greeted with appreciative remarks about how "darling" I was. I never quite realized the meaning of the ministry, but all my family was devout and to them the priesthood was the highest estate possible.

And so, I answered, "Well, yes, I have."

Before I knew it, we were talking about going off to the seminary in Santa Barbara in the fall. He was saying that he could arrange my entry there, sending on the grades and arranging whatever financial commitment there would be. Meanwhile I was watching part of myself carry on this conversation with him while my head part was elsewhere nervously combing through the implications of this decision, if indeed it were a decision.

My mind had already moved on to certain questions regarding my intellectual capacity for the studies that would be involved. I had always managed very well, whatever educational challenges arose. But what about the emotional cost of what I was contemplating? What would my two older brothers think of me? Worse yet, what would they say to me, aspiring to this highest calling despite my numerous, obvious, and profound deficiencies? What would my father say, my father who had bonded so closely with me? My mother, who knew my weaknesses like no other? My classmates, who might greet this decision as pretension? Most of all, what was I to do about my secret life of lustful desires and behavior?

No one knew about these; no one could even imagine where my mind dwelt, especially in those moments of quiet, especially at night. Well, I would have to take the plunge and confess it all in precise detail. To whom? And then what? Would the priest-confessor withhold absolution unless I reversed this decision to become a priest? And in the unlikely event that he would unconditionally forgive my past sins and allow me to pursue a life of vowed celibacy, I would still have to swim against the tide of the seemingly uncontrollable forbidden sexual instinct that tormented me. How realistic was the resolve to be celibate, which I, a thirteen-year-old, was taking in the moment? And without deep thought?

Suddenly, it seemed, Father Brian and I were sealing our agreement with a vigorous handshake and I was strangely excited by our transaction. The idealistic calling was attractive and I felt special.

Then I was plunged into demanding reality when he said in parting, "Go home and tell your parents about our conversation and your decision."

I answered vacantly, "Yes, Father," opened the door into the school yard, and walked pensively toward a cluster of classmates. I would reveal nothing of my decision to them for the time being.

The 3:30 bell marking the end of the school day came much too swiftly. I began my walk home, mulling over what to say to my family and how to say it. The biggest hurdle was how to present my lofty aspirations in the light of my sense of ordinariness. No one in my family had ever gone to seminary. An aunt was a Franciscan nun, venerated not only by the family but by all who knew her.

Her calling, though, was far short of priesthood. Priests were other Christs in the world, forgiving sins in the name of the Father, Son and Holy Ghost, and offering the sacrifice of Calvary in the unbloody form of the Mass. How announce, "I want to be another Christ"? I would deal with my secret, interior unworthiness later, I thought. Right now I needed to unload this burden which pressed heavily on my thin, already sloping shoulders and begin the long journey toward the fall of 1939.

I walked the mile home very slowly. When I arrived, I shouted out a greeting to my mother. My parents' bedroom door was open; her cheerful voice welcomed me home. I entered, drew in a long breath and said, "Are Joe and Henry home yet?"

"No, not yet, mijo. What's on your mind?"

Not at all following the script I thought I had prepared, I blurted out, "Mom, I want to go to the seminary in Santa Barbara and become a priest."

Whatever she felt (I learned later that she received this news "like a kick in the stomach"), she displayed no shock. Rather she heard me empathically, drawing on her extraordinary gift of entering my world without threat. She invited me to tell her how I had arrived at this decision, and I shared with her my conversation with Father Brian. Before I knew it I was confessing my fear, especially that my older brothers would tease me unmercifully.

"Don't worry about this, mijo. I'll tell Joe and Henry to leave you alone and I'll also talk to your father. Let me tell him."

She spoke these last four words slowly, with distinct emphasis on the "me." Then she added, "We will figure out some way to pay for your schooling when you leave home."

I was enormously relieved. She was a formidable ally. True, I still had to live through those first moments with my two older brothers after they learned of my intentions, but my mother was on my side and I was on my way.

As expected, my powerful mother came through. My father was unexpectedly gracious and encouraging. My older brothers, after a few tongue-in-cheek remarks about having a saint in the house, actually expressed their pride in me and their confidence that I could make it.

When I later learned that another five classmates were committed to going to the seminary, I grew more comfortable. And when in the summer the six of us began a series of social gatherings with older teens who were already seasoned seminarians, my decision seemed irrevocable. My fate was sealed.

New German anti-Jewish regulations segregated Jews further and burdened them unjustly: Jews could not attend public schools; go to theaters, cinemas, or vacation resorts; or reside, or even walk, in certain sections of German cities. Jews were forced from Germany's economic life: the Nazis either seized Jewish businesses and properties outright or forced Jews to sell them at bargain prices. In early November of 1938, Germans brutally attacked Jews throughout the nation, burned their Synagogues and destroyed their businesses and homes. This centrally organized riot is known as Kristallnacht.

Alone, I was left with the most serious obstacle of all, the interior unconfessed, unspoken unworthiness of my sullied past. I had serious misgivings about maintaining celibacy. Could I reasonably expect never to indulge deliberately in a single sexual thought, desire, or act? Did I really want to embrace this ideal? And if I did not, how could I withdraw from my now publicly proclaimed intention to become a priest? The calling seemed noble. I valued the idea of service and there was none more exalted than the priesthood, especially in my devout Catholic home. So there were big pluses and big minuses. When in doubt, I thought, confess to nothing and march forward. And so I did.

My decision to go to the seminary upset my piano teacher. Once she realized that she wasn't going to be able to dissuade me from leaving home she asked to speak to my mother. When the three of us got together one afternoon, Mrs. Aronson was brief and to the point.

"I of course have nothing to say about your calling," she said to me. "But I do want to say that you could postpone the start of your formal studies until after high school. That would give us four years to work together and lay the solid foundation necessary for pursuing music as a career if you should want to."

My mother listened intently and acknowledged that Mrs. Aronson was offering us something reasonable. But—she would not intervene. The decision was totally up to me.

"If I stay home for the next four years," I answered, "I may never go to the seminary at all. I don't want to take that chance. So my decision is that I'm going to Santa Barbara in September."

Meanwhile, my relationships with the other candidates and the veteran seminarians who lived in Phoenix prospered and smoothed the imminent transition to life away from home. I was also drawing from a Mexican culture which embraced reverence for the priesthood. This reinforced my resolve to face the impossible.

> *On September 1, 1939, Germany invaded Poland and World War II began. The Polish army was quickly defeated and the Nazis began to destroy Polish culture and enslave Polish people. There were massacres of Polish leaders: university professors, artists, writers, politicians, and many Catholic priests. Thousands, including Jews, were imprisoned in concentration camps. Hitler ordered the death of institutionalized, handicapped patients deemed "incurable."*

In early September I gathered with the other Santa Barbara-bound students at the train station on the south side of Phoenix. My entire family turned out: parents, siblings, aunts and uncles, cousins and close friends, all eager to celebrate the special moment. When the conductor called, "All aboard!" I kissed my mother, shook hands all around, and then turned to kiss my father as I was accustomed to doing. Instead, he gently held his hand to my chest, saying softly so that others could not hear, "You're a man now; men don't kiss one another." Then he took my hand and, eyes brimming, wished me Godspeed.

I was nonplused. Was this passage into manhood on the brink of age fourteen something I should have known about? My God, everyone around me knew this but me. What must they be thinking? And what of this radical change in the norm for expressing my affection for him, from kiss to handshake? Was that a well-known alteration of ritual that everyone was in on?

I interpreted my father's change in attitude toward me as a mild reproof, but I managed it with aplomb and said my goodbye. There was so much jocularity and laughing and so many families seeing their children off that the sadness of departure never really touched me. We boarded the train; the metal doors clanged shut; there was a mighty whistle, and slowly the train pulled away from all that was familiar.

Part II
First Tentative Steps of a Thirteen-year Journey

SAINT ANTHONY'S SEMINARY sat high up on ten acres of land about two miles up from the coastline. From the depot at sea level you could see the long finger of the seminary chapel tower jutting into the sky, and the massive unfinished concrete walls of its chapel. Snuggled up to the rolling foothills and the distant pink-stone mountains, it was an impressive sight.

Off to the right were the twin towers of the Old Mission, which sat on adjoining property and which, though still an active parish, was a popular tourist attraction. Buttressed by the students that I had already gotten to know quite well, my mood was devoid of anxiety as we made our way up to the seminary. We had arrived at the seed bed for the spiritual cultivation of those of us youngsters who felt the call to priesthood in the Franciscan Order.

Saint Mary's, my parochial grammar school, had prepared me well for seminary life. The life of the parish, Mass, Benediction and other devotions, had been like rain gently falling on my young, idealistic soul. The catechism and Bible history classes over the years had given me clear notions of what Catholics were to believe. Among these was the conviction that the priesthood was the highest calling available to man, being the continuation of the saving work of Jesus in the world. The next thirteen years, through high school, novitiate, college and theology, would simply deepen this primer of beliefs. One day, God willing, I would be fit to proclaim the saving word for all the world to hear, and perform the sacred acts that both honored God and gave, restored, and nurtured eternal life to all mankind.

The academic program was rigorous. Four days a week there were six classes and five study halls of varying lengths. On Wednesdays and Saturdays there were four classes and two study halls in the morning, afternoons being free for intramural sports and walks off campus. Sundays were relatively free: there were two study periods, one before dinner and one after, when we were permitted to read or write letters as we chose.

Our curriculum stressed languages: Latin, Greek, Spanish, and German. Of these the queen was Latin, which we studied for six years. In the college philosophy courses and in the four years of theology, the core text books were written in Latin. On occasion a professor might even lecture in Latin. And at the heart of our communal prayer life each day were the Latin Mass and the Divine Office, a melange of biblical readings and prayers.

The spiritual program centered chiefly on the daily Mass, the centerpiece of Christian worship. From childhood I could have told you, though not with much understanding, that the Mass was the unbloody sacrifice of Jesus, meaning that He was present— body, blood, soul, and divinity—in the slender, white, tasteless wafer and in the wine after the priest had uttered the transforming words, "This is My Body; This is My Blood." During this peak moment of our quintessential ritual, everybody in the church knelt in hushed silence and then the server invited adoration by ringing a bell or striking a gong as the priest genuflected and as he held the consecrated bread and the chalice of wine high over his head.

From the first day at the seminary we were introduced to the practice of silence, a difficult but precious discipline which I still hold dear. There was no talking from night prayers until after breakfast the next morning. On some mornings, particularly during Lent, we ate in monastic silence while listening to a student reading aloud from some spiritual work. My hope was always that after blessing the breakfast food, the Prefect might utter the magic words, *"Religiose colloquamur,"* or "Let us converse religiously," and release our adolescent tongues eager to engage one another. The "religiose" part of the permission never concerned us. Our conversation took us wherever our energies and interests directed.

In February, 1939, on the tenth anniversary of the concordat with Mussolini, Pope Pius XI was slated to denounce Germany's anti-Jewish laws. In that very week he died.

Our student days were actually already a community life, although without vows; we lived pretty much the way we would later on upon formal entrance into the Franciscan Order. The same cycle carried us through each day: early rising, community prayers—both oral and then in silent meditation—daily Mass, periods of silence, community meals, study, classes, and carefully supervised extracurricular activities.

True, we had not yet vowed poverty, but the Prefect kept our money for us and on our afternoons off gave us both spending money and permission to go off campus to purchase things. We were also living celibately, trying to avoid thoughts, desires and behaviors sexual in nature. We were obedient to the seminary authority. Most importantly, we cared for one another, performing community chores and treating one another with respect. It was a valuable experience and taught me consideration for those who lived around me.

There were unusual opportunities for everyone. For instance, because the school was small and there was no pressure from interscholastic competition to be the best, there was no undue emphasis on sports. The program was purely intramural and though there was healthy and sometimes charged competition, pleasure and energy outlets were the explicit goals. Thus there was a chance for everyone to participate in athletics at whatever level of skill one possessed or could achieve.

A similar approach to theater facilitated broad, pleasant engagement. Each class was expected to select and stage a play for the rest of the student body. This, too, pulled the reticent and the less skilled to participate in some aspect of theater and to this extent stretched their gifts, dormant or otherwise. Theatrical offerings were always greeted with enthusiasm and appreciation by fellow students. It was quite heady for freshmen to perform for upper classmen and receive their generous, stirring applause.

In 1940 German forces continued their conquest of much of
Europe, easily defeating Denmark, Norway, the Netherlands,
Belgium, Luxembourg, and France.

In my sophomore year, at the annual retreat, I had the first profound spiritual experience of my life. The retreat master was particularly stirring, presenting stories of self-effacing, courageous
ministry and closeness to God. One such story looms large in my
memory. It still carries a powerful message:

"Once a man came upon an angel carrying in one hand a pail
of water and in the other a torch. 'Why carry you a torch and a
pail of water and whither go you?' asked the perplexed man. The
angel answered: 'With this torch I go to burn down heaven and
with this pail of water I go to extinguish the fires of hell. Then we
will see who loves God.'"

In this tale the pure love of God was contrasted with the kind
of love that looked to attain a reward and/or to avoid a punishment. This idealism touched me and I felt called to embrace it in
the deepest part of my fifteen-year-old heart. Deeply moved, I
sought to share my experience with classmates. Some were
touched by my perceptions of the retreat, while others brushed it
aside as an insignificant event. Regardless, I was convinced that
my experience would significantly alter the *way I would organize*
the spiritual meaning of my life, centered around idealistic service to
others.

At about the same time the Franciscans ministering in China
were finally driven out and forced to return to the States. To my
sensitive, idealistic soul these people represented what was most
beautiful about our calling, and manifested a kind of courage that
invited me to respond with similar generosity. My inner flame
burned brightly, confirming to me that I was indeed on the appropriate vocational path. This, despite my continuing nagging concerns about my inability to live a celibate life.

On June 22, 1941, the German army invaded the Soviet
Union and by September was approaching Moscow. In the
meantime, Italy, Romania, and Hungary had joined the Axis
powers led by Germany and opposed by the Allied Powers, i.e.

*British Commonwealth, Free France, the United States, and
the Soviet Union. In the following months Jews, political leaders, Communists, and many Gypsies were killed in mass execu-
tions. The overwhelming majority of those killed were Jews.
Hundreds of new camps were established in occupied territories
of eastern and western Europe.*

On December 7, 1941, in my junior year, the school choir was
performing at Mission Santa Ynez to the north. Some of us who
stayed home had gone to a wooded park in the northeast section
of Santa Barbara to play a pick-up game of touch football. Suddenly we heard a shout and saw one of our classmates running toward us. Japan had bombed Pearl Harbor!

Later we learned that the sneak attack had inflicted devastating damage on American ships, airplanes and personnel. The next
day President Franklin D. Roosevelt delivered his war message to
Congress. From then on, December 7, 1941 would be "a date
which will live in infamy."

One of the seminary staff had a sister on the Big Island. When
he heard the news he exploded in anger and cursed the "dirty
Japs." Fortunately she and her family had escaped all harm.

I grew very fond of several of the staff who became my
confidants. Intimate self-disclosure (beyond the very private confession of personal sin in the sacrament of penance) was unusual
and certainly not upheld as an ideal. But several of the teachers
invited it by their manner of relating to us students. One priest
especially proclaimed his availability as a confidant to the entire
class.

"Some of you with problems should come around to talk
them out with me. I would welcome this. All you have to do is
ask."

It sounded wonderful to me. One day a strange chain of
events led me to answer his call.

I played catcher on one of the baseball teams; what I lacked in
arm strength I made up for with chatter and quickness. At a game
one day, with two out in the bottom of the seventh and final in-
ning of a varsity baseball game, the tying run of the game was bar-
reling down on me in response to a single. I could see that the

throw to me was going to arrive late and I braced myself for a collision as I blocked home plate. The runner clearly beat the throw and slid across the plate. I shouted, "He missed the plate!" and the runner instinctively tried to touch base again. This time I was ready for him and easily tagged him out. The umpire, jerking his right thumb upward, shouted, "You're out!" The ball game was over and we had won.

Some of the fans, seminarians and staff included, exploded at the umpire and at me. They were at the wire cage screaming at his incompetence and my cunning. I held my hands, palms up, shrugged my shoulders as if to say, "It's just a tactic; I'm entitled," and left the field to shower, get dressed, and go to study hall. Nothing more was said, so I concluded that the matter was done with. Not so.

Each month all students were graded on a variety of attitudes; the results were announced to the entire student body assembled in the study hall. One of the categories was "Attitude toward fellow students," in which I had always received high grades. But this day my score in this category was announced: "F."

I was stunned as well as embarrassed. Classmates sitting nearby whispered their surprise and confusion. I had not changed in my behavior toward them or toward any other student. Why this "F"? While their support helped me, it shed no light on what had happened. Then I remembered the priest who had offered a receptive ear. I asked him for an appointment.

After I explained the situation he, with some chagrin, shared with me that a faculty member at the fateful game felt I had "cheated." He felt bothered by it and thought an example should be made of me. Hence the "F," a knock along the side of my head with a two-by-four. This would get my attention and alert the rest of the seminarians that this kind of behavior would not be tolerated, even on the field of play.

It seemed overreactive to me, but I was willing to accept this as a higher wisdom; that is, until the priest told me that the staff person's response was inappropriate, that what I had done on the field of play was not only instinctive and totally without malice, but might even be considered admirable quick-thinking. He was so understanding and so gentle that I treasured the time spent with him. Somewhere in my mind I filed the experience as something I would do for others when I became a priest.

However, it raised doubts in me as to the ultimate, unalterable wisdom of the staff.

The revolt in the Warsaw Ghetto began on April 19, 1943 on the eve of Passover that year. The last of the resistance was not crushed by the Nazis until May 16.

In my fifth and final year at St. Anthony's (the second of the two college years had been moved to San Luis Rey College) I was made student body president. This carried the obligation to be a model to others, as well as to enforce the rules of the school when no staff were around, especially the rule of silence. It was very difficult as a peer to ask fellow seminarians to stop speaking but I did it, perhaps as much to avoid reprimand from the Prefect as to behave responsibly. For the most part classmates were very understanding and seldom presented me with the need to correct them.

In October of my fifth year I turned eighteen. My classmates and I were required to register for the draft. The young men with whom I had studied at home in Phoenix were in the military; some were overseas fighting. In the light of their vulnerability it was difficult to accept that I was classified a protected IV-D, to be called only in the eventuality of desperate need. This privilege made me feel uncomfortable, especially later when I heard from home that one of my classmates had fallen in battle.

Between 1942 and 1944 the Germans moved to eliminate the ghettos in occupied Poland and elsewhere, deporting ghetto residents to "extermination camps" located in Poland. In late January 1942, at a villa in the Berlin suburb of Wannsee, the decision to implement "the final solution of the Jewish question" became formal state policy, and Jews from western Europe were also sent to six killing centers in the East. Between May 14 and July 8, 1944, 437,402 Hungarian Jews were deported to Auschwitz in 48 trains.

Graduation meant not merely the completion of my first five years of preparation for the priesthood but imminent entry into the Franciscan community. School traditionally ended on the Feast of St. Anthony, June 13, and acceptance as a novice at Old Mission San Miguel in San Miguel, California, was to take place some four weeks later. This gave us all a reprieve to return to our homes, near or far, for about two weeks to say goodbye to family and friends, before reconvening at the novitiate for a ten-day retreat.

On July 10, 1944, nine classmates and I were received into the Franciscan Order in the Province of Saint Barbara at a ceremony called investiture, which refers to putting on the special garb of the religious community.

When my turn arrived, I removed my suit coat and handed it to an attendant. Then the familiar brown robe that had once frightened me as a child was pulled over my head. I was given a woolen cord with three symbolic knots to place around my waist. From a loop at the left side of my tunic I hung a large-beaded rosary divided into seven sections of ten beads, each decade commemorating an event in the lives of Jesus and his mother, Mary. A capuche, or hood, was placed over my head. Now my change was complete.

The custom was to mark this radical shift in garb and life-style with a name change. My baptismal "Francis" was now to become my middle name. Well beforehand, each of us had submitted for our new Franciscan identity three preferred names taken from canonized saints in the Catholic Church. My first preference was my father's name, José María, and my third choice was Armand(o). I thought that both these names would be congenial to the Mexican people among whom I hoped to work. The powers that be chose Armand(o). For a long time my family continued to call me Frankie.

The day of my investiture was a proud one, the culmination of five hard years. My mother and father understood my pride and shared their own. My oldest brother, Joe, was warmly affectionate. Everything about the day seemed so right. Nothing, not even the challenge of celibacy, daunted me or dampened my ardor.

The year went by swiftly. Each novice had a private cell, equipped spartanly with a narrow bed, a small table that served as a desk, a wardrobe, and a wash basin. Though spare, this was the very first private space I had ever had in my short life and it seemed grand. At 5:15 each morning we were awakened to a day filled with a round of common prayer, classes, and manual labor or intramural sports. On average we were permitted two evenings a week for recreation. This was an hour or so of snacks, conversation, and listening to music. Every moment of our day was scheduled.

We were extremely fortunate in our Novice Master, Father David Temple, who was eloquent and inspiring both in the written and spoken word. His gifts were critical since he taught us Franciscan history and spirituality, the Rule of St. Francis as well as church law governing life in a religious community.

Of course, with time the excitement of the busy life abated and once again I began to wrestle with the demands of celibacy. And for the first time in my life I began to have serious thoughts about something that should have been evident to me all along: I would never have children. This made me very sad. Coming as I did from a large, loving family where children were treasured, I began to think that I should leave.

I consulted my confessor, who said: "These thoughts are not at all uncommon. They don't necessarily mean that you don't have a vocation to the priesthood. Consider them temptations and pray that they pass."

Typically I dismissed my questions and followed his direction. But when, after the tenth month, one of my favorite classmates left, my doubts returned. I prayed my way through them to a feeling of uneasy peace.

Until April 1945, one of the correspondence courses conducted by the United States Armed Forces included a statement that read: "The genuine American is essentially Nordic, preferably Protestant...the Jew is an offensive fellow unwelcome in this country."

At the end of the year I made so-called simple, or temporary, vows of poverty, chastity and obedience that would carry me through the next three years of college at Old Mission San Luis Rey, California. I was nineteen years old.

*In late 1944 the SS decided to evacuate outlying concentration
camps. The Germans tried to cover up the evidence of genocide
and deported prisoners to camps inside Germany to prevent
their liberation. In May 1945, Nazi Germany collapsed.*

The town of San Luis Rey lay in a sleepy little valley midway between Los Angeles and San Diego about five miles inland from
the coast. The area's chief claim to fame was its Old Mission
founded by the Franciscan, Father Fermín Lasuén, on June 13,
1798, the eighteenth of a chain of twenty-one California Missions. The buildings housed a large Franciscan community: the
parish and college staff, all priests; the seminarians, who were referred to as *fratres*, Latin for "brothers"; and finally all the
unordained support personnel, referred to as Brothers. The College was affiliated with Saint Mary's College in Moraga in northern California; in virtue of this relationship it could issue Bachelor
of Arts degrees upon satisfactory completion of its courses.

Shortly after my arrival I had an unexpected visit from my
brother, Henry, who had just been released from the service. I was
profoundly touched by his coming but my training directed me
away from any expression of softness. In his brief time with me I
could sense his awkwardness in the presence of his little brother in
this "exalted" environment. Nevertheless I was aware of my deep
love for him and grateful that he had gone out of his way to see
me.

In those days many of the college texts were in Latin. Most of
us had no difficulty with this language; we had studied it and
prayed in it for five years. The monastic life provided an ideal environment for study: few distractions, small classes, an excellent
library. The Hellenistic philosophical material laid the founda-
tions of our theological training. It touched material central to
our spiritual lives. We were learning, for example, distinctions
crucial for an understanding of how Jesus was present in the bread
after the priest uttered the words of consecration over it.

Critical to this is the belief that all things are made up of substance and accidents, the substance of a thing being its essence
beyond the reach of the senses, which can perceive only its accidents—those sense-felt aspects that you can see, touch, taste, etc.

In nearly all cases the accidents do point to the essence of a thing, but not necessarily. Nearly always you see a small, round, slim, feather-light, white wafer and can count on its being simple, un-leavened bread made of flour and water. But when a Catholic priest, with a power received at ordination, has pronounced the words of Jesus, "This is My Body," over the bread, intending as He did to transform it, it becomes in essence the body of Jesus, the tangible accidents of bread remaining unchanged.

So where the senses by their very nature fail to note the change, faith enters in and assures us that Jesus, the Son of God, is present under the appearances of bread. Thus this transformed "bread" must be approached with appropriate reverence.

Community life was a rich experience shared with people of similar spiritual ideals and energetic commitment. Most of our waking hours were spent in study and prayer, both communal and private, but there was ample time for recreational activities such as intramural sports and hiking. Our focus as Franciscans was to be deeply prayerful brothers whose simple lives modeled kindness, generosity, gratitude, and respect for the environment. Once a month the students produced a "Louie's night," at which anyone could as an individual or in groups perform for the community. The entertainment was as simple as a reading or as elaborate as a one-act play.

The intense form of prayer to which we had been introduced in novitiate continued to be fostered. Our community retired at nine-thirty and arose at midnight to chant the most lengthy of the Hours of the Divine Office. This was composed of psalms, read-ings and hymns, about forty-five minutes of community prayer followed by a half-hour of meditation. At that hour of the night my level of awareness was usually poor but I did my best. We were all comforted by the fact that this exercise was *"agere contra naturam,"* "acting against nature," a form of discipline that helped one master one's bodily needs and drives.

On July 4, 1946 a Polish mob, its anti-Semitism fueled by ru-mors that Jews had kidnapped a Christian child, besieged a building and slaughtered forty-two Jewish Holocaust survivors.

With the deepening of my intellectual and spiritual life, I grew very fond of the semi-monastic nature of my life, especially the silence. Periodically I wrestled with the notion of transferring to a religious order which was totally monastic. The Franciscan ideal was to be both contemplative *and* active, an ideal that Saint Francis of Assisi had chosen rather than merely contemplative or "in the world." This balance was difficult for me to maintain; the active aspect tended to be dominant.

I was particularly influenced by one of my professors, Father Oliver Lynch, who was personable, intense, challenging, and supportive. I admired his lifestyle and the manner of his teaching. For this reason I chose him as my spiritual director.

From him I learned of a small group of Franciscans in the Midwest and in the East who were trying to deepen their appreciation and practice of contemplation. They produced a small book of their insights based on Franciscan sources. They quoted the much admired and brilliant Duns Scotus, a thirteenth-century scholar who emphasized love over intellectual understanding. This approach suited me perfectly. Moved by their emphasis on experience over theory, I was soon practicing what they advocated, enlivening my understanding of spirituality.

Despite all of this emotional and intellectual richness, I was still in my quietest moments left with the unfinished business of my problem with celibacy. I struggled mightily with the thoughts of never being permitted sexual love, being deprived of the comfort of a loving companion, never having a family. From time to time these thoughts would intrude and disturb my drive toward a priestly ministry. While I continued to discount my normal sexual feelings, they remained a challenge to my priestly vocation.

Then there would pop up the unfinished business of the sexual sins of my childhood which I felt I had never properly confessed. Most of the time I attempted to ignore these intrusions with the thought that I had misunderstood the clear teaching of the Church on sexual morality, or that I had never given true consent to any sexual pleasure I may have felt, or that, since my spiritually blissful moments were so gratifying, my guilt must be without foundation. None of these approaches was adequate.

The three years passed swiftly. On the morning of the solemn vow ceremony, my parents, together with other parents and family members, entered the long, narrow nave of the Mission, filed into the first pews on the epistle side of the ancient sanctuary and knelt. On the other side of the aisle, visiting Franciscans were silently awaiting our entrance. Interested parishioners were also present.

To the sound of stirring organ music my classmates and I marched into the sanctuary ahead of the provincial and his assisting priests. We were eight young men about to take solemn vows to live together in poverty, chastity, and obedience for the rest of our lives. Before speaking our vows we lay prostrate while the priests and brothers prayed over us.

I lay there mesmerized by the mellifluous male voices, strangely at peace with the ideal of a priestly life without marriage, without children, without ownership of life's goods, and perhaps most critically, without the right to make decisions in my own behalf about how and where I would serve.

My turn arrived. I stood up, walked up the three steps to where the provincial was seated, placed my folded hands within his and solemnly promised that I would live in poverty, chastity, and obedience "as long as I shall live." At that moment I was able to set my fears aside and see myself pointed toward all that was best in life, toward the very core of truth clearly delineated by an infallible Church.

By this time the broad lines of my religious beliefs were precise and clear. The world had been alienated from God through the proud rebellion of Adam and Eve. Since their sin had offended the Divine Being, our broken relationship to God was beyond merely human attempts to repair. The only path toward solving this dilemma was a divine intervention on the part of someone who was both God and man. That someone was Jesus.

As man He could represent the human race in the sacrifice of His life for the atonement of sin. As God He could endow this sacrifice with infinite dignity.

The death of Jesus, lovingly suffered in our behalf, provided condign, or completely adequate, satisfaction for the sin of Adam and Eve and for the sins of all of us. In principle we were thereby restored to union with God. The divine life of grace which channeled this saving act to humankind was now dispensed by the Catholic priest, who was an "*alter Christus*," another Christ.

I had just solemnly pledged to live my intent to march on as a Franciscan toward this exalted role. The last four years of this journey were to be in Santa Barbara, the city where I had taken my first teenage steps on a thirteen-year pilgrimage toward personal sanctity and sacramental priesthood. The theological seminary was part of the Franciscan community at Old Mission Santa Barbara, which had been established on December 4, 1786, under Father Junípero Serra.

The summer of 1948 in Santa Barbara was a rare, brief interlude without obligations. The college years were over and theological studies had not yet begun. Our duties were chiefly physical: the gardens were ample and needed tending, as did the long corridors of offices, community rooms, the chapel, and our individual rooms (cells).

Each day there were three to four hours of community prayer. But there were many pleasant diversions such as intramural sports, swimming, and hiking over the rolling hills into the mountains. As a first-year theological student I was on the lowest rung; I had no administrative duties.

At that time, direction of the choir was the job of a third-year theological student. And then one month into the school year the choir director took sick. I grew nervous because staff eyes seemed to be peering my way. One Saturday as I was cleaning a stairwell in the students' wing, I heard a voice at the top calling my name, "Armando." It was Joseph Benedict, a third-year student, a dear friend and gifted musician.

"I've got some news for you."

I stretched out my arms in a cruciform posture. "Yes, yes," I said with a laugh, "give it to me."

I had an inkling of what he was going to say. And then came the unwelcome news: I was to take over as choir director immediately, not just as a temporary replacement but as a permanent job. Joe saw my strained face as I struggled to accept the unwanted burden. I heard him promising to smooth my path, to sing whatever voice would be most helpful, to collaborate in the selection and preparation of the liturgical music. He understood that it might be difficult for me as a newcomer to direct upper classmen, especially fourth-year students who were already ordained priests.

"I'll run interference for you if you should need it," I heard him say.

His presence and kindness calmed me for the moment. For the next two years he was as constant and resourceful as he had promised he would be. He has remained my committed friend ever since.

Father Alan McCoy, the staff canon lawyer, was an extraordinary man. Brilliant, prayerful, he drew many of us to himself by his kindness. Impressive too was his involvement in work with minorities in the community. It was in part his example that spurred me to aspire to contemplative prayer, a particularly attractive aspect of Franciscan spirituality.

The usual form of silent prayer engaged in by the community was called meditation, a structured, busy approach that was easily taught. It consisted of three clearly defined steps.

First, one member of the community read from standard meditative texts. Most often this was a commentary on some aspect of the life of Jesus, such as his betrayal by Judas.

The second step was to ponder the author's thoughts and then attempt to apply his considerations to our personal lives. The author sometimes tried to help us do this by posing questions for our consideration.

Finally, and most importantly, we were to listen to our heart's reactions, express our feeling responses to the God within us and make a resolution of some sort to improve our lives.

Contemplative prayer, on the other hand, was a step beyond this, a radically different form of prayer. In it the mind was quiet and receptive. The goal was to be a wordless presence before the God within.

To arrive at this more advanced state of contact with God, we were presented with a simple but difficult preparatory discipline. As a way of mastering desire, *we were to pursue nothing for the simple pleasure of it.* This norm implied that we would participate only in what was necessary or very useful to preserve life and health. When applied to eating, drinking, resting and sleeping in the setting of a community, this asceticism made it easy to recognize its practitioners. Other Franciscans would not only notice these significantly different behaviors but could easily misinterpret them.

The preparatory discipline of abstaining from pleasure for pleasure's sake could be read as a moral judgment that taking pleasure in something for pleasure's sake was sinful. And indeed some felt judged by those practicing this form of asceticism. I did not observe any overt tension among the students, who were all mutually respectful and considerate of one another.

The tension seemed to be among the priests on the faculty and in the broader Franciscan community on the West Coast. Enough Franciscans concluded that something bordering on heresy was brewing. As a result, we students were abruptly informed that neither Father Alan in Santa Barbara nor Father Oliver at San Luis Rey could serve as our confessor or spiritual director.

The order must have issued from the definitorial board, that is, the provincial and his assistants, but we students were never told. There was no discussion of the matter. One noteworthy thing: neither of the two priests allowed the public embarrassment to hobble them. I considered their equanimity impressive.

The Christian Family Movement was created in 1949 as an American variation of the Young Christian Workers movement pioneered in the 1920s by the Belgian priest Joseph Cardijn.

I continued to study the spiritual literature these men had introduced me to and I lived by it. I felt that this type of discipline would carry me through the so-called "purgative" state (which focused on avoiding sin) to the "illuminative state," which would bring me uncluttered insight into the workings of God. The ultimate goal was the "unitive state," which, as the word implies, would result in a profound union between one's soul and God.

To understand this phenomenon more clearly and to move toward it more purposively, I consulted the professor of spirituality, Father Silvano Matulich, a man in his sixties, balding and slender. He received me warmly and addressed my need very seriously. I said I did not think that I was practicing contemplative prayer. Was there something specific he could suggest to help me?

"Yes," he said, "I have a book by one of the earliest Franciscans, Saint Bonaventure. It's a small volume entitled *Itinerarium Mentis in Deum* (*The Mind's Journey to God*). You can handle it. Here," he said, handing me a worn little book. "When you've finished reading it, come back and discuss it with me."

The volume enchanted me. It invited me into an experience different in kind from the thought-feeling-application meditation in which I had been trained. It taught that the call to engage in contemplative prayer was not an extraordinary one, not uniquely an enterprise for men and women in religious communities. Rather, the call issued from baptism and was available to any baptized person who would submit to the discipline. The mystical experience of God would infallibly follow, touching the soul in a way beyond the power of words to describe.

The method was simple. It required only discipline and consistency. The seminary was an appropriate, propitious place for us to practice this method. The path was smoothed for us: no living to earn, no spouse or children to whom to attend. Time for prayer was abundant. We were provided quiet space without interruption. All that we were required to bring to prayer was openness and willingness.

You sat quietly. As each thought formed, you imagined your mind holding it like a closed fist. Calmly and deliberately, you opened your hand and allowed the thought to fall away. This you did over and over as each thought formed.

With lengthy practice the thoughts formed less frequently and were released with greater and greater ease. The ultimate goal was simply to do all one could to provide an uncluttered, open space for meeting God. Should peace of mind, good feeling, or a sense of accomplishment accompany the union with God, it was to be gratefully accepted as a bonus, an overflow of that state. It was to be enjoyed but not clung to.

I grew to love the discipline and sought the solitude of the chapel whenever I had the time. I shared what I had learned with anyone who seemed interested. Gradually the exercise became a way of being. I could have this quiet awareness under any circumstance, whether studying, conversing, gardening, or playing ball.

But soon some members of the community began to grow

concerned that my behavior was growing strange. One day Father Silvano called me in to tell me that some of the staff had complained. They felt I was being extreme in my asceticism and in my dedication to silent prayer. I responded that for me this way of life seemed essential to my calling. However I promised to be less reclusive and perhaps more attentive to the needs of others.

In my third year of study, the professor of dogma, Father Noel, a priest with a doctorate from the University of Quebec, gave us a lecture on the theological virtues of faith, hope and charity. The way that he presented it annoyed me and some of my classmates. We understood that he was elevating a theological opinion to the level of Catholic doctrine. The former allowed for freedom of inquiry whereas the latter had to be accepted without challenge.

We wanted the younger students to understand that this area was still under discussion in the Church. A few of my classmates asked me whether I, as one who had specialized in the topic, would take on the professor—argue the matter with him.

When I expressed some hesitation because the faculty already had concerns about me, they said, "Don't worry. You speak. We'll back you up." With some misgiving I agreed to present our differing stance to Father Noel.

That night I carefully prepared what I would say in class. I would disagree with the priest but most respectfully. So armed, at the start of the next day's lecture I raised my hand and was acknowledged.

"Father, I would like to return to yesterday's lecture for a moment. I wanted to say that what you proposed as Catholic doctrine about the theological virtues is still an open question among scholars. No Catholic is required to assume a position in this regard at this moment. I've been reading extensively about these issues and feel strongly about our freedom to differ."

Silence fell over the classroom. I could see disbelief and dismay creep over his face. Students began shifting positions in their seats. Now anxious, I looked to my classmates wanting to be rescued. No one spoke up. Not one. My mind was now teeming with the possibilities my contradiction could give rise to. I had probably crossed the line of propriety. I could be refused priestly ordination. I had done the unthinkable. How to extricate myself? My protest could easily be interpreted as a proud attempt to expand myself at the professor's expense. He had a doctorate; I had not yet even completed my four years of theological preparation for the priesthood. Was I presuming to know better than he? Furthermore, I was citing material that could be connected with Fathers Oliver Lynch and Alan McCoy; they had already fallen out of favor and were considered dangerous. Now I would be tarred with the same brush.

In a tone of voice that not too subtly told me to back off, he pronounced, "You are in error."

My carefully planned strategy lay in shambles. We stood *mano a mano*, I a nobody, he a scholar. We were both out of control, both of us defending our beliefs as our voices grew louder and louder, each of us matching the other's mounting intensity.

The promised support from classmates never materialized. It was my fight alone. Technically I could see I had won, because suddenly and unexpectedly I heard him exclaim (I think in desperation): "I don't *believe* what you say but I would *die* for your right to say it!"

He picked up his books, declared class at an end and strode angrily toward the exit. The custom was for the student nearest the door to dip his fingers in the holy water font and offer it to the professor as he left. There was a certain divine irony in the fact that on that day I was that student. I stood up and faced him impassively as he barreled toward me, his hand upraised. As he drew near I offered him the holy water. He took it from me, slapping at my hand like he was giving me an aggressive high five.

Lecture over, my timid classmates clustered around me and thanked me for my courageous face-off. Some mumbled words of approval; others thought I had risked too much for too little. I was so numb I couldn't react to the lack of their promised support. My usual peace of mind was shattered as I pondered the implications of what I had done. Were he to report to the staff what had transpired, I could be in for a rough ride. I had no idea what to expect. On the other hand, had he not said he respected my right to speak my mind, that he would *die* for it? Did he really mean this, or was he posturing?

The following day he entered the classroom, silently fixed his gaze on me, turned to the blackboard and with swift strokes outlined on one side what was theological opinion, and on the other what was doctrinal truth—that is, truth to be held in faith. These were the very distinctions I had made the previous day. In effect, he was implicitly acknowledging that I had been correct.

When he had finished writing, he pointed to one side of the blackboard and said, "*This* is of faith." Then, to the other side, "And *this* is theological opinion. Class dismissed."

This procedure was unheard of. It augured poorly for me. In our system God had spoken through him.

There was no winner in this sorry contest, and surely no celebration of any kind. Both his feelings and mine were stuffed, not attended to. Despite this, I could sense from his abruptness and lack of grace that there were dark clouds on the horizon of my journey toward the priesthood. The fault was not all on his side; I had probably been too headstrong. Or, I could have approached him with this matter in private. Hunkering down, I waited for the next shoe to fall.

I didn't have long to wait. The staff had a faculty meeting. My case was a major item on their agenda. One of the professors, Father John Fowlie, later told me that the discussion among them had been intense. Tempers were frayed. The priest who declared that he would defend to the death my right to speak was demanding I be disqualified from pursuing the priesthood. It was his opinion that I was "stubborn," clearly an untrustworthy prospect as a carrier and minister of the true faith.

Father John Fowlie saved me. He insisted that I was full of promise, that at worst I had been imprudent. Ultimately the staff accepted his moderate position. I was called in to receive a reprimand for my poor judgment, for being argumentative.

The seriousness of their decision, however, emerged some months later when I was told by the provincial, the head of the Franciscans on the West Coast, that I would not be sent to graduate school until I spent several years of seasoning and maturation, offering proof that I could be loyal and true to the teaching Church.

Actually I was relieved; I had no aspirations to pursue a

doctorate in theology. Instead I was bent on an active ministry, preferably among my Mexican people.

This ministerial bent had already equipped me to relieve my parents of a painful burden they still carried. The Catholic theology in which I had been so carefully raised established three possible destinations for the soul.

First, those who died in God's favor, or in the state of sanctifying grace, the life of God in the soul, would go to Heaven, there to behold God forever in the ecstasy of the beatific vision.

Second, those who died in mortal sin, absent this grace, would go to Hell, there to suffer its painful and eternal flames without the possibility of reprieve.

Finally, those who died in the sweet innocence of infancy but without the baptismal event that would have endowed them with sanctifying grace would go to Limbo, a place of natural happiness where no one enjoyed the direct, face-to-face vision of God.

Even as a child, I thought this last provision a terrible inequity, a punishment of the innocent, incompatible with God's goodness. To attempt to make sense of this contradiction, our catechetical teachers provided us with the following limp analogy. A thimble can hold very little liquid. Filled to the limit of its capacity, as full as it can be, it knows nothing of the capacity of a pitcher which is capable of holding much, much more. It knows only that it is as full as it can be. Thus, the soul of the unbaptized infant in Limbo, like a thimble, is as happy as it can be, knowing nothing of what it is missing, that is, nothing of heaven where a soul sees God face-to-face.

My parents early on had had a child who died in the womb without baptism. They grieved not only the loss of this daughter, but, true to Church teaching, mourned the "fact" that she would be in Limbo and that after their death their child would be in one place and they in another. My parents simply accepted this the way it was; it didn't have to make sense. Whatever the Church proclaimed through its priests was God's truth.

They did not know that the existence of Limbo was not a revealed truth like the existence of God or the doctrine of the Trinity. Limbo was opinion and a poor one at that. It was a spin-off of the teaching that baptism was necessary for salvation.

Ordinarily, baptism takes place by water in a sacramental ceremony in the baptistry of the parish church. But what of those who through no fault of their own are ignorant of the necessity of this spiritual birth for salvation? These persons of good will could be saved by the baptism of desire. That is, if an adult desired to do God's will, which was that all be baptized by water and the Holy Spirit, then clearly the person's desire to do God's will implied actual baptism by water.

Infants, however, presented a special problem because they were incapable of any desire or intentionality. For them then there was no back door to salvation. It was actual baptism by water or none at all.

I wrote a letter to my parents explaining that Limbo was just an idea proposed by some Catholic writers. They were not bound to believe that they would be forever separated from the daughter they never knew. When, as expected, they responded with extreme relief and gratitude, I was happy that I could relieve them of a needless, heavy worry. And, though I didn't allow myself to acknowledge it, I grew angry at the mindless suffering this misinformed theology had inflicted on them. The only way to vent my feelings was simply to repeat the story to anybody who would listen.

In the name of religion, my parents were made to endure yet another form of suffering, one having to do with my brother, Joe. After World War II he fell in love with a divorced woman, Carole, who had a new-born baby by her war-time husband. The marriage was brief and fell apart. Because she and her former husband were Protestants and free to marry, their union was *prima facie* valid and, according to the Church's canon law, indissoluble. According to the Church she was not free to marry again unless death took her partner. But her spouse lived.

On New Year's day, 1949, Joe and Carole entered a marriage which the Catholic Church considered invalid. Technically, they were now living in sin; their sexual intimacy was immoral and every sexual act, regardless of the human love it purported to celebrate or promote, condemned poor Joe to hell. He could no longer participate in the sacramental life of the Church (Confession, Communion) unless he were to step away from Carole and confess his delict.

My parents did not understand any of this theology. They regretted not having a Church wedding, but initially their good common sense led them to be lovingly accepting of my brother and his bride.

However, their parish priest told them that Joe was excommunicated and thus prohibited from participation in the Church's sacramental life by reason of this invalid marriage. Only the Pope could lift the excommunication and restore Joe to Communion. He went on to tell them that this penalty rendered their son a *vitandus*, to be shunned, to be avoided at all costs. Furthermore, it was incumbent upon my parents to tell Joe that they could no longer receive him or his bride into their home. In fact, they could have nothing whatsoever to do with him. This meant total severance.

I could imagine their consternation. This was their first son, the apple of their eye, a loving, caring, responsible man without malice. But since through a priest the Church had spoken, they must comply. *"Roma locuta, res finita,"* "Rome has spoken, case closed." My parents adhered to this insane directive regardless of the pain it brought to them, their son and his new wife, their other children, and our relatives and friends. Sadly, the parish priest's directive was in fact devoid of any basis whatsoever in canon law; indeed, in common sense.

Most of this information came to me long after the marriage of Joe and Carole, so the wake of this suffering was long. When I finally learned of the situation, I sought confirmation of my opinion from the canon lawyer at the theological seminary. His response was terse: the priest's directive was rubbish.

I needed to convey this to my parents immediately. I wrote them a letter and a week later I received a response from my father thanking me profusely for the information. They contacted my brother in Chula Vista, California, and arranged a reconciliation. The letter contained not a word of criticism of the priest who in God's name had afflicted them in his ignorance. They were simply grateful that this aspect of their suffering was alleviated; they were once again united with a son whom they dearly loved.

Another serious issue would still remain: for another twenty years, Joe would still be considered unworthy, living in mortal sin because he was still living with a woman who had previously been married. He was still excluded from the sacramental life of the Church.

Meanwhile, my seven classmates and I were steadily moving through a challenging academic theological program that involved course work in moral and dogmatic theology, holy scripture, canon law, church history, liturgy and spiritual direction. A grasp of the principles and directives of moral theology and a facility in applying them were important, even critical, to the Sacrament of Confession. Lay Catholics would be coming to us, submitting their failings, and we would be assessing the kind, gravity and frequency of their sins so that we could impose an appropriate penance—usually prayers.

Should they confess their sins forthrightly and completely and were truly penitent for having committed them, we as priests could absolve their sins in the name of God. This was a priest's awesome role, flowing from his share in the power of the keys that Jesus bestowed upon Saint Peter before He Himself ascended into Heaven to sit at the right hand of God the Father.

For four years we studied the basic principles of moral theology, then in turn each of God's ten commandments as well as the six commandments of the Catholic Church. All sins offended God, but we learned to distinguish mortal sin (that which destroyed our connection with God) from venial sin (that which did not) and, by focusing on the virtues violated by each act, to discern the kind and number of sins committed. For example, patricide was actually a double sin since it violated not only the sanctity of life but the virtue of filiation.

As with all things, there was good news and bad. Some of the material we studied was excellent and concerned practical everyday topics. For example, under the fifth commandment, "Thou shall not kill," we considered the obligation to avoid whatever unreasonably threatens life, and to use reasonable means to sustain life. This morally bound us to use ordinary though not extraordinary means to this end, even where modern technology had made the latter available.

The section of moral theology most troublesome to me was reserved for the fourth and final year of theology, just before we were given jurisdiction to go out into the ministry. This was *de sexto*, the sixth commandment: "Thou shalt not commit adultery." This tract considered every aspect of sexual behavior not as a healthy expression of love but only under the aspect of its sinfulness. The area of study with the detailed clarity of its proscriptive norms made it impossible for me to avoid the troublesome sexual behavior of my childhood. Up to this point I had managed to blur old memories but now they intruded into my consciousness like petulant children demanding attention.

Even though the class material focused not on us but on the penitents who would be confessing their sins to us, every concept, every distinction, every classification, however abstract, bathed my past with brilliant light. What I saw there filled me anew with shame and confusion. Utilizing all my well-developed skills of repression, I applied myself to the course material.

The Catholic Church's approach to the matter of sex proceeded from the assumption that the primary purpose of sexual activity is the procreation of children and secondarily to allay the concupiscence, or disordered sexual desire, of the male partner. His sexual satisfaction was considered important to keep him from straying from his wife. This point of view totally ignored the sexual needs and desires of the woman.

Flowing from the procreative purpose is the inference that the only appropriate *locus* of sexual intercourse is a true and valid marriage, the only natural basis and environment for a family. I was startled to read in our text that even in marriage, sexual activity of any kind, such as touching, caressing, mutual exploration was not tolerated unless intentionally directed to full-on intercourse.

The natural progression of the sex act, the words said, is toward ejaculation of semen, the natural destiny of which is the vagina. Any deliberate obstruction of this natural progression, whether by the male's withdrawal or the use of some contraceptive device for the male or female, is a grave sin. Surgical procedures, too, designed to impede the descent of the ovum to the uterus, or to prevent the sperm from entering the vagina, are gravely illicit.

The couple's sole task is to accept God's disposition in the matter of spousal love-making. Should there be conception, He would provide the grace, the financial support and emotional wherewithal to sustain the child and the family. Even to me, as distant as I was from the adult responsibilities of marital love, parenting and earning a living in the world, this teaching seemed too cerebral, completely out of touch.

Even more obviously, therefore, outside of wedlock any intentional sexual thoughts and desires are gravely wrong. And even if the stimulation is involuntary or unintentional, such as a nocturnal emission, the obligation is to steel oneself against any sexual pleasure and its accompanying fantasies, or to distract oneself immediately upon becoming aware of what had occurred.

Our classes were not totally devoid of humor. In the section on bestiality, for example, after the caution that bestiality—that is, having sex with an animal—was a serious offense against God, the professor noted, *"Sed raro fit cum tigris,"* that is, "But it is rarely done with tigers." In the midst of all these ponderous, dire prohibitions, a funny one-liner was most welcome; we could let off a little steam in laughter.

Father John Fowlie, my recent savior with the faculty, taught this course as well as the canon law of marriage. He had come to us out of the parish ministry, so he had a more realistic, grounded orientation. Beyond the approved Latin text he provided us with a small booklet which was not standard fare. Written by a medical doctor it was realistically descriptive. In two sections it covered first the sexual anatomy of the male and female and second, a description of how to make love, from foreplay to climax. Here was a clear and interesting presentation of normal sexuality. For the first time in our training we read about the sexual capacity of the woman for pleasure and how that pleasure could be stimulated.

The material was explicit and fascinating. Father John explained that as professionals, we were not only entitled but *required* to learn all that we could from this material.

"Don't worry if it stimulates you," he said.

And, indeed, the booklet was almost more than I could handle at the virginal age of twenty-five, even if, as he said, it was professionally required.

Two months later we were abruptly ordered to turn back the booklet. As was the custom, no explanations were given. It was only later that we learned unofficially that although the booklet had been in use in many seminaries throughout the United States, someone in authority had been alarmed by its frankness and reported this to the Vatican. Immediately, the Roman Congregation for Seminaries ordered the booklet confiscated, forbidding its use. As far as I was concerned the intervention came too late; I had already been exposed to a positive, normal, enlightened treatment of sexual love.

A concept in moral theology important to the priest-confessor in assessing the gravity of a sinful act was the notion of *parvitas materiae*, or slightness of matter. This is seen most clearly in the issue of justice, which obliges us, among other things, to respect the property of another. For a violation of this virtue to be considered a serious sin, the "matter," that is, the "amount of damage" needs to be grave. If a child steals candy from a store owner, this is a "slight" amount. If one steals a day's pay or more from another, this is mortally sinful because the amount is sufficiently damaging to the victim and his family.

This concept was also applied to the obligation to attend Mass on Sundays and on other Holy Days during the Church year. To arrive a few minutes late, even up to the end of the sermon but before the beginning of the preparation of the bread and wine, is a venial sin. However to arrive this late and then to leave immediately after the priest's Communion constituted a mortal sin because the aggregate constituted a significant "amount" of the Mass.

On the other hand, a lie precisely as a lie was always a venial sin—unless the lying act violated another virtue. For example, if in addition the lie ruined someone's reputation, the virtue of justice would also be violated and the lie would constitute a mortal sin on that account. The concept of *parvitas materiae*, however, was in no way applicable to the matter of sex. Outside of a true and valid marriage, any sexual thought, desire, sensation, or action is always a mortal sin unless resisted.

In the matter of the Church precept forbidding the eating of meat on Fridays, we learned that the norm of slightness of matter was also applicable. The formal teaching of the Church directed that the eating of meat on Friday was mortally sinful if a sufficient

amount of meat had been consumed. The amount of "slight matter" was fixed at anything less than two ounces. However, we were
not encouraged to ask the penitent confessing the sin of eating
meat on Friday, "How much meat did you eat? Was it less than
two ounces?" Nor were we directed to educate this person about
the distinction between grave and slight matter. Was this, I wondered, because as priests we were not to be seen as encouraging
sin of any kind, including venial?

As fledgling priests, we were learning at a professional level
what had been established and continued to be taught by the su-
preme authority in Rome. Questions directed to the Vatican
about Church teaching were allowed, even encouraged, if designed to solicit information about official interpretations; but
certainly not if they contested a decision that had been solemnly
rendered. Even less tolerated were doubts about the Church's capacity to bind consciences.

In these final days of our preparation for priestly ministry, I
still did not consider these extraordinary ecclesiastical dicta as
overreach. The approach seemed reasonable and verifiable. The
theory, enunciated in the first volume of our moral theology texts,
acknowledged that the primary tribunal or judgment seat for each
person's moral decisions lay within the individual.

This internal forum had two significant characteristics. It was
private, for only the individual truly knew all the circumstances of
the action taken as well as its disposition of conscience at the time,
and it was *sacred*, for here the Triune God dwelt and dispensed His
wisdom and strength to the true seeker.

The conclusion was that we each have an internal guidance
system that carries us to the truth if only we are of good will, ask
for feedback, and listen intently. The fine print, however, reduced
one's personal dignity by stating unequivocally that each of us,
from the Pontiff to the lowliest Catholic layman, is deeply flawed
by the consequences of "original sin."

The guilt of Adam and Eve had resulted in man's alienation
from God and had been atoned for by the condign sacrifice offered in our name by Jesus to His Father. So in our very essence
we had been reconciled to God, sharing His life anew. But four
sequelae of the fall of Adam and Eve remained to taint our nature.

First we are left with a darkness of intellect or a lack of clarity in our understanding of God's will in our behalf. This impediment leaves us open to unenlightened decision-making even when we are at our most open to discerning what God wants from us.

Second, our desires are now disordered and undisciplined. This phenomenon is called concupiscence, and although its strongest expression lies in the area of sexuality, it is meant to apply across the board to whatever one yearns for. Often we eat and drink for pleasure without regard for the nutritional value of the food or beverage. Or we take time off from work even when the call is clear that we must work for a living to maintain home and family. Or we engage in leisure activities beyond our means and then fail to pay our debts. Or we drink intoxicants immoderately, injuring our body, impeding judgment, offending those dear to us, slighting our employers, diminishing our future.

Third, our will is so weak that even when we know the right path to take we often fail to take the proper action. This is a kind of enervating ennui. We float listlessly, wasting time and opportunities, failing to realize the divine possibilities that lie within us. Saint Paul referred to this when he confessed that he found himself at times doing what he did not want to do, and at other times failing to do what he wished to do.

Fourth, our relationships present us with daunting challenges. We do not see in one another the brother or sister we truly are to one another but we see the other as our competitor.

I could verify all of these characteristics, drives and impulses in my own personal experience. They resonated deeply within me. It was true that, despite the insights, the clarity, and the strength I derived from the liturgy and from my private prayer life, I was often weak-willed, imprudent, disrespectful of my neighbor, and at the mercy of disordered desire. But this was no reason for despair, for Jesus after His resurrection from the dead had endowed His first followers, the Apostles, with the "grace of office."

This meant that although they too as human beings had suffered the same fourfold burdensome inheritance from Adam and Eve, they had additionally received a special grace from their position in the Church. Their office had empowered them to overcome this countervailing legacy and to transmit truth to the rest of the Church with a special assurance of purity. This special grace enjoyed by our ecclesiastical shepherds kept them in the truth as they pointed out the righteous path for the entire flock. Because of this absolutely trustworthy guidance, we were to bend our obstinate, proud wills and submit in obedience to ecclesiastical authority in all matters.

I felt safe within this ecclesiastical womb that promised me eternal life for my obedience. True, I might chafe a bit at the constriction, at the abdication of my mind and will, but there was a rich kind of freedom from anxiety in the clarity of knowing when I was in the state of sanctifying grace. At any given moment I could be assured that I was fit for the kingdom of heaven. It was awe-inspiring to know that I would be transmitting this same information to the lay Church at large.

In all of moral theology there was only one reference made to the Jews. It referred to them as the Chosen People from whom came Jesus. In the divine plan He was the fulfillment of the Jews' expectations. Despite the fact that He was the Son of God, the Jews rejected Him. To them He was not the long-awaited Messiah. Instead they dared to cling to what they considered their law, the *halachic* aspects of the Torah.

Catholic theologians had something brief but devastating to say about this. They drew the following distinction: after Jesus came into the world and proclaimed His divine Sonship to His people, the fulfillment of the original revelation to Moses on Mt. Sinai, the *halachic* law was totally stripped of its power to sanctify. It was now *mortua*, dead, devoid of life and incapable of giving life. It no longer sanctified, consoled, instructed, guided, nurtured or sustained. Nothing. It was dead.

Second, after Jesus died and rose from the dead, the Jewish Law was not merely dead but *mortifera*, death-*dealing*. Rather than vitalize those who dedicated themselves to fulfilling the Torah's *mitzvot*, or commandments, it inflicted spiritual death upon them.

Thus the Christian Church, which thought of itself as superseding the Jews as God's chosen people, would bring forth from the "Old" Testament its true and full meaning—to be found in the incarnated God, Jesus.

Not one person among us questioned this mind-boggling,

devastating claim about the Jews. The teaching was ours to accept in obedience and we did. None of us reflected what that implied: by now almost twenty centuries of Jews had supposedly not merely clung to a dead, terminally toxic Torah, but had revered it, kissed it, and unfolded its empty meaning to countless new generations of "morally dead" descendants.

It never occurred to anyone in the seminary, staff or student, to challenge this. No one saw this view as the basis of centuries of hatred and persecution. I prayed that the Jews' current rejection of the Son of God was no longer malevolently chosen (as had been frequently charged by the Church across the centuries) but done in "invincible ignorance." By the grace of the Church anti-Semitism flourished and (*sotto voce*) still does.

In Scripture classes, the Jewish Tanach, that is, the first five Books of the Bible, the prophets and the "writings," was called the "Old" Testament in contradistinction to the "New." The New Testament, now triumphantly seen as fulfilling the Old, was the covenant between God and man mediated by the reconciling death and resurrection of Jesus.

Again, no one among us ever mentioned the arrogant, holier-than-thou anti-Semitic issues this implied. Nor did anyone take notice of the anti-Semitic notions, both implicit and explicit, reflected in some of the New Testament writings, especially the so-called Passion Narratives describing the death and resurrection of Jesus. Whenever this insoluble, ugly dispute between Jew and Christian arose in the classroom—that is, the Christian tenet that Jesus was the only way to our Father in Heaven—we would simply trust that God in His Wisdom would work it out. A kind of "Oops! No malice intended."

Great attention was given to all aspects of the liturgy from the theology of communal prayer to the practical details of ritual acts. I loved the spiritual aspect of my training, particularly since for two years I had been practicing the Bonaventurian form of contemplative prayer. This spirit of union with God gave it vitality.

As did most languages, Latin sat easily on my lips, whether recited or sung. Gregorian chant was hypnotic and entrancing in its melodic, enduring simplicity and syncopated rhythms. It brought great dignity to worship and invited soulful expression of awe, reverence, penitence, and joy. The rules governing our rendition of the chant were based on the work of the Benedictine monks of the Solesmes Congregation in France. There was nothing more inspiring to me than to hear the voices of Franciscan seminarians at 6:00 in the morning singing a Gregorian Mass in the Old Mission Church, their voices reverberating off the ancient walls in musical prayer.

I was ordained to the Catholic priesthood on June 29, 1951, the Feast of the Apostles, Saints Simon and Jude. As was the custom, Franciscans gathered from near and far to celebrate the occasion. Their warm brotherly presence provided special joy, for the bonds we had developed with them in the course of our lengthy training quickened precious memories within us. An intense, silent, ten-day retreat had prepared us for this holy event, sharpening our minds and hearts for the gravity of the transformation that was about to be wrought in us by the consecratory power of the Bishop. We would be forever changed, "priests forever according to the order of Melchisedech," King and Priest of Salem, whose own Old Testament priesthood, offering a sacrifice of bread and wine, had foreshadowed the Catholic priesthood and its mode of sacrifice to God.

I was blissfully happy, eager to join my parents and my three brothers and their families in love and gratitude. My heart was full. I had arrived at this point in my life only because of my family's unflagging support.

We neophytes entered the Old Mission Church and began a slow march up the central aisle toward the brilliantly lit sanctuary. Following behind were the Franciscan theological staff who would assist the Bishop during the ordination. I saw the dear faces of my father and mother turned toward me, their eyes moist with pride and joy.

The ceremony was over in two hours. There were eight newly ordained Franciscan priests joining the ranks of their brethren on the West Coast. We marched down the main aisle, for the first time fully clad in priestly vestments, white amice around the hood of the Franciscan garb, white alb reaching to the floor, cincture around the waist, stole around the neck and shoulders and crossed at the chest, and finally, a fiddle-shaped chasuble over it all. These were the vestments we would don every day of our lives to offer the Holy Sacrifice of the Mass. This was a garb recognizable by every Catholic around the world.

It was a delight to join my parents at the reception held in the parish hall following the ceremony. With excitement I introduced my family to the other families and to all of my newly ordained Franciscan brothers. The reception was brief because each of us would be traveling home, there to celebrate our first Mass.

My brother, Henry, his wife, Terry, their three year-old daughter, Theresa, my parents and I were en route to Phoenix, Arizona, a trip of some ten hours. We started out about 3:00 that afternoon, but brake trouble in Los Angeles stopped us and with time spent for repairs, we did not arrive in Phoenix until 5:00 in the morning. Henry dropped me off at the monastery and took the rest of the family home to freshen up. They returned within the hour.

With only them in attendance I offered my very first Mass. As I looked out from the sanctuary they seemed very small in the vastness of the church, but a sense of great intimacy overwhelmed me as I offered Mass for them. I felt completely fulfilled. Henry served the Mass, spinning off the Latin responses as confidently as he had done as a young boy in this parish so many years ago.

The pure joy of the event was somewhat tainted, however, when my father refused to come up to receive Communion. This confused and pained me. Later I learned the reason. While brushing his teeth that morning he had inadvertently swallowed some toothpaste with his saliva. According to the Church's hard-and-fast directive he judged he had broken his fast. But I had so looked forward to giving my father Communion.

For the moment I was angry and disappointed. But only for the moment; tomorrow at my first Solemn Mass my father and I would then complete our union in the Eucharist. I excitedly gave Communion to my rapturous mother and to my dear brother, Henry, and his wife, Terry. Then, after fifteen minutes of private prayer in thanksgiving for the Mass we had just offered, my family left to get some much-needed sleep. So did I. The first solemn Mass was scheduled for the next morning. We all needed space to resuscitate.

The next day dawned insufferably hot. It was July 1, 1951. As expected, Phoenix had fired up its summer sun for the occasion. Fortunately, the church was air-conditioned and I could don all my priestly vestments over my woolen, brown Franciscan habit without too much discomfort. I could hardly believe that I was now a priest in the very same church where I had been baptized as a baby, and had, in early childhood, been confirmed. Here for the first time I had confessed to sins I did not understand, and here I had received my first Communion.

Now the building seemed so much smaller than when I was a child. The priest who was originally responsible for sending me off to the seminary was my assisting deacon. He hovered over me proudly, reassuring me in my nervousness.

It was time to begin. All the study, training and discipline of the past twelve years served me well. I could focus on the awesome nature of what I was doing. All the rubrics that dictated what to do and how and when to do it seemed second nature. The choral music was contrapuntal to the melody of my prayers as I offered the ultimate sacrifice to God in the name of the Catholic community of believers here and everywhere in the world.

Bathed in the profundity of this event, I moved slowly through the Mass and concluded by blessing each congregant who knelt at the Communion railing. One young woman fainted as I prayed over her; afterward colleagues teased me about my awesome power.

Everyone in the sanctuary preceded me at the recessional. When I reached the front pew where my parents were standing waiting for me, I recalled a sharp childhood memory:

I am in fourth grade. It is the end of the school day. My father finishes a linoleum job early and thoughtfully drives by school to offer me a ride home. He is in his old Durant with its odd front grille. I am filled with shame. It is such an odd and poor car. All the other parents are arriving in Fords, Chevrolets, or Dodges. They park next to his quaint automobile. His appearance, too, embarrasses me. His shoe tips are turned up like an elf's. He smells strongly of linoleum paste. My inner turmoil increases. I am ashamed of my father.

And I am ashamed of my shame, for I love him dearly. I hide from him, successfully eluding his search for me around the playground and the buildings. He leaves without me.

I had never acknowledged this disgraceful behavior to anyone. Now, standing before him as a priest in a crowded church, it was important for me to acknowledge him properly. Now was a wonderful time to express my pride in him as well as in my mother. I paused and with an inviting gesture asked them both to accompany me down the aisle. The three of us exited jubilantly.

Later at the dinner in the parish hall, my emotions overflowed in tears of gratitude for the sacrifices my parents had made. They had made it possible for me to get to this place. It was the first time, though it was not to be the last, that as an adult I had openly cried in the presence of others.

Two weeks later I was back with my seminary classmates at the Old Mission in Santa Barbara. We were to wind up our studies, take a comprehensive examination, and receive faculties to function in the Archdiocese of Los Angeles. The year was even more intensely focused now; daily Mass started each day. I was no longer director of the choir and could now sing when and if I wanted to, freely, without pressure. There was abundant time for prayer. I found myself seeking out moments in addition to those provided by the community routine, to sit quietly, wordlessly, in meditation.

> *In the early '50s research conducted on anti-Semitic attitudes among New York University students concluded that those who were members of Catholic and Protestant religious clubs, "regardless of their religious affiliation, were found to be significantly more anti-Semitic that those not affiliated with religious groups."*

Our lengthy preparation for ministry over at year's end, the excitement now concerned our first appointments as priests. At least I knew where I would not be going—that is, to graduate school. I had been told some time before that my imprudent, impudent, confrontation with the professor in dogma class had effectively botched that possibility. So I waited intently for the list to indicate where I would be stationed and what kind of work awaited me. When I was finally told, it was both good and bad news.

The bad news was that I was to be a high school teacher; I disliked teaching. The good news was that I was to be stationed at my home parish, Saint Mary's, and could therefore see my family on a regular basis.

Besides Latin I, Latin II, and religion, I would be required to teach biology, a science I had never studied. In order to prepare for this I needed to attend summer school at the University of San Francisco and to study physiology. In theory that was to be enough training for me to teach freshman biology. I soon found out differently!

Part III
Early Ministries

IN SAN FRANCISCO I took up temporary residence in the Friary attached to Saint Boniface parish in the Tenderloin. Both the church and its pastor (a gifted beggar to restaurants, supermarkets and businesses) were known nationally for the daily meals they served to the homeless. I took courses in physiology and education. Physiology was particularly challenging; I thanked God for the brevity of summer school. My classmates were all female nurses in training, far more prepared and probably far more invested in learning the material.

For all my ignorance of physiology, however, I was able to pass the multiple-choice exams due to my knowledge of the Latin and Greek roots of the medical terminology. My educated guesses proved sufficiently accurate to earn me a B. But did this equip me to teach biology?

On weekends I was expected to help with Mass and confessions at Saint Boniface. This was an experience I truly enjoyed. In midsummer I was asked to cover for a week as chaplain for an emergency hospital; I was assured calls would be infrequent. That proved to be true, despite the size of San Francisco and the nature of the Tenderloin. However, there was one exception which tested my mettle.

At 2:00 in the morning I got a phone call from the hospital to stand by and await the arrival of an ambulance. This was a new experience for me. Full of trepidation, I donned my Franciscan habit and raced down the stairs to await the medics well inside the iron gate by the side of the church as I had been advised. The streets were dangerous, especially at night. Soon the ambulance arrived, picked me up, and drove the three miles to the emergency room. There lay a woman on a gurney dressed in a long gown, foam bubbling at the corners of her mouth.

"This woman has just died of tuberculosis; she is still very contagious," warned a nurse. "Touch her as little you can, especially in the area of her mouth where you see the foam."

I thanked her for the discomforting information, put on my stole and started to unscrew my container of sacred oils. Considering the illness which had taken her life, I judged it sufficient to anoint her only on the forehead. Just as I began to recite the opening prayers, her hysterical husband rushed into the room. He darted to his deceased wife, loudly protesting his love for her. Sobbing, he cradled her face with both hands and tenderly caressed it.

For a moment I was touched by his love, his profound grief. But then, with mounting alarm, I saw him wipe the foam from her mouth, turn to me, grasp my hands in his sticky ones, and plead with me to pray for his departed wife.

"My God," I thought, "what are his contaminated hands doing to mine?"

However, I was able to maintain enough composure to comfort him as well as I could. As he quieted down and was led away I could envision *Mycobacterium tuberculosis* multiplying on my hands and spreading through my body with lightning speed. My flesh crawled with anxiety. I itched. I scratched. Everything took on loaded significance until, gratefully, I heard through my panic the E.R. nurses urging me to wash up with a special antiseptic solution. I did, but for several weeks I remained only half-convinced that the scrubbing would have been effective.

I had been counting on the time between summer school in San Francisco and the start of the school year in Phoenix as an opportunity to get familiar with the biology textbook which our high school was using. No such luck. I was told to report immediately to Queen of Angels Hospital in Los Angeles for three weeks to substitute for one of the chaplains there. Annoyed, I attempted to explain that I needed time to prepare for teaching biology, a course I had never studied myself.

My provincial superior assured me that since I was very bright I could certainly handle high school sophomores. "When you have time to study some biology," he said, "you can get one of the medical interns at the hospital to help you."

I was disappointed and angry at the provincial's lack of understanding but could not alter this temporary assignment. "You're in the army now," I said to myself. When I arrived at the hospital, the resident chaplain helped to make my three weeks there a rich experience, one that invited me to utilize in the real world much of what I had learned in the cloistered atmosphere of our theological seminary.

Most of the patients were Catholics. It was my job to visit them daily, tend to their spiritual needs, hear their confessions, bring them Communion, anoint the seriously ill, comfort the bereaved. The patients and their families were receptive, truly grateful for my help. Personal contact fed my soul. But, unfortunately, this did not teach me any biology.

The summer over, I headed home to Phoenix, the city of my childhood. I found the Franciscan staff warmly welcoming and eager to help a rookie. Most were seasoned veterans and happy to guide me through problems and crises. The principal, Father Xavier Harris, was particularly helpful. His sense of humor eased me through many awkward moments when as a teacher I learned the protocols of the Catholic high school scene.

Soon into the school year I learned that some members of the staff had reservations about me; my reputation had preceded me. Back in the seminary I had sided with Fathers Alan McCoy and Oliver Lynch, whose spirituality was viewed as extreme, and I was reputed to be one of their followers.

The crux of that duo's questionable beliefs lay in their attitude toward the place of pleasure in Christian spirituality. The two were careful to say that pleasure in itself (unless proscribed under certain circumstances) is a gift from God and should be innocently enjoyed. However, moving to the question of actively pursuing union with God, they held that in the preliminary stages of spiritual life it is important to tame desire by engaging only in those pleasureful activities that are necessary or very useful for one's health.

This would eliminate cigarettes, alcoholic and non-alcoholic beverages, candies and pastries etc. It would discourage naps unless necessary or very useful for reasons of health.

"Control over desire," they said, "prepares us for a special openness to divine illumination and ultimately to profound union with God."

Their theory was quite disconcerting because it challenged the way life was currently being lived by most in the Franciscan community. The majority simply enjoyed in moderation the innocent pleasures that came their way. This in no way conflicted with their silent prayer. This difference between the two sides made it very awkward for them to relax together. The "ascetics," led by Fathers Alan McCoy and Oliver Lynch, were judged divisive, their belief about the use of pleasure only marginally Christian.

So it was that some few members of the Saint Mary's community were voicing their distress to our Superior that, as an ascetic, I might be bringing divisiveness to the community. They complained that I wasn't drinking or eating at our evening recreations. Recently I didn't go swimming with members of the staff when I had the opportunity to do so.

The Superior called me into his office and presented the case for those who had complained. "They [unnamed] say that you will not swim with them."

"I don't like swimming," I explained. "Never have, never will."

That did not satisfy him. With some somberness, as if over an issue of grave importance, he said, "I'm commanding you under the pain of mortal sin to go swimming at the retreat house before the week is up."

"I don't even have a swim suit," I argued limply.

Calmly, magisterially he proclaimed, "Under pain of mortal sin I *command* you to buy a swim suit immediately."

From my theological and canonical studies I knew he was flexing muscles he didn't have; nevertheless, I yielded, bought the suit, and grudgingly went swimming as infrequently as I could.

Good enough to prove to my anxious confreres that I was not courting heresy.

As for my new job as high school biology teacher, the students and I had a love-hate relationship. They tested me relentlessly and forced me to use disciplinary measures I had never developed and had no wish to use. Each day proved a daunting challenge.

The school's rule was that teaching staff give weekly quizzes. While this created additional work for me it proved very helpful in disciplining the class; I could always allude to the forthcoming feared Friday quiz. This served to focus the students.

While biology left me cold, teaching Latin was my forté. I was strong in languages and devoted all my preparation time to making Latin I and II interesting. Often I created simple crossword puzzles. At other times I attempted to build the students' vocabulary by highlighting commonly used English words which were Latin derivatives.

Religion was another area which I was competent to teach because it was a subject close to my heart. However, it proved to be a difficult course because the first year's material was scant, covering little of interest to the students. What made it even more boring was the prescribed method, which stressed memorization and rote recitation of definitions.

It was obvious from the students' disinterest and misbehaving that I needed to abandon the old approach and try to make the religious values themselves relevant in their lives. This took my reaching down deep to find ways to hold their interest. I discovered that if I could stretch whatever we studied to refer to their bodies, especially some aspect of sexuality, the adolescent students' interest was always piqued and led to intense participation.

For example, the sophomores were intensely interested in Christine Jorgenson, the man who was now a woman through a sex-change operation. "How could this happen?" they wanted to know. Our classroom became a forum for intense discussion. I attempted to guide them not only through the physiological aspects of the surgery as it was being described in the press, but through the morality of the process itself.

The Church had taken a strong negative position on the matter. Thus I was able to raise the issue of Church authority in moral teaching. At times we wandered far from the sophomore textbook, but survival pressed me to risk it—as did my own interest in morality and the extent of Church authority to control it.

My bugaboo remained biology. Having never studied this science I was in effect teaching it to myself so I could teach it to the students. I was hard put to remain a step ahead of the class. Again, my linguistic skills saved me. For example, should the students ask me a question I had not yet covered in my reading, I would spew out a response in words that surpassed their ability to comprehend.

"Talk English," they would call out, and I would respond, "You can't understand the later chapters until you first understand this material."

It was easier for me to face my own duplicity than to face their disrespect. However, in my own defense, I would return to give them proper information when I finally learned the answers to their questions. All in all they learned very little science. I doubt that I inspired anyone to pursue a career in biology.

The biggest challenge of all was to my sense of inwardness, which had been flourishing for many years in a monastic setting. There the atmosphere had been conducive to prayerfulness. I was accustomed to silence, to specified times for stopping all activity and gathering for meditation, to abundant opportunities for nurturant reading, to theological study. The three seminaries I had attended were a rich environment for living the liturgical seasons that took us methodically through the year.

In contrast, at St. Mary's I was forced to spend a long, frenetic day with hyperactive sophomores. And there were classes for which to prepare, exams to give and correct, grades to distribute, and long study halls to monitor. When late afternoon prayer-time arrived, my rich sense of God's presence had sadly dissipated over my exasperation and anger with the students and disappointment with myself. Next day I was back in the classroom, disciplining those that had given me a bad time the day before.

My beloved prayer time had been usurped. I was not alone in having problems with prayer. At the community evening meditation I frequently saw the heads of other weary teachers nod off, unable to stay awake.

The severe interruption of "mindfulness" that I truly loved depressed me. In some sense I knew that it was unreasonable to criticize myself for this loss—but not altogether. I began to notice that the fire of spiritual enthusiasm was waning; I feared it might go out. Prayers were becoming routine. I had little time to focus on meditation. My old practice of wordless prayer seemed to be gone.

I was only twenty-six years old and frightened. What might this foreshadow for my spirituality? What did it predict about my spiritual future? What kind of person would I be in five years? Ten? Twenty-five? Would I be insensitive, hard, judgmental, spiritually dead?

I shared my alarm with no one. I had been trained not to share intimately with anyone except my spiritual director. Here, for the first time in my young life, I was without an older priest in whom to place my trust. During the busy days I managed to push my concern out of my mind, but as soon as the quiet of prayer arrived, I slid back into anxiety, pondering my future as a priest and as a member of a religious order.

The only person available to me who could understand and support me was my mother, so grounded was she in the process of being human. She could read my every mood. She was intuitive. When I was a child and practiced the piano, she could hear my feelings in the music as clearly as she could the rhythms and melodies. Now on my visits home she could sense that something was wrong. I would explain that it was my constant dread of facing the tempestuous sea of high school sophomores. There was enough truth in this explanation to satisfy her. I decided just to plod on, trusting that God's help would sustain me.

Slowly I became a seasoned teacher. I could survive my daily teaching load: Latin I, Latin II, two classes of biology and one of religion. I learned how to monitor the early morning study hall and even the more challenging after school "jug" prescribed for students guilty of tardiness, cutting class or disrespecting teachers. Slowly I grew more and more accustomed to being stern when necessary, decisive when facing a challenge, and humorous when that seemed most appropriate. There was one time, however, when I seriously lost control.

On this particular Friday, I passed out a biology quiz and told the students they had thirty minutes to complete it. My announcement was greeted with the usual pained faces and droopy shoulders, but they all fell to—except one. He sat in the front row and, despite our close proximity, shouted to me, "I don't have a pencil or a pen!"

His classmates snickered, looking to me for a reaction. I felt humiliated at his challenge to my control of the classroom. With a frown at his unnecessary volume, I silently handed him a pen.

Then he continued his challenge of my authority, printing his name on the test paper and bellowing each letter as he wrote it: "Capital G, small E, small N, small E." Then, after a brief pause, "Capital G, small A, small N, small O." Seemingly pleased with himself he finished emphatically, "Gene Gano." Then he smiled cherubically at me.

I was livid as I started toward him. Apparently there was more anger in me than I thought showed because he sensed my energy. Melodramatically, he put his hands up to shield the left side of his face and whimpered, "Oh, please don't hit me!"

Before I knew it, I had thrown a hard left hook that caught him on the right temple. The class gasped. We were all startled, I most of all. Then I was appalled.

After a few moments, one of the students smiled approvingly in admiration and gasped, "Wow, Father Rocky."

This broke the tension a bit. I heard myself asking Gene's pardon, and in the next breath ordered him to report to the principal. His temple was already bright red and swelling ominously. What had I done? After he left I again apologized to the class at having lost control. The students joshed a little about my thunderous left hook and went back to their quiz.

The incident quickly became the talk of the school. My impulsive action could have been disastrous both for me and the school. I think what saved me from a lawsuit was that Gene did not tell his father what I had done out of fear of being punished even more severely for his disrespect toward a priest.

One weekend toward the end of the school year, a group of senior students drove to Prescott, the mile-high city to the north of Phoenix. There they "lost their virginity" to some prostitutes.

When this was discovered, the official school posture was outrage. This behavior was not only a mortal sin but a premeditated act, planned to the last detail and carried out without remorse. Privately however among the faculty there were smiles at this rite of passage. Boys will be boys. No big deal.

But personally I was angry. My training had so strongly programmed me against sex that I found it hard to deal with. I was annoyingly and rigidly legalistic: either the senior outing was terribly wrong and shouldn't be minimized, or the Catholic Church's stance on sexuality was mere posturing and her teaching authority suspect. Without my realizing it, this event had touched a vulnerable spot in my fundamentalistic ecclesiastical armor. In one catastrophic leap I bounded from the apparent trivialization of sexual sin to the total collapse of the Church's teaching authority.

Happily, at the end of the school year, the provincial board, formally called the definitorium, transferred me from my unhappy teaching post to Los Angeles. I would be headquartered in downtown Los Angeles and would have three ministries.

The primary one would be work on a radio program called "The Hour of Saint Francis," which broadcast a weekly fifteen-minute inspirational story. The director was a Franciscan priest, Father Hugh Noonan, a warm, charismatic man with an extraordinary writing talent. When a young man, he had abandoned the offer of a professional baseball career in favor of the priesthood.

My second job was to help out with men's retreats. Serra Retreat House in Malibu hosted silent weekends of spiritual lectures and prayer for Catholic laymen from all around southern California. I knew the place well. It sat majestically atop a hill just above the magnificent coast, with the blue Pacific Ocean before it and the rolling hills and shaded mountains behind.

One of my duties was to lead the retreatants in the devotional exercise of the fourteen stations of the cross, those centuries-old images commemorating the stages of Jesus' suffering and His crucifixion. Before each station we paused to read a prayer appropriate to that step in His dolorous journey.

I was also to be available to those men who wanted to go to Confession in the course of the two days. Occasionally I said Mass for them. And I also conducted the traditional, hour-long Question

Box, answering questions the men might pose about various aspects of the Catholic faith.

My third job was to assist the local pastor of Saint Joseph's Church in the heart of downtown Los Angeles. This was where I would reside. The size of Los Angeles frightened me: its vastness, breakneck pace, congested traffic, and the twisting, noisy rivers of cars streaming down the freeways day and night. I was unaccustomed to life in a city this size. Fortunately, when I arrived at Saint Joseph's Rectory on the corner of Los Angeles and Twelfth Streets in the heart of the city, the Franciscan warmth which greeted me calmed me down. Father Hugh was especially gracious.

The Hour of Saint Francis Radio Program was housed, conveniently for me, in a classroom of Saint Joseph Elementary School that adjoined the church and rectory. The heart of its ministry was the dramatization of religious stories, some real, some fictional.

I had previously had little training in English composition outside of exam essays. But initially, at least, my position at the Hour of Saint Francis didn't require me to write. My role was to edit the material prepared by our talented secretary-writer, Juanita Vaughn, and to tailor the stories to fit a fifteen-minute slot.

The radio actors, all skilled professionals with years of experience, worked for union scale. The main performer, known in radio as "the man of a hundred voices," was Pat McGeehan, an Irish Catholic in the twilight of a successful acting career. He anchored each show as narrator and in addition took a variety of roles as needed.

Background music was provided by an organist, Bob Mitchell, whose boys' choir was by that time well known. All those involved with the show had great admiration and respect for Father Hugh's artistic taste. Since I was inexperienced in matters of the real world, I had little to contribute to the story construction at the beginning. Gradually though, under the tutelage of Fr. Hugh, I grew adept at contributing story lines and character development.

Occasionally Hollywood stars came to perform for us. The most famous and memorable was Charles Laughton; he read on tape the Passion and Death of Jesus as recorded in Saint Mark. I remember him lumbering into the studio straight from the beach, dressed casually, hair tousled. His voice was so deep and resonant that it took many minutes before he could get his range up to recording levels.

Asked whether he wanted music in the background, he replied, "If you provide music, I could read the telephone book and the listening audience would find it interesting. No, I want the challenge of silence behind me."

He was easily up to the task; his mood, his interpretation and enunciation were magnificent, spellbinding. Months later, on Palm Sunday, I took a copy of his tape into the county jail. While I read quietly from the Missal in Latin, I played Mr. Laughton's recording to the prisoners. The silence and attentiveness of the prisoners spoke volumes about Laughton's power as an actor.

Most weekends I drove to Malibu to help with the retreats. I truly believed in the power of silence and enjoyed seeing dozens of men gathering quietly, prayerfully at Mass in the morning. During the day they attended talks and various devotions which we provided. The style of the Question Box which I conducted was in the tradition of "Father knows best." Father knows and Father provides answers. Personal sharing was minimal. Focus was on orthodoxy of belief and practice. That is the way it was.

On June 15, 1954, my brother, Henry, called me from Phoenix. He was terse, almost blunt. "Dad was helping me roof my apartment and fell off onto the pavement below. He's comatose and in Saint Joseph's Hospital. He may not make it; you'd better come home immediately."

The crisis with my father brought home to me the blessings of an extended family. My brothers and my mother took turns standing vigil in my father's hospital room. Solicitous relatives would come over after work and spell us to give us a chance to rest. Others cleaned our house and still others prepared food for us.

When after six days my father returned to consciousness, the news spread quickly throughout the family and we received numerous supportive phone calls. The most touching memory that I have came from my mother. She told me that on the day that my father fell, she had been sitting with her six-year-old granddaughter, Theresa, on the front porch of the apartment. She was only a few feet away from the sidewalk where he landed and lay unconscious. She grew hysterical.

Terry, her daughter-in-law, hearing the screams came running out and tended to my father while Henry called for an ambulance. In the midst of all this drama the little granddaughter took my mother's hand and said to her, "Grandma, you shouldn't be watching this. Let's go in the living room and pray." My mother responded, arose, went inside, knelt down and began to pray. From the mouths of little ones....

After two years at this job the powers-that-be assigned me as an auxiliary to the two Franciscans who were county jail chaplains. I was sent to work at the jail farms in Saugus and Newhall. In preparation for the Sunday Masses, I had to write a sermon which, I hesitate to say, invariably proved irrelevant to the inmates. In the comfort of my room, in my own head, distant from the misery of jail life, I found it impossible to write a meaningful sermon. Each time I delivered a sermon I would see the eyes of the prisoners glazing over. But when I broke away from my prepared remarks, our contact would be vastly improved.

Most of the men were incarcerated because of offenses related to substance abuse. I knew nothing about the abuse of alcohol and drugs from personal experience. Everything I knew came solely from my training in moral theology which focused not on addiction as an illness but on the harmful effect of these substances on consciousness, the most precious gift God gave to humankind. In accordance with my training I understood that the sinfulness of substance abuse derived from needlessly disabling this gift from God, trivializing it. Each act of drunkenness or drug abuse was gravely wrong, I told the men. In addition, I added, it rendered the person vulnerable to accident.

I knew nothing then of the powerful, successful movement, Alcoholics Anonymous, which by 1956 was already twenty-one years old. It would take me another twenty years before I learned that AA was the best way known to achieve sobriety.

After detoxification at the main jail the inmates were sent out to the farms at Saugus and Newhall where they grew robust with outdoor work. In truth they seemed like decent folk to me, not in the slightest way intimidating. Unfortunately, some had permitted their lives to become a vicious cycle: binge, arrest, downtown jail-time, recovery of health in Saugus or Newhall, release and repeat of the cycle. Somewhere in this mad whirl could be found a bit of grace and humor. Occasionally I would be greeted on Skid Row by a weaving, bingeing alcoholic with, "Hi, Padre. See you soon out at the farm."

In 1955 Will Herberg in his significant volume, Protestant, Catholic and Jew, *got to the essence of latent prejudice when he described how large numbers of Americans were still anti-Semitic but did not act on it.*

Meanwhile, in my life as a member of the Franciscan community I was trying nobly, with small success, to recapture the spirit of prayerfulness that had dissipated under duress in Phoenix. Early each morning, before community prayers began, I went down to the chapel in an attempt to center myself in the old way. But as I grew more introspective, I became aware that my ministry was really not feeding me spiritually. Worse—it had less and less meaning for me and there seemed to be no realistic hope that I could revive it. This shocked me. In truth I was bored with confessions that I felt were repetitious and most often irrelevant to the penitent.

I have always been capable of intense focus and by nature am patient. These personal traits helped me to pay careful attention to each person and to be understanding and reassuring. Actually, I had taken my theology and plumbed it, looked at it, examined and memorized it. And it felt like I hadn't had a fresh insight in years. From this I extrapolated that I was in deep trouble. If only after a few years of ministry I was "turned off," what would I be in twenty-five?

Consequently, I sought out several of my veteran brothers in the community and shared my angst with them. They listened patiently, respectfully, but each said basically the same thing: "Your feelings are common in ministry; your anxiety will soon pass. You simply have to realize that real work in the world is very different from the days of your being spoon-fed in a cocoon-like seminary." This sounded reasonable enough but did not satisfy me. I shelved my anxiety for the moment and resolved to wait for a better day.

The malaise, however, would not go away. In fact it worsened and drove me deeper and deeper inside myself. The loneliness and unshared terror of my deep restlessness had become too much to handle. However unthinkable the fantasy, I saw myself running away, fleeing to the East Coast, seeking a new life unencumbered by the strictures of the priesthood. And, even more insidious, I wanted to shed what I considered to be a dead Catholic theology. My weakness discombobulated me. I began to drink.

Fortunately for me, I couldn't manage alcohol as a form of escape. I had a strong aversion to its effect; I liked neither the high it produced nor the distortion of my normal awareness. Besides, I didn't like the taste. I found some wines tolerable, but at community recreational gatherings you took what was available, and wine selection was more governed by economy than by quality. Usually I didn't have enough spending money to buy liquor for drinking alone. In order to get money for any form of purchase I would have to lie and I wasn't up to that. Even when some small discretionary money came my way, it was difficult to build up a private stock of palatable wine without attracting a lot of unwanted attention. So I did what I could.

I would arrive at recreation before the group assembled and spirit away a tumbler of wine to my room for later use. Each time I did this I risked an embarrassing moment should someone see me. But I was desperate.

Recreation was a community activity, held each Wednesday and Sunday evening. We would gather to chat about the week, listen to music, read the *Los Angeles Times*, discuss politics, etc. The mood was usually upbeat, a healthy expression of our fraternity. The festivity over, I would retire to my room and gulp the wine I had appropriated. This lonely, gauche enterprise did nothing but sicken me and make sleep difficult. The truth was—and I knew it—I was trapped in a calling that no longer gripped me.

I could see no way out—except in death. The picture was depressing: I was a thirty-year-old man, in excellent physical health, committed to forty or fifty years of service in a task that no longer brought me joy. If I remained alive I would be a drag on the Franciscan community that I loved, a dead voice in the pulpit, a robot in administering the sacraments, an uninspired and uninspiring leader in a Catholic Church I still loved.

This was a kind of slow, silent death—but another kind of death came to my mind. I would kill myself. I would drive off a cliff in Topanga Canyon on my way back from the weekend retreat in Malibu. The thought was terrifying even to my disordered mind, but the accident would be suitably terminal. If I were successful in this attempt, the Franciscan community and the parish would think my death accidental. This would probably spare them embarrassment—but it would also cause them great pain. I did not wish to inflict pain on anybody: not family, not friends, not on the Franciscan community.

But—then there was the doctrine of hell. Hell was unimaginable suffering, represented by a fire that seared every quivering nerve but never consumed. Never. Hell was forever. Hell was eternal separation from everyone I loved and who had loved me, at least the "me" that they could perceive. The hell that I was presently living through was paltry compared to the suffering that awaited me in a suicidal death. God would not be mocked. And I still firmly believed in hell. That was absolute.

So whenever my mind went to the *faux* escape provided by suicide, I would skitter away from the thought. No one suspected a thing. Externally I could banter, discuss theological and political issues, appear to be balanced, even passionate about my life as a priest and a Franciscan. But most nights, when my daily round of activities was over, the veil of denial dropped and I descended into an all-too-familiar darkness.

At this low point in my faith I was reassigned to a post at Saint Anthony's Seminary in Santa Barbara, the place of my Franciscan beginnings in 1939. It was 1957. At first the news delighted me; I was leaving Los Angeles to return to my favorite city. But when I heard what I was being asked to do at the seminary my mood darkened. The provincial board in its wisdom had decided that I would make a fine spiritual director for the teenage seminarians. What irony!

I remembered the spiritual directors who had preceded me as men dedicated to prayer, inspired and inspirational speakers, patient and understanding confessors. By contrast here was I, disillusioned with the path I had chosen, dead in my heart. How could I inspire and lead young people to the priesthood in the Franciscan Order? How inappropriate could an assignment be?

As I pondered my orders I recalled a story that a retreat master had once told. The sudden death of a Franciscan missionary abroad had precipitated a crisis for his provincial superior. Just as the latter was struggling to find a replacement for this responsible and difficult post in a far-distant land, a brother knocked on his door, entered the room, strode up to his seated superior in the United States, took off his own soli deo, placed the skull cap on the table between the two of them and said nobly: *"Ecce ego, mitte me,"* or, "Here I am, send me."

At the time the heroic sensitivity of the man in this story had touched me. Now it guided me to ignore my inner struggle and simply accept my assignment despite my misgivings. Was this not God's will for me? This unexpected change of ministry was probably God's invitation to reenter the world of silent prayer and confident trust. Perhaps it would be my salvation.

The Franciscan community at Saint Joseph's, perhaps sensing my feelings of inadequacy for the new vital post, encouraged me with affirming remarks. Had some unknown insightful superior decided I needed to be sent back to the seminary in Santa Barbara? I would miss my co-worker brothers in Los Angeles, but then Santa Barbara was only a couple of hours to the north. And there could be visits.

At Saint Anthony's Seminary the community was equally affirming. They showed me to my high-ceilinged bedroom in the teacher's wing on the second floor. The room looked out over the playing field and a verdant, residential part of Santa Barbara. Later I was shown my office on the first floor, one flight up from the large study hall that accommodated the entire student body. The spartan room contained only a single book shelf, a desk and two chairs—nothing else—but the view from the window was pleasant. I could look down on the neatly kept lawn of the patio. There stood a single, majestic redwood silhouetted against the imposing concrete south wall of the chapel. Unlike the turmoil in my soul, the view was serene.

My duties at the seminary consisted of teaching a freshman religion class, hearing the confessions of whatever student wished to come to me, providing spiritual direction to those who sought it, and preparing weekly spiritual talks to the entire student body. In addition I was assigned as chaplain to Saint Francis Hospital, the only Catholic medical facility in the city.

This in itself was no small task. It involved offering a daily Mass in the hospital chapel at 6:00 each morning for the Franciscan Sisters of the Sacred Heart, the nuns who ran the hospital. Immediately afterward I took Communion to all the Catholic patients who had requested it. In the afternoon I returned to visit all the patients. Emergency calls were also part of my job description.

Fortunately, these were few and for the most part without the drama of my experience in San Francisco. Overall I liked visiting the sick. Some patients, however, didn't like to confess face-to-face. For those I tried to make it easy to refuse my offer of the sacraments. It was important to announce my availability without intruding on anybody's privacy. Two incidents stand out.

One concerned a man with a terminal illness. His physician was about to release him to spend his last remaining days at home. This patient was a Catholic who had married in the Church, divorced, and remarried civilly. Canonically, he was invalidly married and living in sin. As the appropriate consequence of this condition, were he to die impenitent, he would go to hell for all eternity. These were logical conclusions flowing from rigorous Catholic teaching.

The doctor, himself a serious, practicing Catholic, wanted his patient to have the opportunity to repent and make his peace with God before death. In other words, the patient was to confess all sinful sexual activity indulged in during this second marriage. As a sign of a serious purpose of amendment, he had to resolve either to leave his wife or promise to live celibately with her from then until his death.

The doctor pulled me aside one morning and said, "I'll hold

this patient for one more day just to give you a chance to convince him to receive the sacraments and reconcile himself to God. He's not going to last much longer. This may be his last chance. Good luck, Father."

I was struck by the solicitude of this pious physician whose faith carried him beyond the care of the mere body. I mulled over what he had shared with me. I saw his point of view. It accorded perfectly with what I had been taught in seminary. From this perspective a chance to reconcile him to God seemed an extraordinary opportunity for a priest. On the other hand, the human side of me felt the intervention to be intrusive and disrespectful. However, in accord with what I had been taught, my training won out. I decided to proceed.

I entered the patient's room. Despite his debilitated state he managed a smile and said, "Come in, Father." Overcoming my instinctive resistance, I pulled the chair close to the bed, sat down and began.

"The doctor tells me that you will be going home in a day or two."

"Yes," he responded, "there's nothing more that can be done for me here."

I hemmed and hawed awkwardly and then introduced the matter of his second marriage. His face lit up and he began to talk animatedly about the wonderful woman who had loyally nursed him through all of his lengthy bouts of serious illnesses. Over their twenty years together he had grown to love her more each day. His eyes welled up with tears as he spoke.

I watched him dab at his eyes. What could I say now? I understood that he loved her dearly and she loved him. For two decades, she had demonstrated this love with faithful commitment. How could the sexual expression of this love be sinful, I asked myself?

As gently as I could and with strong misgiving, I launched out into the sea of moral theology: the indissolubility of his first marriage, the invalidity of his second, and the consequent need to repent of the sexual love they had illicitly exchanged. He looked at me in disbelief.

"She has been loyal and true and loving," he said. "She is a splendid wife. And I'm not in the least ashamed or sorry over the love we've shared. That's the way it is. I know I'm dying. If I could make love to her again today, God knows I would. You can bet on it."

I had to admire him. Certainly he was making more sense than I, more in touch with reality than I. I blessed him with warmth, wished him courage and left. Tears flooded my eyes. This dying patient in his love seemed far more a man of God than I.

The second incident involved a youngish man who was being prepared for emergency brain surgery. His prognosis was extremely poor. I was asked to prepare him spiritually for the life-threatening event. Married, with two young daughters, he was agitated with the concern that he might die and leave his family in a financial morass. Also, he told me, he was "flat out terrified of dying."

We talked a long time as he unburdened himself. We prayed together for strength. He confessed his sins; I gave him absolution. Then I went to the door and asked his wife to come in. I told them I would leave them alone to share the few minutes before surgery commenced. And I promised to stay with his wife in the waiting room until the doctor brought us news.

Hours later the surgeon came into the waiting room. From his downcast demeanor I immediately knew the news was bad. The patient had expired on the operating table. The widow collapsed and burst into tears. After a brief explanation that neither the widow nor I heard, the doctor said softly, "I'm so sorry," and left.

I sat with the widow. There was little to say. She had just lost her life partner and would now have to face the world without him. We sat and talked quietly until she felt composed enough to go home. I felt honored to be intimately present at this stark life event, to witness the couple's courage in facing the threat of death, to support the widow who now sat with such penetrating pain. I was startled when she thanked *me* for my comforting presence. Saddened I walked out into the early morning chill and drove back to the seminary for a brief respite before my usual 6:00 A.M. Mass.

The spiritual talks I gave to the seminarians were singularly lacking in relevance to their teenage life. My thinking was dualistic: on the one hand there is the natural life of an incarnated soul that goes about its ordinary worldly business and on the other there is the supernatural life of the soul which we called sanctifying grace. To address the supernatural, I talked about the virtues, theological and cardinal, the former being faith, hope and charity and the latter, prudence, justice, fortitude and temperance. To illustrate this material I interspersed it with stories from the lives of the saints.

Significantly missing from all of this, however, were the issues surrounding adolescent development about which I knew little. I assumed that these students before me were younger versions of who I presently was. What were they doing with their sexuality? I could only address this from the perspective of Church teaching: the idealism of celibacy and the sinfulness of extramarital sex. Not once did I mention that the priestly path in religious community on which they were embarking effectively cut off any experiential way of becoming sexual human beings. The idea of relationships or intimacy was not even in my active vocabulary. Relationship simply meant blood kinship.

I truly meant to inspire these young men to aspire to spiritual greatness, to be ardent lovers of God, to persist in their faith in life's meaning, to hope for a kingdom beyond this world where we would all be transformed and reunited in unending love. I had a sense of humor and I used it to lighten up my talks. I loved to poke fun at human foibles, especially my own.

Whatever I offered, however, continued to reflect the notion that in us there was a kind of supernature lying atop a human nature. It never occurred to me to attempt a satisfactory explanation of how the two related. The preferred theory was that we were to be kind to one another because we saw Jesus in the other, thus elevating the natural kindness to a supernatural level of being which now made it pleasing in God's eyes. And perhaps these young seminarians regarded me as positively and respectfully as I had my priest teachers. But it all seemed so contrived.

Yet down deep at a level of awareness which I avoided most of the time, I still carried the old moral dissonance, the burden of inadequately confessed sexual sins. In the painful moments when

I permitted myself to become aware, I asked myself the challenging question, "How dare you preach to these young men and expect God to move their hearts? You, who are so sinful." I had to
convince myself that, however unworthy, I could still be an instrument of God's grace. Scant consolation, because each ideal I held
high for the students caused me anguish and self-loathing.

The year passed swiftly and in May of 1958 the provincial
definitors held their meeting to assess job needs and to make appropriate reassignments. My immediate superior at Saint
Anthony's Seminary seemed pleased with me so I anticipated staying on as spiritual director. No one in authority evaluated me
face-to-face or confided in me that in their eyes I had matured in
the ministry, that I was being considered for even greater responsibility.

The first indication of a major surprise came in the form of an
excited staff member who entered my office abruptly and with a
grin from ear to ear told me to have a look at the bulletin board.
He would answer no questions and give me no hint as to what he
had seen. I dropped my class preparation and walked down the
long corridor to a group of excited colleagues who had gathered
to read the assignment lists. They saw me coming and stood aside
to make room for me.

"Thanks," I said and started reading down the list of
Franciscan missions, parishes, retreat houses and schools. When I
reached the personnel changes at the Old Mission Santa Barbara,
there was my name on the staff of the theological seminary. The
changes had me listed as professor of moral theology and canon
law! This implied an extraordinary shift in the administrators' attitude toward me. I had matured sufficiently; I was trustworthy.
And they believed that I could teach even without the preparation
of graduate school education. The trust in me was welcome, but I
sensed that the implied professional responsibilities would be
overwhelming; I had already been out of this system for six years
and felt I lacked the depth of comprehension required for the job.

On the positive side, I had two things going for me. The first
of these was that I was not so out of it as I first thought. For five of
the six years since ordination I took annual examinations covering
all the canon law and moral theology we had learned in our four

years before ordination. This had required ongoing studious re-
view. The second was that I would be bringing my pastoral experience to illustrate the textbook material.

The physical move to the Old Mission was simplicity itself. It
involved packing my few belongings in a suitcase and walking
about a block's distance to my new digs, where a welcoming
Franciscan community awaited me. I looked forward to being reunited with Father Robert Pfisterer, a classmate with whom I had
walked the entire thirteen-year path of our seminary training.
Following ordination he had gone to Salamanca, Spain, where he
had received a doctorate in sacred theology in preparation for a
position on the theological staff in Santa Barbara. He and I had
always been very compatible. Not a single unkindness had ever
passed between us. He was a supportive and helpful friend.

I had the entire summer to prepare my classes for the school
year and to adjust psychologically to the idea that I was now part
of the theological staff. Out came the old Latin moral theology
texts written by a Jesuit, approved by the Vatican for use in seminaries throughout the world, as well as the Code of Canon Law
and a voluminous commentary on it by another Jesuit. I wanted to
be as prepared as possible, chiefly for the sake of clarity, but also to
answer the tough questions that could possibly arise. However, in
the area of moral teaching I was certain that I would be protected
from serious classroom disagreement or challenge because fidelity
to the traditional doctrine was paramount in our lives as priests
and members of a religious communiy. I could rely on the old dic-
tum, *"Roma locuta, res finita,"* or "Rome has spoken, case closed."

The rhythm of classes and community routine filled my days.
Spiritually I was once again immersed in the monastic way of life
I loved. The periods of silence and the private time for devotional
prayer began, little by little, to call to me again. Despite the lurk-
ing presence of my old sexual guilt I managed some peace of
mind. I began seriously to consider transferring to a contemplative community such as the Trappists.

*In 1960, in preparation for the Second Vatican Ecumenical
Council, Pope John XXIII commissioned a team under
Augustin Bea to draw up a statement on the Church's relations*

with the Jews. Originally this document was slated to appear in the Constitution on Ecumenism with a focus on the basic unity of Jews and Christians as one people who suffered an internal split. Eventually political considerations forced its transfer to a statement on the Church's relations with non-Christian religions generally. When it appeared in its final approved form, it was known as Nostra Aetate. *In its new place in the document, its intent was to show that in some way non-Christians, Jews implicitly included, could be saved within their own faith. The declaration let stand the clearly anti-Jewish statements in the Gospels and omitted any mention of the infamous charge of Jewish deicide. Nowhere did it call for Christian repentance. Nor did it ask for forgiveness of the Jews as it did of Protestants, Eastern Orthodox, Muslims. Nevertheless, even with these significant deficits it was clearly the Church speaking authoritatively and saying for the first time: Catholics must not blame Jews as a people for the death of Jesus, and Christianity owes a great debt to its "elder brothers."*

Three years later, in 1961, I was informed that the Province of Saint Barbara wanted me to pursue a doctorate in canon law. Their preference was that I go to the Antonianum, the Franciscan school in Rome. Their option offered me the opportunity to travel abroad, experience a different culture, learn yet another language, and share life with an international community. Or, if I preferred, I could attend the Catholic University of America in Washington, D.C. The latter was less daunting.

Although one part of me wanted to dare something radically different, typically I chose safety, closeness to home. My choice respected, I was told to arrange my arrival at the Franciscan Monastery of the Holy Land in Washington, D.C., in time for the fall semester.

Part IV
The Stirrings of Freedom

I LEFT FOR WASHINGTON, D.C., totally unprepared for the weather I might encounter. I was going to the East Coast, which, I reasoned from a Westerner's viewpoint, would be very cold in the fall. I was obliged by the Council of Baltimore to wear a black suit and Roman collar in public. So, of course, I went to the airport in this somber attire and over it all wore a very heavy black coat given me by a friend. The garment was winter-worthy even for the most difficult of climates. I carried two heavy suitcases, and over my shoulder, a camera. A Franciscan colleague had assured me that I had to record the significant moments of my three years at the Catholic University of America.

Actually, my attire was not too warm for that mid-September morning when Brother Cyril, a Franciscan lay brother, transported me to the airport in Santa Barbara. There I checked my bags, and thus unencumbered, visited with my Franciscan brother until time for boarding. My level of anxiety was high, but I did all I could to appear composed.

We went outside. I looked at the mountain range to the north of the airport and admired the deep shadows cast by the slanting fall sun. The rocks glowed pink against the dark green vegetation, seemingly close enough to touch. Ruminating, I thought to myself, "I am leaving my spiritual home. I was received here in 1939 at this very time of the year, twenty-two years ago almost to the day." My heart swelled with fondness for the beauty of Santa Barbara and for my Franciscan family.

In truth I had no interest in studying canon law. In the last four years of my studies for the priesthood, from 1948 to 1952, every semester had at least one course devoted to a portion of the Church's 1917 Code of Canon Law, a five-book collection of ecclesiastical laws governing every aspect of church life. My natural bent had always been toward the philosophical and spiritual.

Conversely, Church law was intensely focused on the practical details of the individual Catholic's internal and external behavior and attitudes. It was still a source of amazement to me that one entire book of the five in the Code was devoted to an elaborate system of ecclesiastical crimes and punishments. This five-book legal compilation, developed over the centuries, was considered a jewel of precision and completeness. Some legal enthusiasts even concluded that its provisions were divinely sanctioned, flowing from an authority solemnly entrusted by Jesus to Saint Peter.

Departure time was fast approaching. We went back inside the small airport. Brother Cyril asked for my priestly blessing. We stood face to face, my hand on his forehead as I blessed him, whispering, "May the blessing of almighty God, the Father, Son and Holy Ghost, descend upon you and remain with you forever." I shook his hand and thanked him for his kindness in seeing me off. Then, with much trepidation, I took my place in line and waited to board.

Fortunately, I happened to sit next to a man who kept himself occupied with a book throughout the flight. On previous occasions my Roman collar had invited the company of some inebriate who had a priest-uncle somewhere in our vast country. On the basis of this slender bond to me he would feel free to regale me with the cute improprieties he had committed growing up Catholic.

Several hours later the plane touched down smoothly in Baltimore. I retrieved my bags and stepped out of the air-conditioned building into the early fall air. I almost collapsed. It was ninety-eight degrees and humid! A little embarrassed, I took off my overcoat and made for the airport limousine to Washington, D.C.

My destination was the Franciscan Monastery of the Holy Land in the northeast section of the nation's capital. This institution's exotic title derived from the fact that the monastery buildings housed various replicas of artifacts and structures in Palestine where Jesus had lived and worked. Even his reputed tomb was reproduced. Visitors from all over the United States flocked here to the monastery to tour the spacious grounds which were truly lovely, especially the rose gardens. A large gift shop at the front entrance greeted tourists, its large bins piled high with devotional items for sale: crucifixes, rosaries, medals, scapulars and statuettes. The commercialism shocked and embarrassed me. It was like a religious five-and-dime store.

Other Franciscans from my province who had been students here before me had told me how well they had been received. This brought me a measure of confidence and allayed my pangs of anxiety. As expected, the host Franciscans whose primary role was the custody and preservation of the holy places in Palestine did in fact receive me graciously. The community had developed a fine reputation for hosting Franciscan students from various provinces in the United States as well as from abroad.

Our student community in 1961 resembled a small United Nations. They came not only from America but from Australia, France, England, Germany, Mexico, Colombia, Peru, Brazil, and Canada. We were all attending Catholic University to pursue degrees in dogmatic theology, moral theology, canon law, church history, philosophy, anthropology, sociology, psychology, or classical languages. Those who had been here for one or more years helped to smooth the entry of the new students into the monastery and the university.

The students in the Department of Canon Law at Catholic University welcomed us and helped us in practical ways. All of us in the first year of graduate work took identical courses. As would be expected, there were no electives. You showed up for the assigned classes, studied, passed examinations, and advanced to the next semester of work. Already having been in the ministry for nine years, I had the distinct advantage of experience over most of the students in the area of pastoral theology.

On the other hand, I was totally out of touch with what went on in chanceries throughout the United States. I knew, for example, very little of the administrative protocols of processing or annulling marriages. I would miss this background back in Santa Barbara in my role as a classroom lecturer.

From the beginning I knew that my strength and only passion would be the philosophy of law, the principles of law. Almost immediately, one canon in the first book of the Code caught my attention. It concerned suppletory law. Its provisions outlined what one was to do in the event there was no law covering a particular case. Such situations were arising more frequently in the wake of industrial, technological and sociological changes. Only in the event of a conflict of rights in an area not covered by law was there a need to arrive at a solution based on principles of law. In these precise cases and only in them canon 20 pointed to parallels elsewhere in the Code as potential resources to settle the conflict. Implicitly therefore, within the canon there seemed to be a preference for freedom rather than restriction.

This might be a tiny area of freedom in a Church that had nearly total control over its members, both internally and externally, but it had strong emotional appeal for me. I had resigned myself to the notion that every aspect of my life would forever be controlled by Church law, so I was surprised and delighted that a part of me was still alive, still responsive to the carrot of freedom. I could resonate to personal space, to responsible freedom, to respect for myself. Principles of Law, Book I, was the first light of freedom I could discern in the darkness of my ecclesiastical upbringing. Autonomy would become more and more pivotal in my life during the next three years of study.

Despite being a newcomer to the community of the Franciscan Monastery of the Holy Land, I became the confessor/spiritual director of the house. I was not asked whether I would agree or like to be; I was simply appointed to the position. Apparently, my reputation had preceded me and once again I was being shown great trust. Unfortunately, I did not share the confidence they showed me. Not that I considered myself lacking in intellectual and experiential training. On the contrary, my preparation had been very thorough.

I simply suffered from the deep conviction that I was a totally unworthy person. While my public persona had proved attractive, internally I was infected by a pervasive toxicity, much of it still sexual. From the time of my pubescence, this inner condition taunted me, seemed irredeemable and irreversible. I did not really know that my sexual feelings were perfectly normal human feelings. I considered them sinful, and since I was inadequately resisting their attraction, I was continuing to commit serious sexual offenses. This tendency to be scrupulously literal in my understanding of Catholic moral teaching was threatening to be my undoing.

My new position as confessor/spiritual director placed no demands on anyone to come to me for either the sacrament of Penance, or Confession, or for any other kind of guidance; it simply made me available to those who might want to see me on Tuesday evenings at 7:30. And indeed, not everyone came.

From time to time the position made strong emotional demands on me, some quite unforeseen. One instance stands out in my memory. A priest in our community developed cancer. The cancer's progress had been arrested by an experimental treatment provided by the National Institutes of Health. Serum was regularly separated from the blood of donors whose cancer had gone into remission. This was then combined with serum separated from the priest's blood and re-injected into his arm. This proved effective as long as the level and frequency of treatment was maintained.

But then, as one by one the donors became unavailable, the priest was left without the donor serum and the growth of his cancer escalated. In a short time he was moribund, facing imminent death. When the doctor informed him that he had very little time left, I was asked to speak with him to help him deal with the devastating truth. I did the best I could with my natural compassion and capacity for empathizing. I do not know whether I helped or not. My personal anguish was that I did not know if I could provide him anything spiritually appropriate. Instinctively, I eschewed pious aphorisms, and that was wise. Still, showing understanding and empathy as one human being to another did not seem enough. The old distinction still reigned within me; my unimportant world seemed merely "natural" as opposed to "supernatural."

Years later, after psychotherapy had helped me integrate my life, I felt disrespect for the constricted person I once was. At least until a wise young nun said to me, "I hope that you don't continue to separate your life into the period before your therapy and after. Don't think you gave little or nothing before and everything after. You certainly gave me and others a great deal before you developed your liberating self-awareness." That has comforted me a great deal over the years.

In 1962, millions of Roman Catholics, especially in eastern Europe, still strongly associated hatred of Jews with loyalty to the faith.

Early in 1962 the monotony of our canonical studies was broken as we heard the news that Pope John XXIII planned to convoke the Church's twenty-first Ecumenical Council, the first since Vatican I of 1869-1870. Bishops from all over the world would be gathering in Rome to pray for wisdom, to confer with one another and to discover new ways to make the Church and her message relevant to our day. *Aggiornamento*, "updating," was a much heard word at the time.

This news fanned my long-buried desire for autonomy. For as long as I could remember, I had without much success been trying to press and mold Catholic doctrine into a form that could elicit something deep within me. I had read that when the renowned Franciscan, Father Junípero Serra, heard that the Sunday that closed off the Easter season would be dedicated to celebrating the mystery of the Trinity (Father, Son and Holy Ghost), he wept for joy. This had puzzled me and humbled me because that doctrine aroused no such feeling in me. I concluded therefore that my faith lacked something critical, that a certain superficiality distinguished my spirituality from that of the truly mature.

As a result I gave myself to reading about the mystery of the Trinity, to praying for its relevance in my life. Eventually I felt I had arrived at a point of appreciating the infinite depths of this mystery. God the Father is ever the essence of truth, the source of all love. When the Father thinks of Himself, that Thought or internal Word reflects His entire being. This Word is God the Son.

The Father and Son then gaze upon one another, behold the beauty of the other. This gaze issues in Love who is God the Holy Spirit. I even got to the point where I could present this central mystery with fervor and a sense of authenticity.

But the excitement I felt about the impending Council was different in nature; the gathering in Rome evoked passion in me. The prospect of renewing and updating an outmoded Church absorbed and excited me; it took no effort at all on my part, as had the Trinity. The thought of reformulating old beliefs, of building new ways of worship and prayer, of restructuring institutional life, of opening our thinking to other ways of believing moved me dramatically.

The fire of my fervor was stoked even more when a local talk-show host with no religious affiliation repeatedly spoke of Pope John XXIII with veneration. He praised the Pope for his fresh compassionate way of relating to all men and women in the world regardless of belief. He raved about Pope John's encyclical letter, *Pacem in Terris*, Peace on Earth.

One of the luminaries in the canon law department, indeed of the entire university, was Dr. Frederick McManus, professor of liturgy. Grounded in both the theology and law governing worship, he made the future come alive for me. His classes were always a joy because they were so open to a new future. While I was not able to put my finger on what was happening within me, I knew I was riding the current to a whole new way of thinking and understanding my faith.

Languages have always been my meat. In my youth I had found Latin and Greek to be absorbing challenges. I had studied Latin for five years, Greek for three. In addition, I had studied German for two years. And to prepare myself for graduate work, I had studied French and Italian. Because of my knowledge of Spanish and Latin, these two Romance languages proved no problem to read and understand. On the basis of language I felt very well prepared for graduate work. As if that was all it would take!

I was allowed to pursue as my thesis topic the one canon that had attracted me from the beginning, suppletory law. When I began to pursue the footnotes to this canon, the research led me to an unexpected discovery: the sixth-century Code of the Emperor

Justinian. The material was difficult at the start because there was a good deal of abbreviation with no suggested way to unlock these codes.

Fortunately I thrive on puzzles; little by little the context began to yield to my repeated readings. In time the abbreviations were as familiar to me as the full text. Slowly but surely I began to realize that much of the law which I had naively thought emanated from the spiritual nature of the Church, the community of believers, was—to put it bluntly—simply Roman law.

Under the Emperor Constantine in 314 A.D., the Catholic Church had become the state religion. This arrangement offered the rapidly expanding Church access to the rich Roman legal mind and its sophisticated principles of organization. Somehow my understanding of the Roman secularity of the Church's religious roots, whatever its practical value, took some of the bloom off the rose. Where once the Church had seemed wholly sacral, now it seemed secular in a very important regard.

That aside, there was the basic preference in suppletory law for freedom of action on the part of Church members unless ecclesiastical authority has explicitly legislated some restriction of that freedom. The notion of liberty within that preference, however limited, intrigued me. No wonder. I had received strenuous training in the opposite direction. Our obligation was to seek guidance from ecclesiastics who by the grace of their office were endowed with special wisdom.

As a result of the sin of Adam and Eve, conscience had been contaminated and desires disordered, easily moving us toward making a decision that favored the satisfaction of unworthy ends. Our minds were darkened; our wills were weakened.

My whole life, therefore, down to the least detail of my being, was governed by the opinions and dicta of Mother Church. She fed me with the purest formula, watched me, graded me, guided me according to her wisdom, rewarded me, threatened me or punished me if I misbehaved, insisted I ask no questions about paths divinely laid out for me, responded to my queries with solemn and unquestionable certitude, and in return for loyalty to her demands promised me lavish rewards in a future life. With that background it was impossible to take the Church seriously when in the fine print she declared that the ultimate forum of decision-making was individual conscience.

Suppletory law presented me with a new notion. There were areas of life which should not be invaded by Church law-makers and should not be entered into except when it was unavoidable and then only to settle a dispute between parties in conflict. What might those areas be? I wondered.

I read commentators on canon 20. They all missed my point completely: they ignored one's implicit freedom to make decisions I thought I had found in suppletory law. They passed over the principle embedded there, that where there is no controlling directive, you are free to make choices except in cases where you might infringe on someone else's rights. Why did they not see my point, when the footnotes which were the source of the law made the case so clearly? Was theirs the same mind-set that had held me in thralldom? Did our training make us perceive reality in a certain way? And was there any way to jettison this attitude and remain true to the Church?

I grew more fervent in my pursuit of autonomy. I read commentators in French and German. Nowhere in the literature, much to my distress, could I find any awareness of opening to the freedom of an individual's conscience. Nevertheless, for the first time in my life I felt empowered enough to believe in myself and the insight at which I had arrived. I longed for someone to discuss this with but there was no one. My few feeble attempts to do this with classmates were met with apathy. While I had made some progress in my thinking, I was not yet ready to take a stand on my autonomy.

On October 11, 1962, two weeks before my thirty-seventh birthday, the Second Vatican Ecumenical Council finally opened in Rome. I was in my second year of graduate study. The Church's bishops, theologians, and scripture scholars had spent four years of intense preparation for this event; I looked forward with great anticipation to the fruit of their work. Pope John XXIII, regarded by some as a harmless octogenarian, was about to launch a revolution with the same good-heartedness and positive outlook that he brought to everything in his life. Unfortunately, he would see only nine months of the young Council's life before death took him.

Many of us at Catholic University began to wonder about the point of studying a code of law that would soon be drastically revised. The theology of the Church would soon be facing radical changes; a new set of laws would have to reflect this altered vision. In the future if all the Bishops in the world were each seen as sharing in ecclesiastical power, and the Pope as the "first among equals" coordinating their efforts, what would the new law look like? The dim and narrow light of self-determination that I had glimpsed in canon 20 paled before the prospect of responsible freedom throughout the Church.

The impulse provided by the opening of the Council in Rome changed the atmosphere both at the monastery and at school. On an almost daily basis, Rome was generating exciting news that became the focus of intense conversation and debate among us at the university.

One of the Franciscan students with whom I often walked to class became an invaluable partner and sounding board. His pursuit of a doctorate in church history made him knowledgeable about councils. Often he would temper my enthusiastic expectations, reminding me that the liberating documents were not yet written, that these would be the result of compromise between dissenting parties, that supportive institutional changes were a long way off. Even those changes, he emphasized, would be implemented by specific individuals, some with conservative, others with liberal leanings.

My desire for change was so intense that I did not want to accept his realistic exhortations. I could see a multitude of possibilities for deep-cutting change, all of them reasonable and in accord with modern understanding. "There is a new paradigm about to be set loose in the Church," I thought to myself, "and there is no stopping it."

Meanwhile in class, except for Dr. McManus, the staff continued as if nothing was happening in Rome. One professor commented gravely that it would be a tragedy were even one canon changed in the Book on Crimes and Penalties.

"This tract in its present form," he said, "is a masterpiece."

For me it was extremely difficult to continue to put energy into most of what was being presented to me. My effort was focused on my thesis for the licentiate, due the end of my second year.

My major professor was a short, prim priest given to detail and precision. I was psychologically ill-prepared to work with him. I had been taught from my youth to discount myself and honor whatever came from a professor's mouth. But I could not agree with his thinking. When he humiliated me with a scornful look and an exasperated sigh, I did what I was trained to do; I "offered it up." This is what one did with any pain or suffering. This would sanctify me and help me walk in the way of Jesus. Any judgment of his behavior would be inappropriate and unseemly. Somehow we made it through, he and I, and I received my licentiate in canon law.

In the summers after my first and second years at Catholic University, I returned to my native province and resided at the School of Theology in Santa Barbara, California. By this time my old classmate, Father Robert Pfisterer, was already introducing healthy changes in the community and in the school.

He was a gentle revolutionary. Multi-lingual, he was able to read broadly in the French, Italian and German theological literature. From these modern theologies he took extensive notes and presented his young students with approaches that ran far ahead of or in opposition to the texts that we were sworn to teach from. A mild-mannered man, his approach was not confrontational, his radical style hardly noticed. In fact he was already far ahead of me.

My insights were progressive but I had not yet thought through their implications for day-to-day life. When I went back to the theological seminary in Santa Barbara, I was shocked to discover that the students there (without permission from Rome!) were now praying the official prayers, the Breviary, in English instead of the prescribed Latin. Because Robert was so grounded in common sense it was difficult not to adopt his stance. His rationale was simply that we had the right to pray in our own language. This he maintained was the direction in which the Council was moving the Church. It seems a trivial matter now, but in the summer of 1962 small differences like these loomed large and stirred strong feeling. I could see the students responding to the new intellectual freedom with excitement. Slowly but surely, so was I.

On November 22, 1963, an unforgettable day, President John Kennedy was assassinated in Dallas, Texas. I was sitting in my small room at the monastery working on my doctoral dissertation, mechanically typing away from my notes when I heard the startling announcement of the shooting. My little transistor radio seemed to shudder. Stunned and confused, I could not believe my ears. Maybe this report is untrue, I thought. I flung my door open and hurried out into the corridor. I had to find someone with whom to share the news. Down the hall I saw an elderly priest exit his room; his agitation indicated that he too had heard the news. I ran toward him.

"Did you hear? Did you hear about the President? He's dead, assassinated!" I shouted.

"Yes," he responded firmly, "good."

I was appalled "This is no time for sick humor," I remonstrated.

"I meant what I said," came the reply, "I think it's good for the country."

I backed away, disoriented at this sick commentary from someone professing to be religious. I needed to distance myself from him and find someone with whom I could share my dismay.

Sometime later, in a quiet moment, my mind went back to my own politically conservative days when I myself opposed the election of John F. Kennedy. The standard Catholic belief on the relationship between church and state was clearly delineated in a two-volume work on public law by Cardinal Ottaviani, the former head of the Holy Office. His reasoning was as follows: A perfect society is one which has within itself all the means needed to reach its goal. Only two societies fulfill this definition. Hence there are only two perfect societies in the world: the church and the state. The goal of the church is spiritual and that of the state is material. Therefore, whenever a conflict of rights arises between these two, the church's rights must take precedence.

During Catholic Kennedy's presidential campaign the Episcopal Bishop, James Pike, had tweaked the nose of the Catholic Church by pointing out that this doctrine would put a Catholic President in an insoluble dilemma. As a Catholic, his conscience would require that he favor his church. As President, he would be required by the Constitution to favor the state.

Kennedy handled the problem with equanimity. His duty was to be true to the oath taken at his inauguration. He would be obliged to follow the law of the state rather than that of the church. At that time I found his position abhorrent. I did not want this kind of uncommitted Catholic at the helm of my country. But I had become a very different person now; significant liberal changes were roiling my old conservative points of view. I now found myself passionately responding to the challenge of the new vision so eloquently phrased by our young President. I grieved his untimely loss.

I felt obliged to attend the President's funeral as a small declaration of my intention to move in new directions. I decided not to attend only because massive numbers of mourners were predicted. So I watched the funeral with the rest of the nation, moved by the solemn ritual surrounding this great tragedy. I was especially touched by the dignified, stricken widow and her two little children. A great man had fallen.

My liberal leanings began to shift from the political scene to the ecclesiastical events unfolding in Rome. I received every new insight emanating from the Eternal City with enthusiasm. I cheered any movement toward deep-cutting change in the Church. Gone was the earlier anxiety which I felt when reading philosophers whose works were on the Index of Forbidden Books.

It was patently untrue that the reading of proscribed works was a threat to my religious beliefs. I knew myself to be trustworthy and discriminating. My breaking free was not from haughty pride or adolescent rebellion. It was simply a normal response to new insight which opened me to modern thought. In faith and practice I was now on the side of those cheering the genie that had escaped the ecclesiastical wine cruet, the spirit that was imbuing the Church with a commitment to enter the modern world.

In 1963, the German Protestant playwright, Rolf Hochhuth, dramatized the moral issues facing the pope and his diplomatic representatives during the Holocaust in The Deputy. *In this*

*play Pope Pius XII is called to account for his public silence be-
fore the moral conscience of the audience.*

Midway in my third and final year of doctoral work I admitted to
myself that I was probably not going to complete my doctoral dissertation. Instead of utilizing my already extensive research and
plodding through the task of writing and submitting it as my dissertation, I would read yet another book on the topic. Ultimately
I exhausted the literature and myself.

Toward the end of my avoidance-driven research I discovered
that someone in France several years before had published a dissertation on my topic, canon 20. With some relief I concluded
that it would be morally wrong to write another book on the same
subject. I took this information to my major professor. He was not
impressed with my sense of morality and urged me to continue
my own treatment. But instead of doing as he suggested, I set
myself to translating the French dissertation, spending long
days until I finished. A meaningless task and completely self-
destructive. Actually the French treatment of the subject was quite
different from mine.

In those days I knew nothing of therapy. It never occurred to
me to ask for help with what was a serious problem of avoidance.
What prevented me from finishing my dissertation? Perhaps
some exalted notion that it was my duty to produce the perfect
work in order to merit a doctorate in canon law. I had written the
first half of the dissertation with a driven fervor. But now I was
clearly lost without the slightest clue as to why I was blocked.

I had strong negative feelings about the professor guiding me
in this task. Consequently, although he intimidated me I never
defended myself in all the years that we spent together. I saw him
as a scolding parent. I did not like him. On many occasions I
wanted desperately to quit the whole scene but my sense of obligation to the Franciscans back home deterred me.

Slowly this inner struggle with the man and the material
drained all joy from my life. My unhappiness was constant. I attended lectures mechanically, heard classmates talk excitedly
about their progress and helped some of them translate Latin
sources. Inside I remained frustrated, frozen, demeaned.

Only the news issuing from Rome about changes in the Church brought me any joy. I was uplifted by the possibility of a different ecclesiastical landscape adapting to modern insights. I sensed the life-giving implications of less centralization and of greater lay involvement in all aspects of the Church. "Perhaps," my heart said, "the ecclesiastical world I am living in now is dying and giving way to something new, relevant, and life-giving."

One night, when a solemn stillness lay upon the monastery, I finally admitted to myself what I had studiously avoided: I must give up the completion of my dissertation. I decided to finish the rest of my course work; that was it. I knew I had a difficult telephone call to make to my provincial back home, Father Terence Cronin, and announce my decision. The next day I made the call, an assertive move for me. Father Terence suggested that I talk to my professor and explain that I would finish my classwork but would complete my dissertation at the end of the summer after my return to Santa Barbara. "Don't discuss your inner struggle with him," he cautioned me.

My major professor did not approve of my decision. He was pleased with my progress, he said, and urged me to finish my dissertation in the more conducive climate of university life. But he could not convince me. My decision caused some initial disappointment among my classmates and my Franciscan colleagues at the Monastery. But they all permitted me to go about my chosen business. As a result, for the first time in months my turmoil ebbed to manageable proportions. I had finally made a firm decision; there was no turning back.

The rest of the year passed uneventfully except for the continuing good news issuing from the Vatican. Changes in the liturgical environment were already happening even in the conservative setting of the Franciscan Monastery. We had turned the altar around and were facing the congregation at Mass. The language of the liturgy was now English. Even more exciting were the explicitly theological shifts being pondered by the Council.

The Church was no longer going to see itself as a pure light in the midst of a surrounding darkness; it was finally acknowledging the presence of God in other faiths. As obvious and overdue as it was, this formally enunciated breakthrough amazed me.

The ramifications were vast: the Church was proclaiming its vulnerability and its immersion in the human condition! As such it could offer a more credible witness to its central doctrine: God has become Man; Jesus, who came to save us from our sins, was truly human. His Church could falter and fail, frankly confess its frailty, ask for pardon, learn from traditions not its own.

This new vision permitted Catholics to move away from the unbalanced picture of the Church as monarchical, a possibility being contemplated a century earlier by the First Vatican Ecumenical Council before its deliberations were cut short by the Franco-Prussian War. Vatican II gave us access to new language in speaking of the Church, language that was refreshing and vital, pastoral and biblical.

Far greater trust was being placed in the basically responsible adulthood of the faithful, evidence of our belief the Holy Spirit vivifies the entire Church body, not just its head. Our God is a creative God and, given room, will guide us to new ways of being Church in the world. This loosening of the grip of ecclesiastical control was long overdue and welcome. The dignity of lay people was finally being honored. The role of the individual Bishop was to be a loving shepherd close to his people rather than a distant hierarch with governing power. The Bishops scattered all over the world together with the Pope, Rome's Bishop, were to be an enduring group or "college" responsible as a single body for the instruction, spiritual maintenance and nurturance of the entire Church.

On June 21, 1964, three Jewish activists, Michael Schwerner, Richard Chaney and Andrew Goodman, who with other civil rights workers had gone to the South to help local African Americans, were killed. They had been followed as they left Philadelphia, Mississippi, then captured and beaten before their execution. Their bodies were found weeks later hidden in an earthen dam site under construction.

My final scholastic year came to an end. I was offered the opportunity to work in several East Coast Chanceries during the summer months but I declined. I was anxious to get home. Canon law was changing drastically and current judicial practices with it. I chose to return to the West Coast with a three-day stop at a national liturgical conference being held in St. Louis, Missouri. This important gathering was to take place in the city's massive basketball arena. It would be an extraordinary opportunity to tune into the most recent changes in worship. The Franciscan Monastery in Washington had not yet introduced them fully.

The conference exceeded my expectations. It was my first taste of the kind of community possible at Mass, a bond that spoke to clergy, religious and lay people alike. I have fond memories of a young African-American priest, Father Joseph Rivers, who led a large group in the new hymnology he was crafting. The words were scripturally based, hence dignified and substantial. The flavor of his ethnic heritage invited us to loosen up and be more expressive in our singing. Smiles, body movement and enthusiastic joy filled the room. The sessions proved so moving that a multitude of participants sat themselves on the floor, pressing in on him, leaving him only a tiny space from which to lead us.

The Masses were true celebrations attended by some ten thousand jubilant congregants. Our voices carried the joy of liberation, the challenge of change and the awareness of the persons around us regardless of race, ethnicity, age, class or gender. "Oh," I thought, "this is heaven." The academic defeat I felt I had suffered was forgotten in the joy of those few days. I understood this way of being a faith community. I resonated to it. The fact that I was not a priest-leader at these gatherings was also significant to me; it brought me close to lay people. My appetite for more of this sort of connection was growing.

Shortly after my return to the theological seminary at Old Mission Santa Barbara, the pastor invited me to speak at the Sunday Masses about the Christian Family Movement. I knew almost nothing of the program's origins except that it had started in the Midwest and was designed to give married couples an opportunity to develop spiritually. At their meetings they were to read and discuss passages from the New Testament and learn how to apply its principles to their everyday lives.

What an exciting notion! The groups actually belonged to the lay participants; the priest assigned to them was to sit silently by until the meeting's end. Then and only then was he to speak. His humble task was to summarize the discussion. Following the meeting the host couple would provide refreshments.

A good number of couples applied for acceptance; I was assigned as chaplain to one group. My intuition proved to be on the mark—the experience was transforming. Though my role with them has changed, my relationship with them has lasted for over thirty years. It would be difficult to overstate the healing, grounding, supportive influence these people had on me and one another both as they listened acceptingly to my story and revealed their own. By what they did and said they taught me the beauty of married love and their dedication to family and children. Their love for me was a singular grace that touches me even today.

Before the start of our theological school year I accompanied a group of Franciscans on a week-long retreat/seminar hosted by the Congregation of Saint Joseph. The setting was idyllic: a group of rambling buildings amid fir trees on the shore of Puget Sound between Tacoma and Seattle. The presenter was the internationally known, highly regarded theologian, Father Bernard Häring, the author of a new book that approached moral theology from a spiritually positive rather than a sin perspective. Fr. Häring made himself completely available to us. He said Mass for us daily, gave all the talks, shared our table, and spent some of his leisure time with us. He was genuine, profound yet approachable. As he spoke I sensed a new world dawning for me, the parameters of which were only faintly perceptible.

Häring's approach to the subject of marital sexuality was revolutionary, surely for that time. He had obviously taken great care presenting his teaching so as not to alarm the Roman authority. I could not understand how he managed to speak as he did without being muzzled by the Vatican. The opinions of American liberal theologians far less dissenting than his were almost immediately reported to Rome and were treated swiftly and severely.

I was amazed that what he shared with us in this protected, semi-secret environment on Puget Sound he had already shared publicly with the country's young marrieds in the Christian Family Movement. He dared to tell us that though ignored in the 1917 Code of Canon Law, the sexual expression of a couple's love is one of two primary purposes of marriage. Making love is critical to the maintenance and nurturance of the marital bond. Man and wife grow closer to one another when they express this love physically.

"Reproduction," he said, "is the other primary goal of marriage. However," he continued, "the responsibility and freedom to decide when and how often to have children rest with the couple themselves."

This means that should a husband and wife after prayerful consideration decide that they should not have a child, they can use birth control. They can consider this as God's will for them. I compared Häring's approach with the old belief, "We will accept as many children as God sends."

He did not specify what means a couple should use to avoid pregnancy, but indicated it might be not only by rhythm but also by withdrawal or the use of contraceptives.

I couldn't believe my ears. Not only was he inviting us to look inside ourselves for solutions to moral problems, he was indicating that we should do this even in such a grave matter as sex. I had been taught that these issues were not negotiable. The determination of what was sexually sinful was determined solely by the teaching authority of the Church. In the matter of birth control the truth was clearly defined, brooking neither doubt nor dissension: the practice of birth control was intrinsically and gravely evil. It was to be repented of with the sincere resolve never to do it again and immediately confessed to a priest. Only then could the sin be absolved.

I found Häring's daring to think for himself attractive and inviting. Our Masses celebrated together were marvelous communitarian acts of truly maturing individuals. If this was the new direction of the Church, I wanted to grow in it. I was ready and eager to disseminate this Good News to anyone who would listen, particularly to those who felt disrespected by ecclesiastical authoritarianism.

Our holy scholar-in-residence gave us another gift, a new approach to the sacrament of Penance, popularly known as Confession. The established routine had been for the priest to listen to the narrative of the penitent, judge the kind, gravity and frequency of the sins presented, share a few pious words of encouragement, assign an appropriate penance (usually prayers) and grant absolution in God's name.

In a very short time I had grown bored with the whole idea; nothing about it seemed to matter. The dialogue between priest and penitent seem contrived. Nothing hit on the reality of life, on genuine concerns and failures. And furthermore it was totally sin-oriented. It gave the person confessing no room to tell his story fully.

Totally left outside the focus of the two persons in that tiny chamber were the feelings and thoughts of the penitent. What had led up to the moral failure? What was the impact of his sin on his self-image and on his relationships to those touched by it?

Father Häring encouraged us to probe the fuller picture. He urged us to get a sense of the penitent's attitude that had set him up for failure. We might ask the penitent to apologize to the person offended rather than simply to ask God to forgive the sin. We might suggest that an offended spouse express anger directly to the offender. We might enlist the penitent in our search for an appropriate penance. Thus we could be realistically helping to solve a problem rather than escaping into pious, rote aphorisms.

Before the week was up I went to Confession to Father Häring. It was the first time in my life that the sacrament of Penance was a fully human experience; God was present in our interaction. If I were to minister to others in this manner, Confession would be a real cleansing. Certainly not the bore it had become to me.

When classes began in September I was feeling much more confident about my teaching. My outlook was now much broader than that offered by the standard seminary text. The new approaches in moral theology were more in touch with the actual human condition. I could bring the student a new, more human way of hearing confessions. I could teach him to bond with those confessing and encourage his creativity in bringing them new directions and possibilities for living a holy Christian life.

Articles and books propounding new insights abounded. Even in canon law drastic changes were expected, changes reflecting the new ecclesiology, fresh approaches to Church as a community *semper reformanda*, always needing reform. One important area needing immediate attention was highlighted by Pope John XXIII in his disturbing dream of thousands of divorced and remarried Catholics lined up outside the Church asking to be readmitted to the sacraments.

The Pope's loving observation moved me like few others. It truly hit home because my brother Joe was in just such a marriage. My parents ached to see Joe and Carole married in the Church so that he could return to full sacramental participation. Now it was possible to feel more hopeful for their situation. The Council, under the gentle, visionary leadership of John XXIII, was redrawing the contours of Church life, rendering it compassionate and respectful of dramatic cultural differences.

Even Book V of the Code of Canon Law, "Crimes and Penalties," perhaps especially Book V, was undergoing drastic revision. After all, more than any other book it dealt with a heavily juridical, even punitive treatment of human failures, bristling with definitions, threats, fulminations, procedures and protocol.

Enthusiastic and excited, I walked into my class to teach *De Matrimonio*, the various laws governing the sacrament of marriage in the Catholic Church: who had jurisdiction to preside at a wedding, what was the parties' capacity for marital union, what conditions of marriage had to be accepted by the parties for it to be valid, what were the impediments to marriage, both "impedient" (sinful if you proceed without episcopal authorization), and "diriment" (invalid if you proceed without episcopal authorization), how to "heal" invalid unions, how and where to record the facts of marriage. Still glowing with the St. Louis and Tacoma experiences of the summer of 1964 I opened the class with a brief overview of the material we would cover. After about fifteen minutes one of the students raised his hand. I recognized him.

"Pardon me, but do you really believe all of this? We've been talking to you during the summer. We know you no longer think in these terms."

His remarks froze me for a moment. To put it gently this was not an auspicious beginning to the forthcoming semester's work. But he had a valid point and I thought for a moment before replying.

"You're absolutely right; I don't. So the question remains,

how shall we approach the Church's current archaic law on marriage? I propose that we treat marriage law as rules to an esoteric game. You may or may not choose to play when you go out into the ministry. I can teach you the rules of this game and how these rules are currently being interpreted by the various dioceses that you may find yourselves working in. I can teach you how to navigate the system, give you ideas on how to narrow the gap between what the Church demands that you do and what you are moved to do. But I will also inform you what consequences may follow upon your disregard of the rules. Finally, I will outline for you how to talk to couples living in the modern world about the life that they are embracing. Deal?"

Lively discussion ensued. We settled on my suggested approach and began a trek through the canonical terrain of *De Matrimonio*. Whenever the legal prescriptions seemed particularly antiquated we would grind to a halt, remind ourselves of our compact and proceed gingerly.

Some concepts that proved particularly nettlesome had to do with the Church requirement that the validity of a marriage depended upon the couple's being open to the creation of new life. You could not enter upon a valid marriage with the explicit intention of never bearing children.

"So," asked my students, "if this is true, how then is the marriage of Mary and Joseph valid? She conceived by the Holy Spirit (virginity *before* birth), gave birth without injury or pain (virginity *during* birth), and remained virginal forever (virginity *after* birth)."

I had no answer. I knew couples who for valid reasons—for example, poor health, career considerations, or personality traits they judged incompatible with parenting—had chosen to marry solely for spousal love and companionship. They knew beforehand that they did not want a family and would do everything to avoid a pregnancy.

Clergy, friends and acquaintances knew nothing of their intention and experienced them as a loving couple. How could anyone consider them living in an invalid, sinful union? What of those people who, having entered into a sacramental marriage judged indissoluble by the Church, subsequently found it necessary to divorce and wished to be remarried? And if they remarried and seemed to be living in a loving relationship, how could one say that this was an invalid and therefore sinful union?

On the practical level the arrangement I had made with my class worked out. The students appreciated our interchange and were cooperative. But even with the amount of freedom this style afforded me I was by year's end increasingly disaffected with the institutional Church. The fatherly loving visionary Pope John XXIII had been dead for a year; canon law would be a long time in revising. There were growing tensions between the liberal and conservative members of the staff over how much freedom our theological students should be permitted.

This problem proved to be unusually divisive. The liberals argued that in the past our students, ages twenty-one to twenty-six, were treated like minors, despite their age. We were still protecting them from the world as if they lacked the capacity to make judicious decisions, and this despite the fact that we had trusted them to take their final vows. Led by the quietly progressive dean of students, Father Robert Pfisterer, they were encouraged to take classes at the University of California at Santa Barbara, where they could be in touch with their secular peers and develop a more realistic sense of what was going on in the outside world. To do this they dressed in "secular clothes" when they went to UCSB. More and more often they remained dressed that way even when they returned to the seminary. The university milieu at the time was aboil with controversy sometimes attended by violence, mostly over the Vietnam war.

The Church conservatives looked at these new freedoms with alarm. The seminary world, once secure, seemed to be in flux, slipping away. Indeed process, movement, and action were now idealized. Gone, they lamented, were the good old days of predictability, of protected orthodoxy, of fidelity to the sacred Roman prescriptions concerning seminary life. No longer were there simple and clear norms for deciding who among the students should advance to Holy Orders. No longer were there tight safeguards against encroachment by the "world" with its music, its popular literature, its films, its dangerous ethos of individualism and autonomy, and especially its sexual allure. The relationship between the liberal and conservative factions on the staff grew even more strained as the students received and sometimes took more and more freedom. The split staff was finding decision-making about seminary policy almost impossible. On most votes staff was evenly split three to three.

Even in the pulpit the same divisiveness was evident. Liberals thought conservatives irrelevant. Conservatives judged liberals sensationalists. The problem of irrelevant sermonizing was central to Father Robert, my classmate, and to me. Moved to address real issues and emboldened by the pronouncements of Vatican II, we took the question of modern war to the pulpit of the Old Mission Saint Barbara's parish. We were convinced that most Catholics would never think to question the morality of the war.

The Church's "just war" theory did not play a prominent part in its teaching at a popular level, in its catechisms or its pulpit teaching. Nor did the Bishops emphasize the obligation of Catholics to apply this theory to conflicts of our own era. The council, however, in its recent document on the Church had pointed out to all nations that since "every kind of weapon produced by modern science is used in war, the fierce character of warfare threatens to lead the combatants to a savagery far surpassing that of the past."

And later in the same document, "All these considerations compel us to undertake an evaluation of war with an entirely new attitude."

Our current concern was about the morality of the Vietnam war. It seemed to us that this conflict in particular offered an opportunity for us to point out our parishioners' ethical obligation to evaluate it morally as the Council had indicated.

The Catholic "just war" theory teaches that there are four conditions for a war to be considered moral. It is the obligation of the individual Catholic to verify the presence of these conditions whenever one's homeland takes up arms against another country or people.

One of the four is the proportionality between the ends intended and the means utilized. Some theologians were saying that modern technology had so advanced the possibilities of destruction and death that it was impossible *ever* to wage a just war; the means available were so devastating that no purpose could justify them. Others thought that there were still situations where a just war could be waged; it behooved everyone to study each war on its own merits and then take a moral stand.

We planned to speak as a duo at the Sunday Masses, which were best attended. We would first explain the Church's just war theory, then apply it to the Vietnam war. Both points of view we felt must be presented fairly and neither side slighted. Our main point was to show that each Catholic must set biases aside, openly study the issues, and come to his or her own conclusion. In the post-conciliar era the layperson in the Church was finally being regarded as adult, responsible, and capable of forming moral conclusions, especially of this dimension. The sensitivity of our challenge required more thorough preparation than usual. We stressed the personal obligation of each and every person to study the problem conscientiously. Most congregants at the Masses seemed receptive. A few walked out, distressed at what they perceived to be an unjust attack upon our country's decision to wage war in Vietnam. But over all, Robert and I were pleased with what we had presented.

Another group that impressed me with their courage was the community of the Sisters of the Immaculate Heart of Mary, whom we called with some affection the IHMs. They were headquartered in Los Angeles, where they ran hospitals and schools, the most famous of which was Immaculate Heart College. One of their staff, Sister Corita, was an established artist whose fame helped to spread the school's notoriety. Locally they ran a retreat house and conference center, La Casa de Maria, which also served as their novitiate.

Responding to new theological paradigms, they reconsidered the role of superior in their convents. The superior had always been invested with ecclesiastical authority, could bind the consciences of their subjects, and was the ultimate arbiter of all matters. The community changed this vertical, hierarchical role to the horizontal one of coordinator of a group of equals. Her function as such had more to do with service than with rule. In addition, the IHMs decided to allow members to choose forms of community service rather than channel everyone into the traditional ones of hospitals and schools.

Another change, perhaps not as substantial as the first two but more dramatic, was their decision to abandon the traditional garb. There would no longer be a compulsory "habit"' to wear; they would dress conservatively but in the style of contemporary women. As a group they were a light year beyond what my own community was willing to do. Their willingness to risk, however, got them into trouble with ecclesiastical authorities. Not surprisingly.

Not all the IHMs were willing to make such deep-cutting changes. A minority group was strongly opposed and wanted to stay with the traditional structures and garb. The tension between the two groups caused concern for the community's future. Each side made arguments that their point of view was vital, critical to survival. The liberals argued that without adaptation to the new theological insights of Vatican II, a status quo stance would soon render the sisterhood obsolete and ineffective. The conservatives insisted that what liberals called "changes" would actually destroy the very identity of life in religious community.

The majority of the community went with the changes which sought to blend a strong, respectful connection to their past with a moderate step forward into the contemporary world. I had a deep personal respect for their new direction.

They invited me to teach a course in the principles of moral theology to their novices at the Casa de Maria, a group of some ten bright young women from the Los Angeles area. The experience was a joy. The novices were receptive and challenging, and I found myself very grateful for my summer's exposure to Dr. Bernard Häring. It gave me permission to humanize the material, to take their input very seriously, and to let stand opinions not entirely my own.

Down south in Los Angeles trouble for the IHMs was brewing. Periodic complaints were being filed with the conservative cardinal, James Francis McIntyre, and he was beginning to take these dissenting voices ever more seriously. His Chancery officials were also concerned with reports that throughout the diocese, clergy and laity were experimenting with the liturgy (Mass) and hymnology. Contemporary music and lyrics that spoke to the values of the '60s were being used not only in casual settings but even in the parish churches.

One favorite, for example, was the scripturally based, "Turn,

turn, turn" (Ecclesiastes), which began, "For everything, turn, turn, turn; there is a season, turn, turn; and a time for every season under heaven."

Perhaps because it was set to a folk melody and sung by the popular trio, Peter, Paul and Mary, the Auxiliary Bishop to the Cardinal, John Ward, grew alarmed and sent out a letter to all the parishes of the archdiocese of Los Angeles. In it he condemned the song's use as secular, yet at the same time blessed spontaneity in worship services—with one critical caution. He welcomed spontaneity, he wrote, "as long as it is a *structured* spontaneity."

This was further evidence that we were living in a pre-Vatican II outpost with little hope for meaningful change. This isolation from a Church in movement invited underground activity and home Masses where we could to our hearts' content sing whatever expressed our honest sentiments.

The home Masses that I presided at or participated in were largely in the residences of my CFM couples. Without invitation or pressure, their teen children were likely to be present at our gatherings and share their response to the evening's scripture. On special occasions they would request their own Mass. At times the home community would swell with other invitees who would contribute to our understanding and application of the readings. I loved the experience.

In the midst of these seminary and parish tensions I received word that my father had died. On an insufferably hot August day I stoically presided at a solemn high Mass at his funeral at Saint Mary's Church in Phoenix. I felt so much for my widowed mother who was feeling both the sadness of saying goodbye to her husband and relief at seeing his suffering end.

In their 1966 book, Christian Beliefs and Anti-Semitism, *Charles Y. Glock and Rodney Stark report that a majority of American church members were prejudiced against the Jews. They found that 60 percent of Protestants and 40 percent of Catholics thought that "the Jews can never be forgiven for what they did to Jesus until they accept Him as the True Savior." They added that a majority of observant Christians still thought Jews were materialistic, dishonest and vulgar.*

Among the staff in all three of our seminaries, tensions between liberals and conservatives continued to increase. In our theological school any excess or misstep on the part of one of the students was interpreted as evidence of the recklessness of our new policy. This placed me in a vulnerable position. As dean of students, I was in a role of special responsibility and influence. My liberal decisions about the students were seen by conservatives as jeopardizing the future of the province. This tension to which I was seen as contributing blinded me to what was about to happen.

Part V
Psychological Awakening

THE WEST COAST was the geographic location of the Saint
Barbara Province of the Observant Franciscans in the United
States; there were several more provinces to the east of us. According to the structure outlined in the Constitutions of the
Franciscan Order, each province had four definitors, assistants to
the provincial and vice provincial, and a secretary/treasurer. Our
provincial definitorium had just met to consider the manning of
parishes, schools, missions and provincial seminaries at the high
school, college and theological levels. Out of curiosity I went
down the hall to the bulletin board where the personnel changes
were posted.

As I approached, one of the friars shouted to me, "Congratulations!"

"On what?" I asked.

"You're a definitor," he said with a big smile.

"No fair teasing about things like this," I remonstrated in
disbelief.

"Who's teasing? Come look."

At first my heart sank; I considered the definitorium a conservative body. If this were true, I would be a lone liberal among
them. I could already see that on issues important to me I would
be the only dissenting vote. Not only that, but I would doubtlessly
be subjected to constant quizzing and complaining about the new
look in our theological school. Unflattering rumors about our

abandonment of control had already circulated around the province. It was enough to deal with the conservative wing at home; I didn't need additional carping. On the other hand, I told myself, this was an opportunity to express clearly and firmly what I stood for and why.

Then I noticed on the list of definitors another name below mine, that of a classmate, Carroll Tageson, who had received a doctorate in psychology from the Catholic University of America. He was a liberal who taught psychology at the College Seminary at Old Mission San Luis Rey. He knew the necessity of adapting the seminary policies to a new generation. We had known one another since we were fourteen. At the thought of his support I sighed with relief.

At our very first meeting Father Carroll and I heard several complaints about our respective schools. In Santa Barbara we had begun to hold late afternoon Mass in the students' large recreation room rather than in the Church or the community chapel. As reverently performed as this service was, the setting was unorthodox as were the vestments worn. The celebrant or celebrants utilized only a simple surplice and stole. In addition the homily was frequently a dialogue between the priest and the congregants. The conservative definitors saw our style as erosive of authority and as inviting unhealthy spontaneity. Where was the control? Where would this approach take us? What kinds of liberal expectations were we planting in the minds of the students that would later conflict seriously with Church directives?

On the other hand, Father Carroll and I viewed our students as maturing, as still receptive to sound ideas from others even when these conflicted with their own. They were bringing in fresh new approaches and perspectives that might never have occurred to us who were so accustomed to direction from above.

To illustrate my approach, I shared that Father Carroll and I had been on a team that conducted a different kind of retreat at our house of philosophy at the Old Mission San Luis Rey. We gave talks on the new Church based on the documents of Vatican II. The students responded in ways that we could never have imagined. They displayed strong interest in what we said, and responded with refreshing enthusiasm, creativity and honesty.

At the end of the retreat as we were saying goodbye, the students burst out into a joyous rendition of the hymn, "When the Saints Go Marching In," and began a spontaneous march around the large hall where we had met, out of the hall and into the courtyard. I had never seen any outburst like this but let myself go, setting aside my usual reserve.

I admitted that I did wonder what the rector of the seminary might think and say because at the time he was much less receptive than I. Later I heard that he had frowned on the "chaotic" outburst but had offered no other criticism. I related this to the definitorium to explain how delighted and excited the students had become over the perspectives outlined in the new documents issuing from Vatican II. This, I said, was a positive sign that should please us. Unfortunately, the example only served to confirm the conservative stance of the definitorium.

By the spring of 1967 tensions on the staffs of the various seminaries had mounted and become quite serious. Now we heard rumors that a plan was in place to heal the split between the liberal and conservative sides. A team from the Western Behavior Sciences Institute in La Jolla (later The Center for Studies of the Person) would be arriving to work with all of us at a three-day seminar at the Franciscan Serra Retreat House in Malibu, California.

The team's background and training was Rogerian, that is, stemmed from the research and work of Dr. Carl R. Rogers, an internationally known, highly regarded psychologist. That was all we knew. I imagined that this was to be a kind of mediation run by professionals in an effort to bridge staff differences, a forum for each of us to present our point of view in a safe atmosphere. Perhaps we could thereby be reconciled and resume our life of brotherhood in its deepest sense. I had never heard of Carl Rogers before, but Fr. Carroll had while in the pursuit of his doctorate. Though the idea of such a meeting was a bit scary, it seemed promising and gave me hope.

Twelve of us gathered awkwardly at Serra Retreat. No need for each of us to announce our biases regarding seminary policy; our respective positions had been well scrutinized, were well known. We were all cordial and smoothly superficial. The La Jolla team, I thought, must wonder what all the fuss was about. We would be polite. We would negotiate smoothly. We would generously make the necessary compromises. That would be that. Or so I thought. In a very few hours I would find that my life had changed forever in a kind of B.C./A.D. way. For the moment, however, in full Franciscan garb we meditated, recited the hours of Prime and Terce, then co-presided at the morning Mass. Breakfast afterward was quiet and uneventful.

As we finished our meal the schedule for the day was announced and thanks were expressed to Father Carroll and the others who had arranged this important "coming together." After a brief thanksgiving prayer for the daily bread our Father in heaven had provided, we were dismissed. We were to meet in the large retreat room at 9 A.M.

Fifteen chairs arranged in a circle awaited us; seating was random. I had expected liberals to be positioned on one side of the room, conservatives on the other. In the absence of any announced structure I waited for my side to be seated and when some of them sat I quickly plopped myself down next to them. The La Jolla staff simply sat wherever there was an empty chair.

Bill Coulson was the Catholic of the threesome; he had a double doctorate, one in psychology and one in education. He was cordial, easy to meet. Another of the team, Melinda Sprague, also had a doctorate in psychology. Blond and fair-skinned with a charming hint of a Southern drawl, she was equally warm and friendly. Doug Land, the third staff person, was a retired Protestant minister. He was a large man with a disarmingly simple manner.

Bill Coulson began the meeting. He and his staff needed to know what was going on among and between us to cause such anguish. He invited each of us to speak so the staff could understand our issues. Afraid that our anger toward one another would soon be spilling out I opted to play it safe and remain quiet. Little by little some few risked comments but only warily and with multiple qualifications. Despite deft staff interventions to draw us out, we priests managed to keep the environment as sterile as an operating room, masks over our faces to hide pain, gloves on our hands in case we should touch one another.

After a bit, Doug Land ventured, "There's no way that you people can negotiate anything. You choose to keep your deepest thoughts and feelings hidden from one another. The truth is perhaps you don't even know who you are."

No response.

An hour of restrained sparring and intermittent silences went by. No movement. Bill Coulson spoke up in a soft voice, "As I sit here and listen to the little you have to say, as well as how you say it, I'm getting a strong image. I would like to share it with you. Get comfortable in your chairs, please; close your eyes; relax and listen to me as openly as you can. Okay?"

We all nodded assent. He began: "I'm walking into a very large, formal garden. It is a perfect square. The area is divided into four perfectly equal quadrants, each quadrant bounded by a perfectly trimmed boxwood hedge standing hip-high. From each side a path leads to the absolute center of the garden where the four meet at a fountain flowing with pure, lustrous water. Only the soft, somnolent sound of the gently cascading water breaks the silence. In the exact center of each quadrant, placidly looking down on the beauty below is a tall, beautifully sculptured, faintly veined marble male statue, each flawless and perfectly proportioned. The garden paths of small creek-washed pebbles are immaculate and perfectly raked; not a footprint has disturbed them. Ah, the silence! Ah, the perfection!"

He waited. Then concluded, "Whenever you are ready, please open your eyes; stretch a little to get the kinks out."

We did. The change of mood in the room was remarkable. Each person looked soft now and pensive, seemingly ready to engage. I was surprised how this altered demeanor in the room drew me, yet repelled me. On the one hand, as one of the perfect statues I was impelled to leap off my pedestal, shed the marble of my perfection and be real. I wanted to kick the hell out of the path's perfectly placed pebbles as a sign of my anger at my years and years of restriction and constriction. I yearned to roar and shatter the God-damned silence I had kept through all the years despite the many signals my God-given common sense had been telegraphing to me.

The "now what?" of this outburst frightened me to death. I

intuitively sensed that on the other side of my "coming to" and "coming out" there was a world most attractive and unpredictable. To reach it would require disclosures about my inner self I had never yet had the courage to make to anyone. But these disclosures might lead me to an autonomy and intimacy I had never known. Would such an unveiling bring burdens it its wake, burdens I could not handle? Fear gripped me.

Many of us seemed to have been moved by Coulson's image of perfection. Many were eager to respond. Now I was rapt and listening intently. My brothers of many years were speaking up, coming out for the first time, revealing a humanity I did not know existed. Now that I heard the person beneath the views, I no longer saw him as the enemy.

Through all of this self-disclosure I was assessing the group dynamic. Once you began to speak, all eyes turned toward you, their charged gaze pressuring you to continue. So whenever I was tempted to open my mouth, fear overtook me and I stopped. For yet another hour I kept my silence. Then abruptly and without conscious decision I dove in. Two of the Franciscans were expressing anger toward one another. Their charged words came slowly and awkwardly at first but with the support of our facilitators they came cleanly and clearly. I was moved by their honesty and mutual respect.

Someone else seemed annoyed and said, "So what's the big deal here, anyway?"

"Can't you sense the high drama?" I blurted out.

"High drama?" he echoed. "What the hell is that supposed to mean?"

"These two men are finally being open and honest with one another; that's a big deal," I explained, my enthusiasm somewhat flattened. What I wanted to say was, "The issue is not what they are saying but the process. Maybe this is what our brotherhood is all about; maybe this is what has been missing. New and exciting stuff. Daring to be ourselves, warts and all. Mutual acceptance and support." However none of this got to my lips.

But before I knew it, all eyes were trained on me. I knew intuitively that when I spoke my life would be changed radically and forever. With a deep breath I began, "Though this whole thing has been scaring me, I have to say that I was particularly moved by the perfect garden analogy. I'm embarrassed to admit it, but it describes my behavior here—up to this point." They all listened intently and respectfully as I went on to share the pain buried beneath my years of silence.

When I paused one priest spoke up, "Your sensitivity and the courage of your openness really touch me." Typically, I responded by discounting his compliments. He took offense.

"Much as I care about you," he said, his voice rising, "that's the one thing that bothers me a lot about you. Directly or indirectly, you always manage to discount yourself whenever you are complimented."

I flinched. He spoke a painful truth; that was my usual pattern. "I need to play it safe," I said, "so that in case I fall short of your expectations I can say, 'See, I told you you were exaggerating. Don't expect much from me.'"

With the understanding help of the facilitator, I grew in my ability to release my defensiveness and listen receptively to what I was being told. The feedback was respectful but relentless. One after another said that whenever they consulted me, I took great pains to inform them that I wasn't an expert in any area. One priest recounted that when he attended a conference in Washington, D.C., he had gone out of his way to take me to dinner only to hear me talk and talk about my ineptitude in canon law.

"Frankly, it spoiled the evening for me," he finished.

His memory was true and on the mark. As this picture of my self-deprecation was exposed, I found myself overcome with shame. There was concern in the faces of the three facilitators as they gently helped me not to catastrophize but to accept this side of myself simply as part of my persona and my history. The faces in the group now seemed accepting and encouraging, rather than challenging or intimidating.

"Have you had enough?" Bill Coulson asked me.

I knew exactly what he meant. The group's message had penetrated my armor. I accepted it as the truth. "Yes," I answered, "I get it. I've learned a clear lesson. Thank you."

That was it. With this initiation the group held no more terror for me. I became a spontaneous, active participant, openly reporting my feelings to whatever was going on but with respect for the sensitivity of the other. During our three days together only one of the men could not or would not break through his extraordinary caution. It was as though a loud, menacing, authoritarian voice inside him permitted him to speak only in the most tentative, hesitant way. He would second-guess everything he said, take it back, try again, then repeat the same process. We all tried to reassure him but to no avail.

Melinda Sprague was a godsend. By the third day she had become an inspiring mentor to me. Without sexual overtones she affirmed both my masculine and feminine sides. She was particularly insightful and spoke in ways that I could easily permit in. I had never before allowed a woman so close to my feelings (except for my mother), nor had I ever imagined that I would dare to feel this close to one. I could receive her perceptions of me, even invite them, without fearing the intrusion of sex.

All of us were now showing signs of a remarkable closeness and mutual respect. Could this be the same group that had arrived a short time ago, splintered, alienated and fearful? What had happened to the differences we had each held with such passion? We offered our concluding Mass slowly, savoring a new expression of unity that had been forged in our three-day journey.

A period of three days was a biblical metaphor for death-resurrection. We understood that difficult days still lay ahead, but I was convinced that we could sit and work through our differences without hostility. I began to cry softly from my very depths. My life had changed; a new and exciting insight had been revealed and I thanked God for the miracle. On the way back to Santa Barbara I couldn't stop crying for joy at my liberation. It may have been awkward for my fellow passengers in the car but they were understanding, probably feeling much as I did.

When we arrived in Santa Barbara, the seminary students were quick to note the change in us and pressed to know what had happened. It was difficult even with carefully chosen words to convey what was essentially a process. But their curiosity was intense; they wanted more. Somehow I knew we would have to provide them with a similar experience.

The minor seminary staff members who had not been invited

to the encounter group asked us to come over and give them an account of what had taken place at Malibu. Fathers Keith Forster, Robert Pfisterer and I accepted their invitation. I was still having difficulty controlling my emotions; I cried through most of my sharing. Two of the minor seminary staff thought this was much ado about nothing. I couldn't blame them. A verbal description couldn't carry the power of the experience; it was an inadequate way to spread the word. So I resisted involving myself in extensive rational explanations when other groups of Franciscans asked me to talk about the experience. Awareness and understanding would best come through a person-centered group itself.

In 1967, the Department of Public Science of the Presidium of the Soviet Academy of Science established a Permanent Commission for the "disclosure and analysis of the history, ideology, and practices of Zionism." The torrent of anti-Semitic books that ensued were all grounded on the fraudulent Protocols of the Elders of Zion.

As a result of my new openness, a miracle happened almost immediately. A member of the Old Mission community, an eighty-year-old priest whose entire life had been spent in parishes, showed particular interest in what had taken place at Malibu. Father Andrew Bucher and I had never been particularly close. In fact, some months before my encounter experience we had clashed over what I perceived to be his rude treatment of some of our students. I had spoken firmly to him in defense of the students, politely but firmly insisting that he first deal with me before criticizing a student's behavior.

There was still tension between us, yet he was asking politely that I talk to him about our group experience at Malibu. I went to his room in the infirmary wing where he lived. He had a life-threatening aneurysm and a serious bladder condition which forced him to be near a bathroom at all times. This limiting physical condition jarred his sense of propriety; he found it embarrassing and humiliating.

I began by telling him that our experience was called an encounter group. The goal was twofold. First we were to set aside our reservations and inhibitions and share our thoughts, feelings, and beliefs just as they were in that moment. Second we were to listen to others precisely as they revealed themselves, acceptingly and without judgment. Beneath this process is the belief that your thoughts, feelings and beliefs are your own creation for which you must take sole responsibility. Personal change is possible and is most likely to occur in this atmosphere of trust and acceptance.

"For instance," I said, "when I discovered how my brothers and colleagues felt about me, I swiftly came to realize that for most of my life I had been discounting, if not totally repelling, compliments."

This had annoyed other people and might seem a trivial matter but it was a riveting revelation to me. Most important in this group process was the intimate experience of a respectful, intimate exchange between participants. Instead of alienating one from another it actually brought people closer together.

Then I took the further step of saying, "Andrew, for a long time I have wanted to be your friend. I was drawn to you, your depth, your passion about life, but I have always instinctively pulled back because of your brusque manner. I'm sorry I've never said this to you until now."

He seemed intent upon what I was saying but he spoke not a word. When I expressed my feelings for him, his eyes moistened. We sat together for a long time. I patiently waited for a response.

Finally, he spoke. "I understand what you went through," he said pensively. "And I heard what you said about me. I want you to know that I'm mostly bark, not bite. You see, I'm extremely shy. It takes a lot for me to pull out of myself what I want to say, especially if I anticipate any opposition. So I huff and puff to hide my vulnerability and I end up intimidating people." He managed a weak smile, tears still in his eyes.

"I see," I replied. "Without knowing what was in your heart I easily assumed the worst. I concluded that fundamentally you have little respect for others, especially if they aren't ordained priests, simply students. It makes such a difference knowing this about you. I feel compassion for your shyness. I'm basically shy too. You can trust that I'm your friend."

This was the beginning of the first intense friendship of my life. Over the subsequent weeks Andrew poured out decades of his story, complete with fears, hopes and disappointments. He spoke of past misunderstandings over some of his ideas considered radical by his Franciscan brothers. These conflicts had pained him and he had isolated himself. He shared with me his love for a woman, love which he never expressed, never acted upon.

Andrew proved to be a gifted listener and I continued with him the interactive process I had begun at Malibu. His transformation was remarkable. Once unburdened he was now joyous, bubbly, loving and vital. He was even willing to overcome his embarrassing bladder condition and leave the safe confines of his room to travel with me to Phoenix to visit my family. His doctor thought the trip was good therapy. We managed the practicalities of frequent bathroom visits as Andrew grew comfortable enough with asking to be excused. My family gave him a warm welcome. It was amazing to see him emerge from his cocoon and share with them old memories of his young priesthood, which coincidentally had been in Phoenix.

The vacation and the new mood that had allowed him to risk leaving his room revitalized him. Upon our return I took him to his doctor who greeted him in the waiting room with amazement.

"Fr. Andrew, what's happened to you? There's a new look about you. You seem more alive!"

Andrew's blood pressure and pulse were much improved.

Several of us who had been participants in the Malibu encounter group were invited to La Jolla for a two-week, mid-June training in encounter group facilitation. I welcomed this opportunity to hone my skills. We resided at Old Mission San Luis Rey and commuted daily to the University of California, San Diego campus in La Jolla.

About a hundred people arrived in La Jolla that June morning. We were directed to a large hall where we were introduced to the core encounter staff. We were divided into groups of ten, each led by two facilitators. We started with a three-day encounter with a core group. We would return to this group to process whatever other activities we had engaged in.

My experience at Malibu had given me the confidence to dive right in from the very first. The facilitators had subtly taught us the nature of group experience by modeling it. I learned by seeing what they did, responding to their prompting and trying out what they exemplified. Because of that training I could now risk identifying my emotional response to whatever was going on, report these feelings and be open to whatever anyone said to me about theirs. I had not theorized about any of this; I just knew the process experientially. It wasn't until the didactic sessions which came later that I realized there was solid research behind what we were doing.

For many years Dr. Rogers had recorded his sessions with clients and had painstakingly sorted through their interactions with him. This study provided clues to what prompted client change in valued directions. For Rogers these desired directions consisted of the following: a growing awareness of feeling responses, an increasing non-judgmental acceptance of them, a capacity for expressing these feelings openly while taking responsibility for them, a sensitivity to and respect for the feelings in others, a growing belief that the locus of evaluation is within oneself and that one's behavior is appropriately driven from this inner place, a growing zest for living creatively, a greater comfort in challenging beliefs and in living without the support of old orthodoxies.

I could see that this autonomy posed a serious threat to authoritarian systems that proclaimed rigorous, unchallengeable religious and moral truths. In my bones I could feel my tensions and disagreements with the Catholic Church worsening. In the secure environment of the encounter I could safely share my new attitudes, certain that the participants would unconditionally accept whatever I revealed of my interior world. Thus I was able to place more and more confidence in my own experience even when it conflicted with the formal Church teaching I had been steeped in. The training in group facilitation ended too quickly. Before I knew it we were heading home to Santa Barbara.

When we got back to the theological seminary, we encountered a major disappointment. Those of us who were envisioning an emerging Church in which power was shared had been heartened when a group of papal commissioners was first appointed to study the morality of contraception. Evidence of a new day dawning: the panel included lay people! It had been even more exciting to hear the panel's majority conclusion that preventing pregnancy was permissible, even appropriate, under certain circumstances.

The upsetting news that greeted our return to Santa Barbara was that Pope Paul VI had rejected the one-sided majority vote and had sided with the minority, closing off any further discussion. My thoughts returned to our week with Father Bernard Häring, whose teaching squared exactly with the opinion of the papal commission majority. Rome's attitude and action as far as I was concerned issued from pure avoidance, cowardly timidity, and was an obvious face-saving strategy to uphold an antiquated belief. Ultimately, I was sure it would backfire. This soon became even clearer to me when, shortly after the conclusion of Vatican II, there was an explosion of activity in the Religious Studies Department at UCSB, headed by Dr. Walter Capps.

A number of internationally respected religious thinkers and writers accepted Dr. Capps' invitation to come to UCSB to lecture. The public's enthusiastic response made it abundantly clear that the Pope's attempt to control beliefs even in the matter of birth control was too little, too late. Those of us who attended heard the German theological scholars, Hans Küng and Johannes Metz; the Canadian, George Tavard; the German theologian of hope, Moltmann; and the Jewish theologian, Emil Fackenheim; to name a few.

During Hans Küng's stint at the university, he stayed with us at the Old Mission Theological Seminary. This gave me an extraordinary opportunity to talk to a major ecclesiastical scholar whose opinions, based on vast and rigorous research, were offered confidently and without the fearful over-the-shoulder glances toward Rome I was unhappily accustomed to living with. With him and the other scholars I could sound out opinions on the so-called Dutch solution, a practical response to a thorny problem.

Prompted by the plea of Pope John XXIII in 1963, it offered Catholics who had re-married (after being divorced from marriages considered indissoluble by canon law) restoration to the sacramental life of the Church. The bottom line, these scholars assured me, was that the right to marry was based in natural law, whereas the right of the Church to intrude into this sacred institution was not.

The Dutch solution was a theory evolved by moral theologians and canon lawyers in Holland to provide a solid rationale for bringing divorced and re-married Catholics back to the sacraments. First they called upon the accepted distinction between internal and external forum; that is, the arena of conscience and the arena of public law. Apart from its standing in law, they said, a relationship between two people based on mature love is real. Because of the quality of their committed love for one another, the couple can in good conscience consider their marriage to be as healthy as any other. When this union fails to measure up to the legal norms for its validity, the law from its point only states the obvious: there is no canonically acknowledged marriage between these people.

What to do to resolve conflict between the internal and the external forum where the former says there is a marriage and the latter says there is not? The Dutch theologians and canon lawyers concluded that if reasonable people, unaware of the absence of the canonical necessities in this couple's marriage, got to know this couple over time and saw in their mutual love a sign of God's love for his people, the marriage bond would *in reality* exist. Therefore they could be considered to be living in God's grace and receive the sacraments.

This solution still left a problem for the Church. How could the couple participate in the sacramental life of the Church which was, after all, public? Might this not create a scandal in the parish? The answer was: not necessarily. There would be no scandal if no one knew their canonical status. What if they simply went to a parish where they were not known and could not be judged? Their loving attitude surely would not be one of flouting the law and flaunting lawlessness. It would be simply the desire to participate in the life of the faith community. Their mutual, caring devotion might even be an inspiration to other couples.

So the Dutch solution lay first in acknowledging the canonical brokenness of their marriage and second in honoring the wholeness of their spousal love. And finally by sacramentally celebrating that reality in a parish geographically not their own.

It made sense to me. And when I heard that throughout the United States many priests were instituting its practice, I decided that I would too.

On the morning of August 6, 1967, as I was preparing to go to the Casa de Maria to say Mass for the IHM novices, my intercom phone rang. Father Andrew was in a medical crisis and calling for me; the doctor was by his side. I raced down to his room in the infirmary wing. Through the open door I could see him writhing on his bed attended by his physician. As I entered he asked me in distorted and halting words to explain to the doctor what medicines he had been taking. I was explaining it to the doctor just as the medics arrived to take him to the hospital.

Fearing the worst, I asked to be kept informed about his condition. With Father Giles, the superior of our community, I waited at the front desk of the Old Mission for word. Within a few minutes the phone rang. The news was bad. Andrew had sustained a ruptured aneurysm and had died on the way. I was standing against the wall when the news came. The next moment I had slipped down to the floor like butter melting in a pan. The pain was unbearable. I wept.

I had been through a number of deaths of Franciscans who were dear to me. I had even lost my father. But no loss had ever pained me like Andrew's. Our friendship had grown very swiftly in three months because his infirmity had made him totally available for our sharing. Plainly we were both hungry for all that our shared experience offered: an open acknowledgment without fear of judgment of our deepest beliefs, attitudes and feelings; a description of pivotal events in our lives; an avowal of doubts about our religious beliefs; and finally, feelings of human love for one another.

This friendship, though brief, was a transformative event which taught me the beauty of intimacy. In my growing up we used the word "relationship" only to refer to a consanguineal bond, such as parent-child, siblings, or cousins, but never to a psychological, emotional, intellectual and spiritual connection between two people. But now I had seen that one could feel closeness with any number of people, and that this kind of intimacy promoted the growth of the people involved. Why could we not have some degree of this in our Franciscan communities? After all, we were brothers who shared a common life.

Deep-cutting changes were occurring in society in general, and in the Church in particular, changes that were challenging, distressing, promising, disconcerting, elating. It seemed natural to call upon one another, especially one another, for support and encouragement.

Open and respectful communication between us all could short-circuit the conflict that had already begun to reappear. It would make us aware of what we had in common beneath the differences. Neither side might have everything it wanted, but at least we each would have the satisfaction of knowing we had been heard and taken seriously. This show of respect could help maintain our fraternal bond.

At another level of my being I was finally acknowledging that as long as I remained in religious life I would never have the full intimacy that I had now glimpsed. I would never have the loving companionship of a woman, one that could be " 'til death do us part" and could be expressed sexually.

My grief over Andrew's death was severe. Several members of the community grew concerned about me. I know that I was a burden to many of my brothers as I explored with them the burgeoning of this remarkable friendship and its effect on me. Within the month, however, the sharpest edges of my wound finally grew less acute and I set my mind on preparing for two upcoming encounter experiences, one with the Immaculate Heart community and their students, and a second with our own theological seminarians.

The group with the teaching nuns and their students was to take place within a week. The Center for the Studies of the Person staff had invited the four of us who trained with them to help co-facilitate encounter groups at the Casa de Maria. Actually, I was to have been a co-facilitator, but my prospective partner got sick and could not attend. When Melinda Sprague explained that the staff wanted me to go it alone, I asked in my usual self-deprecating way, "Do you really think I can do it by myself?"

"Did you hear your question?" she answered.

"Yes, I heard," I replied. "If you're inviting me to do it, you must think I can. Case closed."

Before separating into groups of ten, all of the staff and participants gathered in the large reception area of the retreat house. Carl Rogers briefly explained what encounter groups were about. Because words were inadequate to the task, he said that the staff would provide a fish-bowl experience, positioning ourselves in the center of the large group and sharing for about a half-hour in the manner of an encounter.

One of the teens raised her hand and after Carl acknowledged her, she innocently asked, "Dr. Rogers, what are your credentials for doing this kind of thing?"

Carl laughed good-naturedly, commended her for asking an important question and offered, "I've done groups like this for years and professionally studied their nature."

She seemed satisfied.

My group was made up of teenage women. As we began, I allowed myself some moments of silence. Immediately I noted in myself the familiar signs of grief over the death of my friend, Andrew. I had to share this from the start.

"A few short weeks ago," I began, "I lost a very close friend. Actually, he was the closest friend I have ever had. He was a Franciscan priest, too. And I can't seem to stop weeping. Even now as I speak I'm about to break into tears. That shouldn't stop me, but I will share whatever is going on within me. I'll make every effort to get beyond my own feelings and listen to what you have to say. I've been learning that love exacts a heavy toll."

The group's response was immediate. Despite their youth, the teens showed uncommon understanding and were unafraid to express their concerns. A few identified with me, sharing losses they themselves had suffered. This opening exchange primed the pump and we moved ahead rapidly, staying remarkably close to the present.

As in Malibu and La Jolla, once again I experienced, this time in teens, the raw power of this deceptively simple process. There was a kind of sustaining, nurturing, human wisdom in the group that emerged to handle each disclosure that was made. It was accepted that feelings have no moral tone; they were seen simply as clues to each one's identity. Daily debriefing sessions with other staff members served me well as each of us described what was going on in our respective groups. At the end of each day one of us Franciscans would preside at a Mass where we could celebrate our individual awakening within the supportive community we were becoming.

It was clear to me that encounter groups were an invaluable environment for people to discover the beauty within themselves. I had been praying Psalm 139 for two and a half decades without being moved. It now sprang to life. In it the psalmist realizes that regardless of how hidden he thinks he is, there is One who knows him "through and through." That One knows him standing or sitting, up close or far away, walking or lying down. There is no escaping God's penetrating gaze. Then the psalmist, exhaustively known, cries out: "O God, for all these mysteries I thank you: for the wonder of myself, for the wonder of your works."

Of the two encounter groups the second was to be far more challenging and life-changing. It had been two months since in response to the request of the theological students I had organized a three-day encounter group for them. My Franciscan colleagues who had trained at La Jolla with me were encouraging and supportive. Together we had decided that the three staff leaders from the Center for the Studies of the Person at La Jolla were to be in charge, but that we would be leading groups as well.

As soon as I announced to the students that the arrangements were in place, three of them became wary of participating. They frankly feared intimacy. One by one I took them for a long walk, carefully explaining what the encounter was, answering their questions, listening to their fears. As a result all three came around. One of the three said that if all went well for him he would bring me a single rose when the sessions ended. This was to be a sign between us.

To bring more depth to the experience, my staff and I decided we would include three women from the parish and a nun as participants. While this was a departure from our accustomed separation from the opposite sex, it seemed important to us. The women we invited were delighted to be included.

The encounter with the theological students began in our community chapel. First we prayed in silence. This gave me a chance to focus on what we were about to do, on how radical a

step we were taking. Our students had been living in unquestion-
ing obedience to an authoritarian system. This experience might
be—probably would be—explosively liberating.

This best guess of mine was not based solely on my experience; it was reinforced by a large number of priests and nuns who
had been at La Jolla with me. There at our evening Mass each day
we used to share how powerful an experience it was to be taken
seriously, to be invited to regard conscience as the ultimate forum
of decision-making, and to face the frightening intimacy of sharing. What would we, the seminary staff, do with thirty awakened
young men eager and ready to live out what they had learned? My
reverie was interrupted by Father Robert who prayed aloud for a
successful outcome. Our prayer over, each of the four groups re-
paired to the room where the drama was to begin.

I had learned to open a session with a brief statement of what
was going on inside me at that moment. I shared both my fears
and excitement about our three days together. Then I sat in silence, hoping that someone would follow my example. The only
woman in the group spoke up. "I want to thank you for inviting
me to this encounter. I am feeling quite awkward as a lay woman
among all of you." Of such a simple beginning the group slowly
took shape.

All the other participants were theological students, ten of
them. They had grown up together at Saint Anthony's Seminary,
the residential high school just a hundred yards away. Before coming to Santa Barbara they had lived for four years in community as
religious brothers. Now in their early to mid-twenties, they were
discovering that through all those years together they had remained virtual strangers. Not one had known the other's deepest
fears, doubts, joys, aspirations.

As each man shared his life, however, the particularities of his
experiences and reactions gave him shape. The cumulative effect
of getting to know one another in depth was powerful. At times
tears flowed freely.

With the palpable growth of trust in the room each participant felt increasing freedom to be more and more self-disclosing.
Occasionally a formative experience from childhood might
come rushing to consciousness and help the person understand a

lifetime of self-doubt. Once out on the table, the early issue could be understood and released. Now the repressed energy could be re-directed into living positively.

At mealtimes my task became trying to explain the sometimes unusual behavior of the participants to the rest of the community who were not involved. In the middle of their busy day they were being confronted with strange sights: young men from the encounter group, newly come to appreciate one another, might be standing together, gazing into one another's faces, deeply involved in conversation. Some of them even had to be coaxed to eat.

Our Mass at day's end was unusually celebratory. What had happened in group that day filled the scriptures and ritual with new and special meaning. The Church was seen as a community of caring, supportive people, the Holy Spirit as a creative presence working wonders among us, the Franciscan Order a fraternity called to prayer and service. We were now brothers who not only prayed and studied together but who contributed to one another's spiritual growth by open and honest interchange.

Not much to my surprise, by the last day some of the students felt trusting enough to express strong doubts about continuing on the path toward the priesthood. In the encounter environment of acceptance they were realizing that they had long repressed substantial doubts, or that their motivation had been faulty, based as it was on an incomplete awareness of all the factors involved in their decision.

I had feared this but I also welcomed it. My fear concerned the province's likely reaction to young men suddenly leaving the community, especially at this late juncture. My joy was that young men could now make informed decisions based on awakened awareness.

Our last session ended quietly with each of us summarizing what the group experience had meant to us and expressing any special appreciations that we were feeling. Then we headed for the chapel for the Mass that would conclude our encounter.

From across the patio I could see Tom coming toward me. This was the student who had had severe doubts about his participation and had promised me a flower if he managed it. He was wearing a soft smile and carrying a rose.

Physically and emotionally exhausted, I entered the sacristy and vested for Mass. I knew that I was too close to my feelings, too overwhelmed to give the homily. When Bill Coulson entered the sacristy I let down my guard, put my head down on the counter and started crying.

He put his hand on my shoulder and asked, "Can I help in any way?"

"Yes," I said haltingly, "I don't know exactly what I'm feeling, but I know I can't trust myself to put two sentences together without sobbing. Would you speak?"

"I'd be delighted," he responded.

And so we concluded an experience that would have profound repercussions and consequences for all those who had participated, as well as for the Franciscan community at large. This was immediately apparent. Those who were to receive minor orders from the bishop that evening manifested very little interest in the matter. Faculty members reminded the ordinands at dinner that since the ceremony would begin at 7:30, they would need to be in the sacristy by 7:15. The students seemed to be living on another planet. They nodded assent but nothing we said seemed to penetrate. With only minutes to go we finally corralled them and marched them down to the chapel.

This was an ordination like no other I had ever attended. It brought together two distinct worlds that hardly touched at any point. First there was the universe of this resplendently dressed hierarch, one built on an understanding of the supernatural that set aside "merely human" awareness by damning it with faint praise. The inhabitants of that world would therefore be unaware of and disinterested in what had been going on in our hearts and minds for the past three days. That was a heavily institutional world where taking an inward psychological look was reserved only for those with obvious mental health problems, a world that honored and rewarded obedience to authority and carefully defended orthodoxy.

On the other side there was the fresh world of these young ordinands who had just moments before come up from the baptismal waters of human contact. Newborn, they had taken a giant step away from the *persona* or façade that they had thus far shown the world and with which they had been over-identified. In the new self which they were just glimpsing there beat the healthy heart of a God-given autonomy. They could now responsibly challenge anybody's notion of who they ought to be, however much this stance might frighten those in authority, including me.

Henceforth while they honored the agreements they entered into, they need not respond to another's expectations of them, especially when these issued from a world view alien to their own. The encounter had given them the experience of abandoning rigidity, allowing fluidity in their beliefs and in their way of being in the world. This would undoubtedly frighten those obedient to a system requiring strict dogmatism and submission. Their new self-perception had revealed to them how complex they were in actuality, opposing traits often sitting side by side within them. They had begun the process of accepting this reality in themselves and in others. Now they were more able to experience their cowardice as well as their courage, their disinterest as well as their zeal, their selfishness as well as their otherness.

The two worlds were colliding in the Friars' chapel that night. In the sanctuary sat the bishop, promoting young men to orders that had lost all significance in their world. Facing him were eight ordinands moving as if in trance—kneeling, standing, praying at the appropriate moments. The ritual duly performed, we left the chapel with all due grace. The ordinands received the congratulations of the bishop and his assistant, and of the Franciscan community. One aftermath of the encounter however hung in the air. It would require a lot of attention.

The next day when I got to my room after breakfast there were four students waiting for me. Others were lining up outside the rooms of my brother priests who had facilitated the three-day group along with me. The impact of the intense sharing was just settling in. I listened carefully to them, trying to discern mere venting of feeling from the tentative formation of a serious doubt. The catharsis was intense and ongoing. This continued for an emotionally draining week leaving me exhausted and in need of a physician.

I told the doctor about the three-day encounter and that it had left me feeling like my bone marrow was quivering. He took my vital signs, asked me some questions and then, with a stern face said, "Get out of town. You need a complete rest."

"I'll go on Sunday, after my Masses," I said.

"Listen to me," he insisted, emphasizing each word of his orders. "Go home and pack now. Leave town immediately."

And so I did. I sought refuge at San Miguel, the provincial novitiate. It was just a two-hour drive to the north and the novice master was a close friend. That night I slept for ten hours. Three days later I felt refreshed and returned to Santa Barbara.

It was weeks before I heard the first clicks of a typewriter in the students' wing. Taking this to be a sign that they were returning to some normalcy I allowed myself a deep sigh of relief. With the three-day rest I was able to hear more easily the doubts of some of the students about continuing in their religious vocation. Several did ask to leave. Since they were in solemn vows, this required a special dispensation from Rome. I grew worried because many more might soon be reaching this same decision. I called Father Alan McCoy at his Oakland office and expressed my concern.

He reassured me. "I trust what you and the others are doing. As long as the students give careful consideration to what they are doing, so be it. If there are only five left at the end of the year, that's the way it will be."

This was the solid support I needed; I was relieved and grateful. And I felt even better when he invited me to call him on a special line, day or night, should I need to consult him again.

Our Christmas definitorial meeting was held in our Scottsdale retreat house in the desert on the outskirts of Phoenix. For the first time I would be without Father Carroll, my chief supporter on the board. At the end of summer, just one week before school was to open, he had precipitously left the Franciscan community. It was a shock to all of us.

While I had heard second hand that he was very disturbed by the high-handed, imperious behavior of some priests toward nuns whose friendship he valued, I knew little else. I had no idea that he was angry enough to abandon priesthood and community life. I realized I would miss his supportive presence at the meeting. Now I would stand alone when questioned about the disruptions in the

Santa Barbara School of Theology and my part in it. This had disturbed many in the province.

One elderly priest summed it up, "Armando has ruined the Franciscans on the West Coast."

I was expecting fireworks. I could really use a friend on the board.

The issues that surfaced centered on freedoms we in Santa Barbara were taking with the ritual of the Mass. We were offering our daily Mass in the students' recreation lounge, rather than in the Friars' chapel. We were not wearing the full array of prescribed vestments. Some of the music we were singing was that of the pop culture, featuring the Beatles, Bob Dylan, Joan Baez, Peter, Paul and Mary and others. At the time of the homily everyone was invited to comment. At times some non-Catholics were receiving Communion along with the Catholics.

I responded to these criticisms with reasonable calm, explaining that what we were accused of doing recklessly was in fact a careful attempt to adapt to the changing culture of our age. We were scandalizing no one; everybody who attended the liturgy welcomed and encouraged this experimentation. Those that did not want to join us attended liturgies in the Old Mission church, which might be more to their liking. Everything we did in the lounge was done reverently and only after due consultation among the staff. Each innovative change was examined for evidence that our efforts were bearing fruit. Proof that we were connecting with people was abundant. They were coming daily, freely, not out of obligation. Young people were attending and joyfully participating. The music chosen for the liturgy was not simply pop music but pop music with a contemporary message about our brotherhood and sisterhood, about peace in the world, about social justice, about respect for God's creation, about the process of death and resurrection, about discovering the beauty of each person in the world.

In the end, a definitorial vote was taken on whether to form a committee that would draw up directives to guide us in our liturgy. The tally was five to one in favor of the resolution. I was the lone dissenting vote. I knew that a monitoring board would stifle creativity and lay participation. Despite my defeat I was proud of having stood up to the other definitors. Later that week I told my mother about the vote, saying, "Mom, for the first time in my life, I felt a strong sense of being a full-grown man."

Some time elapsed before the liturgical committee met and issued its guidelines. Meanwhile, our Saturday Masses were growing more and more popular. People feeling disaffected with their own parishes came to worship with us and seemed so taken by the celebration that they brought their friends. Families came with their children, babes in arms, tots, pre-teens, teens. Some of the young people played guitars and sang. The mood and setting were informal and inviting. Participants felt free to call out for support for causes they were championing or to announce a joyful personal or family event.

The Episcopal bishop, James Pike, came with his wife; later he brought his aged mother. Some UCSB professors joined us, bringing with them a wealth of understanding and support. A few priest-celebrants even took liberties with the canon of the Mass, generally regarded as its sacrosanct and untouchable heart. They familiarized it, using terms more understandable to the young. Prayers for the sick and for other special intentions were offered by those present without self-consciousness. Faith perspectives on significant current events, political and ecclesiastical, were the focus of some of our liturgies.

Toward the end of May my classmate, Father Robert, told me of the special plight of a Jesuit priest whom he knew. The man had fallen in love and wished to marry his fiancee. The couple was going to Texas where the priest had been offered a university position. Two obstacles stood in his way: his religious vows, and the priesthood. Each calling entailed the obligation of celibacy.

To clear his path toward marriage he first petitioned his Minister General in Rome to be released from his religious vows of poverty, chastity, and obedience; this was granted.

Next he asked Los Angeles Cardinal McIntyre to petition Rome for a dispensation from the impediment that arose from his priesthood. The cardinal refused.

The priest was told to wait for at least a year to ponder the wisdom of his decision. In effect, this prohibited a Church wedding for an inordinately long time.

I considered this a clear violation of the man's natural law right to marry, a flagrant injustice. Since Father Robert was about to leave for vacation he himself could not preside at the wedding. I volunteered to do it in his stead. Even though the Church would consider the union invalid it would at least be recognized as a true and valid marriage by the state of California.

The bride and groom were jubilant at my offer to marry them. An elderly couple who lived two blocks from the theological seminary offered their spacious home for the ceremony. This was icing on their wedding cake.

The wedding day arrived. To enhance the ceremony I asked four of our students to come along; they played and sang beautifully in the style of Peter, Paul and Mary. A close priest friend accompanied me.

As soon as I entered the home, an alarm went off in my head. I had been told that the assembly would be small and that I would know everyone in attendance. But it was still a half-hour before the wedding and a large crowd had already gathered. Five Jesuit priests from Loyola University in Los Angeles came to celebrate their brother's happy moment. How to control the notoriety of this ceremony? Cameras were everywhere. Entirely too many people would come to know about this event. It would almost certainly come to the attention of Church authorities.

Before we began I announced that we needed to be careful about with whom we shared news of the wedding, and even more importantly, the identities of those officiating. Photographs could create problems for me and others present. Hoping for the best at this late stage I cautioned, "Remember, discretion is the better part of valor."

The ceremony was warm and participative. Everyone attending was educated and accustomed to speaking. Each felt free to comment at the time of the homily. Just before we concluded the Mass many offered eloquent best wishes to the couple.

At the reception, held in the back yard of the house, the couple generously expressed their gratitude to me for a meaningful ceremony. The five Jesuits gathered around me and thanked me for presiding at their brother's wedding. Why, then, was I feeling sick in the pit of my stomach?

Mulling it over I understood my fears were due to the fact that almost certainly I would have to answer for the ceremony I had just performed. Though as a civil marriage it was not explicitly forbidden, Church authorities would interpret it as a significant violation of canon law deserving substantial consequences.

On the walk back to the Old Mission I poured out my anxious heart to my priest friend. He didn't think me melodramatic at all and assured me of his support should anything come of this. That was as much comfort as he could offer me and it did help to calm me a bit.

It was the middle of June, 1968. I was delighted that my teaching obligations were behind me for the summer. I was returning to the Center for the Studies of the Person in La Jolla, this time as an unpaid trainer. The experience would be invaluable. My new role offered me an opportunity to utilize the skills I had been developing during the year. This time I was paired with an older, more experienced man. Supported by him I could relax into the work.

Midway through the training, instead of returning to my quarters at Old Mission San Luis Rey, I went to visit my brother, Joe, and his family in Chula Vista, a few miles south. After a hearty dinner I lay down on the floor of the living room to visit with the children, Jean, Mike, and Jennifer. I was feeling physically, emotionally, spiritually and gastronomically satisfied. Things were going well. The encounter experience was not only teaching me new skills but, more importantly, it was radically changing the way I viewed life. Then my sister-in-law called to me from the dining room.

"A call for you," she said.

"Stay there," my nephew, Mike, said, "I'll bring you the phone."

I was surprised that someone had managed to track me down here in Chula Vista and needed to talk to me on the weekend. Perhaps it was one of my fellow Franciscans going through the training with me at La Jolla. "Hello," I said. "Who's this?

"This is Kenan. I'm calling you from Santa Barbara with some important news. I thought you needed to hear it right away."

Father Kenan Osborne was a professor of systematic theology at our Santa Barbara seminary. He had always been very supportive of me, though, at times, he enjoyed teasing. So I said, "Are you serious this time, Kenan?"

"Very serious," he said. "Are you sitting down?"

"Better than that; I'm lying down."

"Well, stay there," he said firmly. "We received a letter today from Cardinal McIntyre in Los Angeles. It concerns you. I want to read it to you."

Immediately a bell went off. This must be about the marriage I had just performed in Santa Barbara. My premonitions at that time were about to be verified.

"Shoot," I said.

He began to read. It was a very formal letter, first greeting my superiors, then detailing that it had come to his attention that a Franciscan of the Saint Barbara Province, Father Armando Quiros, had recently performed a canonically invalid, unsanctioned marriage between a woman and a priest, formerly a Jesuit, who had not yet been dispensed from his obligation of celibacy. This was an invalidating impediment; the marriage was invalid and illicit. For this act of ecclesiastical recklessness and disobedience he was herewith divesting me of jurisdiction to function as a priest in the Los Angeles Archdiocese.

In terms of its practical effects, I told myself, the sanction was not extreme. The cardinal's action was limited to his jurisdiction, which included my parish ministry in Santa Barbara. So it was only within this area I was no longer permitted to preach, join Catholics in marriage, and hear confessions. I could still minister to members of my religious community. The letter was signed "Yours warmly in Christ Jesus, Cardinal James Francis McIntyre."

For some time I was dumbfounded. Even if the practical consequences of the cardinal's action were quite limited, there were far more important considerations to look at. I was a definitor in the province. I was a professor and the dean of students at the seminary. These were positions of importance, which implied that the province trusted me to play by the rules, surely not to embarrass the community.

On the other hand, I wasn't really sorry that I had provided for two worthy people an appropriately spiritual experience to celebrate their coming together as husband and wife. And I thought I had taken reasonable steps to control the wedding's notoriety. Obviously, I had not been careful enough.

Father Kenan's concerned voice broke into my thoughts, "Are you still there? Are you okay?"

I assured him that I was. Then he continued, "Actually the cardinal first telephoned, wanting to speak to you. When we told him that you were in La Jolla leading encounter groups he was very upset. He had just seen a *Life* magazine centerfold of a nude encounter group and assumed this was what you were doing. This obviously aggravated his mood. When he calmed down he told us that a letter would be arriving, formally withdrawing your faculties to function in the archdiocese."

"We'll talk some more in a couple of weeks when I return," I said.

"Indeed, we will," he said quietly.

Then I told my brother and his family the plain facts and their implications. I did not worry about "offending their pious ears," as we used to say about sparing lay people. They knew nothing about the ecclesiastical world and were more curious than judgmental. Perhaps sensing my concern over the gravity of the situation, my brother assured me that their house was my house if I were in really serious trouble. I was grateful for the family's kindness but even more for the grounding their reality provided me.

The third week of training at La Jolla provided me a perfect opportunity for processing my reactions to the cardinal's letter. With the help of my group I scrutinized myself, especially for the catastrophic thinking to which I knew I was prone. All were supportive, not so much of what I had done—all agreed it was high-risk—but of my willingness to look at myself.

Clearly a whole host of events had freed me of rigid adherence to the directives of authority. My present focus was self-discovery. At the point where my new self conflicted with ecclesiastical norms, I needed to make decisions true to the self I was discovering, even if this moved me further and further away from my calling.

However, I had to reckon with reality. My "ecclesiastical

recklessness" had extra repercussions because of my leadership position in the seminary and in the province. What I did in this role cast either light or shadow upon the Church and those whom I represented. Our encounter group drew close to me around my dilemma. At the end the group awarded me a purple heart, precious even though it was a hastily assembled cardboard replica.

Needless to say, my ecclesiastical delict split the faculty anew. Three professors were quite vocal in my defense. In their minds I had simply helped a priest who had been treated inhumanely by the archdiocese, which, despite the openness of the Vatican to dispensations, chose cavalierly not to process his case. Besides, there was nothing in canon law forbidding me to act as a civil minister in a marriage. However, the three faculty members on the other side thought my behavior not only intolerable in and of itself but exacerbated by my position as definitor and dean of students.

Not to diminish the gravity of the situation, my own opinion was that the repercussions were mainly internal to the Franciscan community, with little practical effect outside of it. Well before this crisis occurred the provincial definitorium had decided to move the theological seminary to Berkeley to join the Graduate Theological Union. This was in the Oakland diocese where the matter of the wedding was unknown. For the asking I could receive priestly faculties to function in the Oakland/Berkeley area.

When I shared my predicament with my supportive friends in the CFM group, one of the men asked me whether he could give me a little advice. I readily nodded assent and he said, drawing from his military experience, "Never crap in your own mess kit."

This expressed my situation accurately if graphically. How better to point out to me that my situation in Santa Barbara would be uncomfortable for a good while? However, what was done was done. So be it.

I wasn't quite finished with the L.A. archdiocese. One Saturday evening I got a call from the IHM community at the Casa de Maria in Montecito. Three archdiocesan monsignors had descended upon them unannounced and were completing an unscheduled site visit of the novitiate.

Apparently, rumors were rampant that the young novices were watching either too much or inappropriate television. These clerics came to ferret out the truth. The nuns' questions to me poured out. Do the monsignors have a right to conduct an unannounced site visit? Do we have to comply? As a canon lawyer would you please advise the administrative staff on this matter?

I studied the law carefully and concluded that the invaders were just that, violating the rights of the community through intimidation by virtue of their honorific position in the archdiocese. Their arrival should have been scheduled in advance and the reason for their visit made clear to those they wished to interview. At 11:00 that night I went out to the Casa and advised the nuns that their canonical rights had been violated. They chose not to confront the trespassers but did alert their charges to the fact that the monsignors were using bullying tactics.

No apologies were ever proffered the nuns, nor reparations made. I noted that in this instance the Chancery violated canon law for an unworthy, illegal purpose. Yet it had condemned me for the dubious impropriety of performing the civil marriage of two people in love.

I left Santa Barbara and arrived in Berkeley a little ahead of the rest of the staff to help get our new house in order. It was there I heard that Father Robert, before beginning his farewell Mass in Santa Barbara, had invited the Episcopal Bishop Pike to come forward and concelebrate with him. A further scandal!

While the students and laity present were moved by this friendly ecumenical act, a few members of the Old Mission community considered this *communicatio in sacris*, a strictly forbidden co-mingling of Catholic and non-Catholic participation in the most sacred act of the Catholic Church.

When word of the "travesty" reached me in Berkeley I winced. Another member of the theological faculty had stomped on a provincial open sore; there would be no peace for a good while. Word of this fresh and insolent delict swiftly swept the province. The Friars were divided even further.

From provincial headquarters I got word that one of the definitors had selectively polled some members of the province. The results of his informal study led him to propose to the definitorium that Father Robert and I be required to resign from

the seminary staff. When the definitorium followed his recommendation and issued their order for the two of us to leave, I went
back to Santa Barbara to consult with Father Robert and the other
three liberal priests on staff.

That evening we gathered in the musty library on the second
floor of the old wing of the Old Mission to plan our strategy. As a
canon lawyer I saw serious flaws in the procedure followed by the
provincial board. Our canonical rights had been violated. Whatever the truth of the charges against us, all the evidence was hear-
say. None of the definitors had been present at either of the two
Masses in question, my wedding Mass or Father Robert's
concelebration with Bishop Pike. Thus they lacked first-hand
knowledge of both occasions. Nor had they interviewed us
personally so that we could render our own account of what had
transpired.

In my case, they had not even spoken to anyone present at the
wedding. Cardinal McIntyre had moved against me because the
five Jesuit priests present at the wedding had discussed the matter
in the presence of yet another Jesuit who saw fit to alert the cardinal.

In Fr. Robert's case, apart from the rumor about what had
taken place at his Saturday Mass, there was only one letter of
complaint and that was from an unidentified Franciscan. The law
required that a formal invitation be issued to us to appear before
the provincial board. We were not even privy to the identity of
our accusers. On the strength of these legal considerations, we decided to send a formal letter to the provincial definitors. Together
we five composed a document which detailed all our objections,
insisting that if officially requested to resign, Father Robert and I
would press for our legal right; we would demand a formal ecclesiastical trial.

To make certain that every definitor knew exactly what we
were saying we made several copies of our letter and sent one to
each member. On we worked into the night, feeling right was on
our side, our mood in no way somber. By the time we finished it
was quite late. In our exhilaration we decided to take the letters to
the post office immediately, middle of the night or not. Giddy
with weariness, someone began to sing a bawdy lyric set to the

music in *Bridge over the River Kwai*, substituting names of definitors for the originals:

> *Alan has only got one ball;*
> *Terence has two but they're quite small;*
> *Martial has something partial*
> *But poor old Gratian has no balls at all!*

A week later the provincial, Father Alan, informed Robert and me that the definitorium had agreed to drop the whole matter if we would allow him to apologize to the province in our name for any offense that might have been given. We agreed and there the public consequences ended. Or so I thought.

Six months later Bishop Ward, for whom the issue was still of pathetically great moment, sent the provincial a letter in which he said that the matter of the wedding I had conducted had been referred to Cardinal Seper of the Holy Office, the doctrinal watchdog of the Vatican. In this letter Bishop Ward quoted from the cardinal's response. His Eminence considered me obliged in conscience to reveal the names of the other priests who had been in attendance. The provincial, with admirable restraint and respect, consulted me about how I wanted him to proceed.

I responded, "Tell Bishop Ward that if he pursues this matter any further, I will call a press conference and reveal the injustice of this whole matter." I never heard another word from Bishop Ward.

Before I left Santa Barbara for Berkeley, I needed to provide a so-called Dutch Solution for my brother's canonically invalid marriage. At my invitation Joe and Carole drove up to Santa Barbara from Chula Vista. I led them to the chapel off the sanctuary of the Mission Church. Father Keith Forster, a fellow Franciscan and dear friend, heard my brother's Confession. Then he brought Joe to join his wife at the altar. We went through the renewal ceremony after which I gave my brother Communion—his first Communion in twenty-five years. No sooner had I placed the host on his tongue than he was in my arms, sobbing in gratitude.

Part VI
Berkeley and Beyond: Steps Toward Freedom

THE GRADUATE THEOLOGICAL UNION (GTU) was located on Holy Hill in Berkeley at the northern edge of the University of California campus. The Franciscan School of Theology was joining two other Catholic schools, Jesuit and Dominican, and a number of Protestant schools: Episcopal, Congregational, Presbyterian, Lutheran, Unitarian. Each institution offered courses that prepared students for ministry and cordially accommodated applicants from all faiths.

Our move to GTU was exciting and challenging. Suddenly the atmosphere was no longer monastic; our large home, two blocks from the UC campus, had at one time been a fraternity house. We were now "in the world." Young men and women surrounded us in throngs wherever we went. There were twenty-eight thousand students at the university itself. At the time, Berkeley was a hotbed of all that was revolutionary, enterprising, high-risk, and strange. Young people from all over America were streaming into the city as well as Haight-Ashbury in San Francisco to "tune in, turn on, and drop out." The use of drugs was commonplace. Word was that you couldn't go to a movie in Berkeley without getting high from the second-hand pot smoke.

Despite all the tensions I had experienced that summer, the newness of what lay before us revived the hope that we could yet develop a new way of being Franciscans in the modern world. Yes, we might make mistakes, but together we would examine our decisions and make appropriate accommodations. Usually we wore our Franciscan garb only on formal liturgical occasions; otherwise we dressed like everyone else in the larger community. Like their contemporaries, some of our students sprouted beards and let their hair grow long.

As a sign of our fraternal democracy, faculty and students alike accepted house duties equally. This new emphasis on a totally shared life presented its own problems. It meant that as faculty members of the Franciscan School of Theology we were uniquely challenged with multiple roles: we were brothers to the students, their teachers and their mentors, sometimes their confessors. Our greatest challenge was the burden of evaluating and voting on the readiness of the senior students to move toward ordination.

In the real Berkeley (not the city of that era's myth) on the real Holy Hill (not the neighborhood of wicked compromise) the staff and students of the Franciscan School of Theology were dealing well with seminary life. The situation, although challenging, was quite manageable. But away from Berkeley, where fear-driven stories sprang up like toxic mushrooms, some Franciscans were regarding the new seminary setting and our liberal arrangement with panic. Some alleged that we were fostering and promoting sexual experiences for our celibate students. Others thought we were heading off into the horizon without a plan. Still others felt we had wantonly jettisoned tradition.

It was true that things had changed radically. Our students were now studying with women of other faiths as well as with men. Friendships between them began to develop. People visited beyond class hours. Some female seminarians even came to our Franciscan school to pray with us or to chat over coffee. Our Catholic theological students attended other seminaries, utilized their libraries, wandered over to the University of California campus, shopped at bookstores in downtown Berkeley. All of this went on without the strict tracking to which old school Franciscans were accustomed. While this system was risky and required trust, it was certainly a far cry from an unholy accommodation to a wicked world.

Early on I suggested to the faculty that one day a month be spent sharing in small groups and as an entire community. In the encounter group model we could discuss how all of us, faculty and students alike, were responding to one another, to the larger community outside our own seminary, and to the challenges presented to our faith. I wanted this experience built into our class schedule as an important part of our curriculum. Since we were preparing our students for ministry, their preparation should of necessity include training which made them sensitive to their own feelings as well as those of others. I was convinced that openness of this kind was imperative for all of us as individuals, as members of a brotherhood, and as spiritual ministers.

Unfortunately, our first day of sharing in this fashion was our last. Though most came to the groups and spoke with candor and respect, there were those who considered the process intrusive and irrelevant. Once again, on a very important issue, the staff—although mostly liberal—was newly divided. One insisted that what was shared among us on that day was more appropriately the stuff of spiritual direction and so should remain a private dialogue between a priest and his student. Others expressed alarm that we were back-pedaling, retreating from the gains of the past year. But to no avail. The groups were dropped. Perhaps I had been too idealistic in pushing for community encounter groups. Though this dream was dead, I still had two new ideas I wanted to launch.

My first idea centered on my course in sexuality. My own training in this area had focused on the confessor's need to distinguish the kind, severity and frequency of sexual offenses. This had totally ignored the meaning and beauty of sexuality. I decided to offer a course for our Franciscan seminarians with the goal of remedying this situation. I would utilize materials developed by the Unitarians.

Geared to sixth-graders, its candor was still quite advanced for Catholic seminarians. It would make our students confront their own sexuality head-on. There would still be plenty of time to consider the old moral theology and its confessional aspects. The course was an excellent package of slides, tapes, and questionnaires that explored issues of sexuality, sexual orientation, genderidentity and sexism.

The feeling in the room was intense; voices were muted; speech was slow and deliberate; questions were frank and short. At a coffee-break early in the semester, some of the staff remarked to me that my students looked like they were mildly anesthetized. This pleased me because it indicated progress was being made toward ensuring that our seminarians were facing their deepest, most secret selves. This was necessary before they ventured out into their ministry.

The second of my endeavors was to move the students toward genuineness and inwardness. To achieve this I would offer a course on pastoral counseling open to seminarians of all faiths. Rather than lecture and theorize, I would provide a mixture of experience and theory. Each class would be four hours long. The semester would conclude with an eight-hour encounter around the issue of operant faith—faith as actually lived rather than faith as doctrinally confessed. Classes were offered in two segments, two hours each.

The first two-hour segment was to be a group experience in which we each shared what we were experiencing at the moment. Here we could be therapists to one another, practicing the skills proposed by Carl Rogers for a helping relationship: genuineness or being real, unconditional positive regard for or acceptance of the other, empathic listening and appropriate self-disclosure.

In the second segment we would theorize about what had occurred in our mutual sharing. This approach was very close in nature to my monthly encounter group idea for the Franciscan community. But I thought it had even more relevance for anyone preparing to do pastoral counseling.

One student, a Lutheran in a year-long marriage, spoke up. He objected to my design. "Your process is flawed. Not everyone has problems," he declared. He implied that he was at peace with himself and with his significant other. I assured him that we would consider whatever problems arose, small or large. But this group was designed to be more about sharing our present reality, whether that included personal difficulties or not.

Some time later when the trust was high in the group he let us know that in fact he and his young wife were struggling with their poverty and with a failing marriage. In truth, they were quietly planning a divorce.

Slowly the group built enough trust to enter deeply into the theme for our last class, an eight-hour encounter around the issue of the operant faith beneath doctrinal Confession. These two could differ greatly; I wanted the students to explore this. In the case of Sheila there was just such a dichotomy. She did not share her Unitarian contemporaries' belief, which exalted sexual love and did not allow for the choice of celibacy as a life path. Up until now she had kept her dissent to herself. And yet in the safety of our pastoral counseling group she grew enough in courage to share in the presence of two other Unitarians in the group that during her recent stay in India she had vowed celibacy for a five-year period.

Turning to the Catholics in the group, she said, "In the matter of celibacy I feel much closer to you than I do to the students of Starr King Theological Seminary. I've been ashamed to share this with my Unitarian friends for fear of being ridiculed as isolated and out of touch with modern insights."

Her two Starr King classmates heard her, thanked her for her painful admission, and assured her of their sincere respect.

Evan, a Lutheran, remarked, "The deeper we get into the reality of who we really are and how we respond to what each of us is sharing, the less sense our religious 'turfiness' makes to me." We all shared his sentiment.

Carl, a Catholic, spoke up. He told us that on his trip from San Francisco that very morning on the Bay Area Rapid Transit he sat next to a man who eyed him in what he thought a strange way. When the stranger put his hand on Carl's thigh he froze. A flood of feelings washed over him, some pleasant, some unpleasant. Then came a second flood of judgment, blame, condemnation of any part he may have played in this. He said nothing; he simply moved his leg away as naturally as he could. He was spared any uncomfortable confrontation when the man turned away without saying a word.

This precipitated another hour of frank talk around a variety of very personal sexual issues. All of it was accepted by the group without judgment, all of it respected and welcomed precisely as it was shared. Despite the openness of that time in Berkeley, most of the participants had never really allowed this personal and close a look at their sexuality. My Catholic tradition, burdened by the powerful fifth-century pronouncements of St. Augustine, had labored mightily over the centuries even to admit that sexual love between spouses was a beautiful thing in and of itself without needing to be redeemed by an intention to procreate.

The semester ended well. I was certain that these young men and women had taken a big step toward becoming proficient, caring, pastoral counselors. Having done this work, there was a much better chance that they would be aware of their countertransference and would not permit it to intrude into their work in an unhealthy way.

> On June 25, 1969, in a letter to Archbishop Leo Binz of St. Paul, Bishop James Patrick Shannon announced his resignation as priest, pastor and bishop. He gave as his reasons the following: "I have repeatedly found myself at odds with the timidity, secrecy, studied ambiguity of the curial style and the heavy-handedness of many persons in authority in the Church."

In mid-year I was invited to join the staff of the Berkeley Center for Human Interaction housed on Holy Hill. The facility consisted of three large well-landscaped buildings sitting on a block-long piece of property stretching down to the university campus. Formerly it had served as a theological school for Episcopalian women. Now that women were permitted to enter the seminary and study side by side with male seminarians, the diocese had converted the buildings into a growth center under the direction of Trevor Hoy.

Trevor was an Episcopalian priest whose main work was to administer, develop and direct its various programs. He was widely travelled and experienced in the various psychological movements and centers of the time, including the well-known Esalen at Big Sur. A gifted, enthusiastic leader, he was seemingly delighted to discover that I had trained at La Jolla with Carl Rogers and his staff. He invited me to utilize his facility. Not only did the center offer me the opportunity to continue to facilitate encounter groups, but it took care of whatever program promotion was necessary.

At the end of our first year in Berkeley, much to my chagrin, Father Robert, my almost constant companion since we were fourteen years old, resigned in disappointment from the theological staff. He had hoped that in this ecumenical atmosphere we would move toward becoming a sharing community, eager to discuss not only theological and pastoral changes but our own personal faith. Instead, though there was much freedom of choice and movement, he found the interpersonal element lacking. The loss of his support further weakened my own desire to continue as a member of the theological community.

A deeper understanding of the growing conflict within me came in the mail. The Center for the Studies of the Person sent me a copy of a letter dated May 8, 1953 from Carl Rogers to a psychologist who was consulting him. I read with fascination something that Carl had never pointed out to us at La Jolla. He had serious concerns about the relationship of Catholicism to client-centered therapy and had made a point of sharing thoughts with a small group at the Catholic University of America.

His issue was that the bishops' approval of client-centered therapy might lead Catholic counselors to a superficial acceptance of his approach without realizing the implications of the deeper assumptions upon which it was based. These assumptions might be incompatible with Catholic thought and might present Catholic therapists with a difficult dilemma.

On the one hand, if they simply used client-centered therapy as a technique, it would lead to superficial work—an unacceptable outcome. On the other hand, if they personally engaged their clients out of the deep implications of the theory, the outcome might create a severe conflict with their Church. He made three telling points, each of which spoke eloquently to me.

The first was that as the client rises to awareness and accepts all of his experience, he grows in the ability to make his own choices, to find within himself an inner guide. The client thus grows less willing to be guided from without even in matters of faith and morals. This would include even authoritative pronouncements. Would not this orientation be opposed to the way the teaching authority of the Church sees and proclaims itself?

The second point lay in the view of the client-centered

approach on the nature of man. Carl had come to see this nature as basically positive, moving toward the good when provided the appropriate environment, learning from its missteps, as well as creative and trustworthy. Would this conflict with Catholicism's teachings, especially on the consequences of original sin?

The third point was that these realizations or shifts in attitude would arise subtly out of the *experience* of the therapist-client contact, which had mutually transforming power. Therefore, regardless of where one stood on these issues intellectually, the experience would provide a relentless push toward a position at odds with Church teaching.

Carl's typically clear insights shed abundant light on the changes that had occurred and continued to occur within me. A conservative Catholic would probably say that in the Rogerian system of therapy I had swallowed a toxic substance and was on my way to certain spiritual death. My personal view was that God had sent me a light that was inexorably dispelling the darkness.

In June of 1969 I was invited to join the La Jolla staff at the University of Illinois in Champagne-Urbana. We were to do one of our month-long encounter group trainings. This was a priceless opportunity to continue my training, not only with Carl Rogers and his staff but with other well-known psychologists who made presentations each year.

In my two summers at Champagne-Urbana I met such greats as Albert Ellis, the founder of Rational-Emotive Therapy; Clark Moustakas; and the Gestaltist, Jim Simpkin, successor to the mantle of Fritz Perls. There were many others whose names I cannot recall but whose fields of expertise included body therapies and psychodrama.

I remember clearly a distraught psychiatrist who waited patiently in the lobby of Bramson Hall for Carl Rogers to arrive. When Carl finally entered, the psychiatrist rushed up, threw his arms around him and thanked him again and again. He explained that in his long professional life, with the detached distance he had been taught to bring to the therapeutic encounter, his work had been growing less and less rewarding. In fact until he participated in an encounter group with Carl he had seriously considered suicide. After his new experience he revolutionized the way he related to his clients. Now he found his work exciting and life-enhancing both for himself and for them.

During these summers my desire to leave active priestly ministry intensified. So did my thoughts of leaving my community. Two unresolved personal issues demanded attention.

The first issue was my increasing desire for autonomy, for the freedom to pursue whatever theological and ministerial directions my experience led me to. Increasingly I understood that what I had been taught in the seminary held little relevance to my daily life. Yet what I learned by being open to whatever crossed my path, whether a relationship, a book or an event, engaged my energy intellectually, emotionally and spiritually. Furthermore, *by trusting my inner self rather than Church directives I had not lost a scintilla of trustworthiness or respect for myself and others.* If anything I had grown on every level. The feedback of the people that really knew me from the inside kept me centered.

My second issue was my attraction to the experience of intimacy. Were I to remain a Franciscan priest I wanted to be the person I was in the groups with the staff members that I had grown to know and love. If this were not possible in community life, what was I to do? My solemn vows committed me to live "in poverty, chastity and obedience for as long as I shall live." But the direction of my current experience was away from that paradigm. I was torn. Could I arrive at the point of inner freedom required to abandon my commitment?

The idea of leaving religious life and seeking marital intimacy was looming large; it was demanding a lot of soul-searching. My ongoing groups provided me with the opportunity for this work. I was face to face with a major decision, perhaps the biggest of my life.

I found myself fantasizing about pursuing a relationship with a nun, Sister Carolita, whom I had known for almost twenty years. I had first met her in the hospital where she was a surgical nurse, and I the new chaplain. We were exactly the same age. Her mother, now deceased, was Mexican and her father, Caucasian. She was dedicated to work with Latinos, something I also shared. We were highly compatible and enjoyed one another's company.

For a long time we did not discuss our friendship yet I sensed she knew I considered her special.

When a new appointment to Chicago took her away from the local scene, we kept our relationship alive by letter and an occasional phone call. Recently when she had come to the Bay Area to see her brother, I visited her at Saint Joseph's Hospital. In vague terms we spoke of our special friendship and our "interest" in one another.

As I was leaving she said to me, "I could understand if you decided to leave your community and the priesthood. It's reasonable for you to change your mind. After all, you joined your community at such an early age. But I entered religious life when I was older, more mature. I can never leave my community."

I got the meta-message and a little hurt answered, "We'll discuss this more at another time," and left.

Shortly after the theological seminary set up shop in Berkeley, four Franciscans in the province formed a new experimental community in a very poor area of East Oakland. Their mission was to reach out to young men in the military about their right to object in conscience to the Vietnam war. They leafleted the local army base about conscientious objection. They helped objectors state their convictions in a way that would be honored by the draft board. The four men rented a small, three-bedroom apartment and designed a life that was overtly secular. They wore ordinary lay garb, had no superior, had no chapel, and did not even pray in common. As time went by the belief system of two of them was scarcely theistic. All of them eschewed theology. Their life was almost purely an intense involvement in their ministry, a work requiring great stamina and courage. Its effectiveness soon pushed Congress to pass a law forbidding groups such as theirs to access military bases. To their credit, in all matters religious they stayed in constant contact with our very bright, committed and liberal provincial, Fr. Alan, sharing with him their grave doubts about institutional religion.

Soon after our arrival, many of us at the Graduate Theological Union began to participate in the local peace movement. It was in full stride; we responded emotionally to every protest that took place in the nation: the October 15, 1969 Moratorium designed to expand the peace movement off the campuses and into the cities; Nixon's "silent majority" speech; the second Moratorium march on Washington on November 15; the 1968 My Lai massacre of civilians; the conviction of Lieutenant William Calley for his role in this atrocity; the Kent State University demonstration in which four students were killed. Tensions were therefore understandably high at the air base in Fairfield where the staff from the Franciscan School of Theology helped the chaplain with weekend Masses.

In 1970, three members of the experimental community in East Oakland abandoned their conscientious objector enterprise and left the apartment. Only one remained, Tom McEneany. Tom had been pursuing the priesthood, but dropped out to join the little group that had recently formed. He loved the work and was determined to continue it. I left the seminary residence and joined him in Oakland to provide emotional and financial support for his work. This was an obvious step away from the Franciscan community and toward the freedom that had been beckoning me for some time. Tom and I were joined by a Canadian Franciscan, Father Sigismond LaJoie, who in middle age had decided to pursue a master's degree in pastoral counseling at the Graduate Theological Union.

Our little three-man community was known simply as the East Ninth Street house. It was an upstairs apartment with three bedrooms, a bathroom, a small kitchen and tiny pantry. The neighborhood was very poor and heavily industrial. Not far away a redolent Del Monte tomato canning factory sometimes made it difficult to smell anything but tomatoes. Fortunately, the freeway and BART were nearby, easily accessible. Directly across the street was a small, humble neighborhood parish church staffed by Franciscans. The parish hall served as a gathering place for a diverse group of Catholics involved in the anti-war effort as well as in a number of other social justice causes. Below us lived a family where domestic violence frequently erupted, due mostly to alcohol abuse. Police were frequent visitors. At times the brawlers spilled out into the street where the local pastor and others tried to separate the sparring partners and restore order.

Never having cooked, I now set about learning. I bought a small paperback appropriately titled *The I Never Cooked Before Cookbook*. Slowly I made my way into the mind-boggling intricacies of food preparation. The burden was not solely on me, of course. Tom, Sig, and I took turns. The three of us kept a modestly appointed but nevertheless neat home. I continued to teach at the Franciscan School of Theology, led groups at the Berkeley Center for Human Interaction, did family therapy at Saint Elizabeth's parish and occasionally helped out in Tom's work with conscientious objectors. Periodically I would be invited to lead encounter groups in various locales away from the Bay area.

One such three-day group took place in Grass Valley, not far to the north of Oakland. The participants were second-generation Japanese who wanted to come to terms with the new emphasis on awareness and expression of feelings in relationships. We also travelled to Vancouver Island, Canada, to work with parish teenagers in encounter groups.

In the summer of 1970, my religious brother, Tom, was ready to take his solemn vows. He asked to do this in a small, private ceremony in our apartment, instead of in the local parish church. To my surprise his wish was granted; the provincial agreed to come to our home and receive Tom's vows. Just a few other Franciscans would be present.

For the occasion we prepared the apartment carefully. We scrubbed the living room walls, vacuumed thoroughly. In the center of the room, atop a small table, we placed a floral bouquet flanked by two festive candles. The ceremony in the ritual needed some adaptation, so we rephrased it to convey its meaning in a modern way. Since ritual was sacred and usually followed rigorously, we could only hope that the provincial would approve.

The day arrived. We began the ceremony. Everything went smoothly until we came to the vows themselves. Tom had rewritten them to say that he was promising life in the Franciscan community, a life lived in poverty, celibacy and obedience "for as long as I am able," rather than the prescribed "for as long as I shall live." The provincial made several gentle attempts to nudge Tom toward the standard wording, but Tom was resolute.

So on a Saturday evening in July, in our small ghetto apartment in East Oakland, with the scent of Del Monte stewed tomatoes hanging in the air and the distant hum of freeway traffic in the background, unbeknownst to all the world we made canon law history: solemn vows, by their legal nature "for life," were accepted "for as long as I am able." A fitting end to the era of the '60s when nearly every traditional limit was tested.

Meanwhile I was developing a substantial counseling practice, thanks to the Saint Elizabeth's parish staff which allowed me to use their offices. I saw individuals, worked with couples and families, ran groups. Though I charged very little money for my services I still made more than enough to carry most of the financial obligations of our little East Oakland community, especially when this was combined with money I earned at the Berkeley Center for Human Interaction.

As a Catholic priest I was permitted to offer therapy without a state license. The licensing board in Sacramento reasoned that preparation for the ministry was in effect preparation enough to do therapy. As far as I was concerned this was a flawed assumption.

Seminary training, especially in my young adulthood, totally neglected insight into the human process. It was disinterested in the facilitation of psychological wholeness in others. The irony was that as a priest, however unprepared, I could secure a state license to do therapy for a mere twenty-five dollars.

But now after intense group training, whether licensed or not, I knew I was capable of good work; I began to understand that if I so chose I could make this my life's work. I was especially interested in helping couples in serious trouble; some were considering separation, even divorce. In many cases I was able to get them to the point of honest sharing with one another rather than blaming and judging.

That same year I was introduced to the work of the theologian, Father Gregory Baum, an Augustinian priest on the faculty of Saint Michael's College in the University of Toronto, Canada. I first became familiar with his thinking when he wrote a book in response to the English theologian, Father Charles Davis, who had just published a widely publicized attack on the institutional Catholic Church. But it is what Baum had to say in 1971 in his book, *Man Becoming: God in Secular Experience*, that intrigued me.

It became monumentally important to me because it precipitated a new way of thinking about my personal and professional life. Its appearance on the theological horizon was a synchronous event, entering my life precisely at the moment I needed it—at the very point of my groping to understand my growing excitement. He was eloquent and precise in his enunciation of my experience. It was by expressing the message of Christianity in the language of human growth that he provided what I had been missing, a synthesis of my religious beliefs and my psychological convictions.

As I read I realized that indeed I had not been at all histrionic at my first encounter group experience when I had noted the "high drama" of a heated, honest exchange between two Franciscan colleagues. It was the presence of God that I was sensing in their genuineness and in their efforts to transcend their fears. The Franciscan who thought I was exaggerating came from the perspective of the old theology.

What then was the great difference between the old theological viewpoint and the new? The most fundamental difference was that the old theology, having first defined the divine and the human by emphasizing the chasm between them, then faced an overwhelming task. How to bring the two into a relationship? The theological attempt to do this was a purely intellectual enterprise, heavy with intricate Hellenistic distinctions and explanations. For me it failed utterly.

The new approach on the other hand stressed that the human contains the divine in its definition. To be human is to be divine at one's core. The task of the new theology, therefore, is not faced with restoring to the human a participation in the divine which was lost by sin.

If this new approach were a recent phenomenon, I could have understood why I was ignorant of it. But I was astounded to learn that the shift in approaches from the old to the new had actually begun three-quarters of a century earlier. The founder and chief figure of this new development was Maurice Blondel, who published his doctoral dissertation in 1893. It was a masterpiece. An epochal man, he dared to think his own thoughts and publish his own insights despite the fact that they conflicted with the approach of the Catholic Church of his day. Because of his openness to the new ideas and thought patterns of his era, he succeeded in expressing the essence of Christianity in ways that the contemporary culture could understand and relate to. Indeed, he believed that it was impossible for the Church to speak relevantly to the modern world, unless it entered into respectful dialogue with the ideas at the heart of current thought. Isolation from the modern world, he said, had inevitably left the Church disconnected from modern experience. And thus it had become irrelevant. A revolutionary change! And as early as 1893!

Why then had my professors not mentioned it? Even if they had considered it heretical or dangerous, they could at least have listed it among other movements condemned by the Church. But there seemed not to have been even the faintest glimmer of awareness. True, much of the material was in French, but our professor of systematic theology had studied in Quebec and read and spoke French fluently. Yet he had said nothing.

The position papers written at Vatican II from 1962 to 1969 finally evidenced the shift from outsider to insider God that had begun with Blondel and developed after him. But there had been no similar movement among my theological professors in Santa Barbara. Why not?

I began to realize how critical it was for me now to think for myself, to challenge the rigidity of Mother Church and of conservative theologians. Now I wished to open myself to all the currents of thought available in the world. No more would I allow someone else to decide what was safe and what was dangerous to think, to say.

The grim truth was that during my eight years of philosophical and theological studies I had allowed myself to be limited to the texts provided us, texts which had been approved by the Congregation on Seminaries in Rome. I did not know that a significant, even critical, development had begun within the Catholic Church even before the turn of the century, first in the new way some were experiencing the Gospel, then in the way they understood this experience and put it into words.

The fertility of such an approach, based as it was on modern experience, spoke to the person I had become. I had changed in significant ways since my graduate studies in Washington, D.C.

Vatican II had planted in my mind the seeds of autonomy. I wanted my beliefs to be pertinent to life as I knew it—whatever I believed and professed had to be dynamic, open to endless unfolding, trusting of the individual's worth and orientation, dialoguing with differences in the world, growth-oriented rather than sin-forgiveness oriented.

Roman authorities and the majority of bishops on the other hand were still living in the old paradigm of the outsider God. From that perspective, the human being precisely as human did not share in the life of God. Man as such was merely a "rational animal." However beautiful a creation of God, this merely natural creature needed elevation to a supernatural state, exclusive access to which was provided by the Church.

Through baptism she gave supernatural birth; through the other sacraments she brought to adulthood, nurtured, and sanctified. In things moral she was the solicitous parent of a toddler incapable of perceiving danger and taking proper steps to save itself. In matters of faith she was the keeper of divine revelation (which had ended with Saint John in the first century). In this role the Church was to maintain God's word intact against the attenuating, even polluting, influence of modern thinking.

The more I entered the realities of human life, the more transcendence I discovered there, the more irrelevant I found the old approach. In both my personal and professional life, the evidence was that individuals from other religious systems or no religious system at all were offering profound insights into life, were ecumenical, were involved in the struggle for social justice.

I remembered that in 1970 at an encounter training at the University of Illinois, Jack Winthrop, a professor of psychology, had sought me out to discuss the astounding similarity between his values and mine. He was a professional man, an avowed atheist, who without recourse to religious beliefs had arrived at an understanding of the sacredness and uniqueness of the individual. Here was a person committed to promoting respect for the person both as an individual and as a member of society. It would have been disrespectful to diminish his sensitivity and openness to the sacred in human life to call him a "hidden Catholic," the clever hypothesis that, implicit in his good will was a desire to enter the Church.

He was fascinated by the way I spoke theologically about our mutual experiences. He wished to pursue our discussion further. Beneath our apparent differences we both touched on the same dynamics in human life, dynamics which flowed from a mysterious inner invitation to know, respect and love ourselves and one another.

Dialogue was life-giving, life-enhancing. Refusal to respond to this invitation, we both saw, locked us up inside ourselves with all our petty secrets, with all our unmentionable impulses and feelings, and thus with an increasing sense of helplessness and hopelessness.

Jack said that he had been in despair until he entered therapy and dealt with the emotional wounds inflicted by parental abuse. The strength to enter this past darkness had come through a personal encounter with an empathic person whom he trusted. At the concluding session of the month's intense training, Jack was scheduled to give a lecture, an analysis of the psychology of the group movement. A few minutes into his talk he realized that his intellectual presentation was not meshing with the emotional mood of the community, a mood created by an entire month of interpersonal sharing.

"I prepared hard for this talk," he said, "but I can see in your eyes and in your faces that you aren't with me on this. I don't feel disrespected by you. Not at all. But I feel very sad. My place here at a podium separates me from you who have become my community. I'm going to stop this now and sit with you in silence. I will go with whatever needs to happen."

Silence. Fertile silence.

After several minutes a man spoke up, "I could best express my feelings about our month together by singing a spiritual." He began to sing, "Oh, freedom."

Gradually everyone joined in celebrating our liberation from the slavery and oppression of once carefully guarded secrets. Then individual participants began to share the critical moments of attitudinal change they had made in the safety of our encounter.

One young man, having recently received his doctorate in psychology discovered that his new hard-won degree did not open life up to him. He had come to the group in despair. But now he was telling us that he had been able to identify and express feelings for the first time in his life.

After about an hour I had reached a point which was now familiar to me: with the gentlest nudge I would begin to sob in response to the month's pain and healing.

Another silence. Glen spoke up. He was a male therapist in a wheelchair, paralyzed from the waist down. "I want to read a poem I wrote today. It's titled, 'Jason.'"

Jason was the five-year-old son of one of the staff. He and his mother had come to pick up his daddy. The child's uninhibited ways had touched Glen, particularly when the boy approached him, pointed to his withered limbs and with innocent simplicity asked, "What's wrong with you? What happened?"

Glen contrasted this child's spontaneity with the avoidance we had all displayed. His poem described the power of the boy's directness and acceptance at every level: his innocent gaze, his simple words, his fearless proximity, his uninhibited gestures. Jason untied the last knot of my emotional resistance.

I was having a very hard time with all of this. My body began to shake. I bit the inside of my cheeks to stop the process. I tried to divert my attention. I let my eyes roam around the room, trying to focus on the details of everybody's clothing. Despite all my efforts to contain myself the dam broke. Putting my head in my hands I wept. Before I knew it I was on the floor.

There were hands massaging me with sweet gentleness. I could hear others around me crying. I lost track of time. When I finally sat up I could see that the persons consoling me were the members of my core group. I thanked them and we returned to our chairs.

When I looked around, I saw that the members of all the core groups, some one hundred people, had constellated. They were sitting very close to one another, supporting one another.

Finally I spoke, "I think I'm finished now. Words would be redundant. I want to say goodbye to all of you and leave you with my feelings of closeness, gratitude, and awe. Thank you very much."

For me this episode solidified the emergent new paradigm of the discovery of the divine, a transforming power in ordinary, everyday life. From that perspective, the primary locus of God's presence is in what the Church calls, somewhat derogatorily, "natural." And as Baum says, the mode of that divine presence is by its transcendence. That is, the immanent, or indwelling, God within us calls us to transcend or overcome our ego and move to a higher level of awareness.

If the ecclesiastical community could clothe this mystery in terms that helped me to understand and pursue it, so much the richer. But I was no longer willing to allow membership in an ecclesiastical institution to deflect me from my new direction. I had already seen the marvels attendant upon enlarging personal awareness.

I could accept that I was my doubts as well as my convictions, my cowardice as well as my courage, my alienation from others as well as my connection to them, my timorous dependence as well as my healthy autonomy, my body as well as my spirit. I was committed to this calling for myself and any others who might want to share in it.

I made a conscious decision to move into therapy as my ministry, particularly with couples and families. For some time I had increasingly distanced myself from practices of the priesthood such as saying Mass and hearing confessions. I was even seriously entertaining the idea of leaving the Franciscan community where the healthy intimacy for which I yearned was frowned upon.

With this change in perspective I rejected the hierarchical aspects of the Catholic Church. No longer could I accept edicts purporting to bind the consciences of Catholics, or assuming a capacity to define reality as a complete entity. I had found it insupportable to keep looking over my shoulder to see whether someone would be reporting what I said and did to a Church authority at whatever level. The Church's stance on sexuality was particularly insensitive. Especially its insistence on the intrinsic immorality of homosexual behavior.

Despite my best efforts to exorcise them, I am sure there were still homophobic remnants in me. Nevertheless I was increasingly accepting of gays and lesbians, particularly in the open Berkeley environment. I found it refreshing that gay Franciscan students were finding it easier to come out even though a painful dilemma now confronted them.

Formerly, an openly gay orientation would not have been tolerated in our seminary system. In this intolerant environment they understandably had to stay in the closet. Now many were convinced that psychological and spiritual recovery required not only that they openly acknowledge their sexual orientation but that they explore every aspect of that life. For some that might even include participating in gay sex.

But as Franciscans solemnly committed to celibacy, this path of sexual exploration was theoretically closed to them. We never managed to formulate a policy about this serious issue. The reality was that no gay student was ever excluded from advancement to the priesthood, nor were gay priests in any way restricted.

In a television inteview with Carl Stern in October, 1972, Abraham J. Heschel said that he would rather go to Auschwitz than give up his religion. But he also shared his belief that "...religious pluralism is the will of God."

Perhaps the most moving experience at the time was the urgent request of a friend, a former priest (he had come out a year before), that I say a funeral Mass for his gay lover who had died of an accidental drug overdose. The couple had been very active in gay and lesbian politics in San Francisco and had made a large number of friends. A Catholic pastor, when apprised of the situation, said that while he would allow the Mass to be offered in his church he would not himself preside.

When invited to offer Mass in his church, I accepted immediately. My only concern was what to say on such an occasion. I learned from friends of theirs that the lover suffered severe depression, for which he was being medicated. Despite this burden, they were a loving and committed couple who found their relationship fulfilling.

The sexual expression of their love, whatever homophobes might say to the contrary, drew them close to one another and to God. Courage to come out and take pride in their identity came from their mutual support—clear evidence, the former priest maintained, that God was in their love. They prayed together, went to Mass together, and looked forward to a long life together.

Ultimately it was his lover's depression that had been his undoing. My friend had been away at a training workshop when his
partner's depression grew particularly relentless and he overdosed.
Upon his return, my friend made a tragic discovery; his lover was
seated at the desk in the hallway, slumped over, his hand holding
the phone. Obviously his call for help was never placed.

From our talks I pieced together a eulogy which I delivered to
hundreds of mourners. My words were a paean to their love and
courage, and a call to the Church to set aside its prejudice and pay
attention to the reality of healthy homosexual union.

In my second year at the East Oakland community, one of my
former students, who had just graduated from a master's degree
program in counseling psychology at Santa Clara, approached me
with the idea that I pursue the same degree there. Because of my
experience at La Jolla, he thought the degree would be exciting
and professionally enhancing.

"If you have any doubts, let me walk you through the necessary paperwork," he offered.

I thought back to La Jolla and to a conversation that I had had
with Melinda Sprague, a significant person at my first encounter
and a source of courage for me all along my path. After a year and
two summers of groups, I told her about my wish to go back to
school to lay an educational foundation for the work I was doing.

She looked at me tenderly and said, "You should know that
you are already an effective facilitator of movement in people,"
she began. "My only fear about further academic training is that
you may come to believe that these skills come from books. Yours
are natural. Please don't go back to school *until you don't need to*.
Understand?"

"Apparently you think I want to go back to school to remedy
what I perceive as inadequacy in myself. Actually I need the credentials to move toward state licensing and decent employment
opportunities."

"You got it," she said.

Now that the opportunity of graduate school had been laid at
my door, I reflected on Melinda's words to me. Yes, I was now
ready. I really did not need further training but I needed credentials. I could go back to school, deepen my understanding of my

years-long group encounter experience and move toward licensing. The Santa Clara program was very appropriate for me because classes were offered in the late afternoons and early evenings and I would have time for my other jobs.

I suppose that at some level I understood that I was preparing myself for the day when I would no longer be working under the aegis of the Catholic Church. At that time licensing by the state of California for the agencies would be essential. At any rate, the master's program would reassure me that my training by the staff at the Center for the Studies of the Person in La Jolla was sound.

As word spread of my willingness to preside privately at unorthodox marriages, I continued to receive a wide range of invitations, each involving a potential collision with the Church. Perhaps the most satisfying one was a request from a Catholic couple. Each had been previously married to another Catholic in the Church; both unions were therefore sacramental and indissoluble. They requested that I receive their wedding vows at a private Mass I would offer for them and two witnesses.

The groom was an African-American who had fallen away from Catholic practice and declared himself an agnostic. The Caucasian bride on the other hand was a practicing Catholic for whom ritual was still important. I spent several hours discussing their request with them and decided to proceed, but only after lengthy and intense preparation. They were delighted and relieved.

Throughout our preparation time I found them to be thorough, tough, honest, mutually respectful, and loving. I knew they were on the right path. The community of the Franciscan School of Theology graciously allowed me to use their small chapel for the wedding Mass. When we assembled there I learned that the best man was the groom's dear friend and colleague, a young Jewish psychiatrist. The matron of honor was a former baptized Catholic, now a Buddhist. This presented a problem. How were the five of us going to share a Mass when we professed such a broad range of beliefs?

I decided to explain what I thought to be the essence of the Mass and how this related to the celebration of a couple uniting in married love. The Jew, because of his experience with the *seder pesach*, said that he understood, and that he was quite familiar with the ritual of the communal blessing and sharing of bread and wine.

The Buddhist matron of honor thought she could authentically participate; she liked the notion of our coming together beyond our illusionary differences. And so we proceeded: an agnostic, a Catholic, a Jew and a Buddhist, all sharing in a Mass offered by a Catholic priest seriously considering abandoning his ministry. The union among us was profound. All four of them were reverent in their participation, especially at the moment of Communion.

Following the ceremony, the Jew approached me and asked me to translate the Spanish on a gaily painted wooden cross that hung on the wall near the door. It was an ancient Aztec Indian prayer written in Spanish.

I translated, "It's a lie! The last survivor will not be left alone on earth! He too will die and be reunited with us."

Suddenly he was embracing me, crying softly, his head buried in my shoulder. Everyone silently waited. Finally he stopped and explained his grief. A short time before, his dearest friend had died suddenly. As a survivor he was left with a sense of inexplicably painful loneliness. And in addition he said, "I've just been informed that I have cancer."

The French Bishops' Committee for Relations with the Jews issued a statement in 1973 that stressed the eternal validity of Judaism and the Jewish people.

In the summer my good Franciscan brother, Father Sig LaJoie, having finished his master's degree in pastoral counseling at the Graduate Theological Union, returned to Vancouver Island to resume his parish work. In his stead a young Franciscan theologian, Pat Groves, came to live with me for his final year at the Graduate Theological Union. The staff wanted feedback from me about his suitability for the priesthood.

I was reluctant to assume the task. First of all, I no longer believed in the sort of top-down evaluation that was traditional in the Church. I believed that all of us who were in solemn vows

owed the solemnly vowed petitioner honest dialogue about the issue. A staff decision should be arrived at only after due discussion
that included him. Besides, I knew in my heart that my own bonds
to the Franciscan community and to the priesthood were growing
weaker with each passing day. I didn't want to manifest an enthusiasm that I was not feeling.

Pat was a splendid housemate—bright, energetic, and incred-
ibly creative. He could inspire the least inclined in the local
Catholic high school to read and to study. He wrote and directed
plays. His students created an exciting design for the senior year-
book. His spontaneity encouraged me to put more trust in my
own instincts and talents. While both of us abandoned the standard forms of prayer, we shared our changing insights into spirituality more deeply than I ever had before. He reintroduced me to
the power of poetry to express the inexpressible. I began to write
again.

> *In its December 1972 and January 1973 issues, the* National
> Catholic Reporter *disclosed the existence of an "unpublished
> encyclical of Pius XI attacking anti-Semitism." Jim Castelli
> editorialized that "the story of this encyclical draft means that
> the question of the Vatican's failure to denounce anti-Semitism
> at the proper time in the prewar period involved not an over-
> sight, but a conscious refusal to work with a document outlined
> by a pope himself." He added that this failure raised "many
> questions about the internal workings of the Vatican during
> World War II."*

As a result of our conversations, I realized that I really did not
want to continue teaching at GTU. Nor did I wish to lead intensive groups at the Berkeley Center for Human Interaction. What
I wanted was to return to Santa Barbara and be a therapist for the
high school students at Saint Anthony's Seminary. In addition I
would develop a ministry to the aging Franciscans in retirement at
the Old Mission. My periodic visits there had convinced me that
the busy members of the larger Franciscan community were not
attending to the psychological and spiritual needs of these elder
brothers. After a lifetime of intense engagement in ministry, they

rightfully wanted to remain in touch with the ecclesiastical mainstream. I could keep them abreast of the wide-ranging changes in the Church, changes that sometimes bewildered them.

Even as I came to this decision, however, I knew that I did not want to live with the Old Mission or the Saint Anthony's Seminary community. But why this conviction? Was it simply because I had grown accustomed to an informal way of life and wanted to continue in it?

I was not yet ready to go deeply into this question and the provincial definitorium did not ask me to. They agreed to let me live on the seminary campus in a building that housed the school library and a recreation room for the high school seniors. The move was to take place at the end of the school year in the summer of 1974.

I did not make the move to Santa Barbara; instead, my plans began to unravel. My choice not to live in community was saying something that I needed to face, something that was becoming painfully clear. I entered therapy with a psychologist at the Graduate Theological Union to face the state of my relationship to the Franciscan community.

With the therapist's help I realized that for some time I had been drifting away from the theological framework for the priestly calling. I was already finding in my therapeutic life a far more relevant and satisfying service. What truly weighed so heavily upon me, I realized, was my life in community. I had lived twenty-nine years of brotherhood with a group of men whom I truly loved, but had I not already begun my separation from them? Could I muster the courage to step away completely?

In the midst of pondering this dilemma, the provincial definitorium asked me to organize a three-day training on mental health for a select contingent of West Coast Franciscans. About fifty to sixty men would be in attendance. I accepted the task with the condition that I would work with a committee of my brothers and in addition could hire two professionals in the Berkeley community. I wanted help with both the planning and the training itself.

One of the professionals was the wife of an Episcopalian bishop, a veteran trainer who could provide unusual insight into the mental health stressors of our community life. The other was a Presbyterian theologian/psychologist whose expertise lay in group dynamics. My requests approved, we began the planning.

This offered me a great opportunity. I could now place before the community my vision and experience of how we could minister to one another in the challenges that we faced personally, professionally, and as a community. We chose a format designed to maximize personal input from each individual. Our focus was on how to revitalize our Franciscan calling to live in a community of prayer and service. It seemed critical to take a fresh look at this ancient ideal in the light of modern experience.

To increase our chance of success, we asked those who were slated to attend for any ideas they might have. We also sent them articles to read that would prepare the ground for our presentations. The committee members also spent pre-workshop time getting to know one another. We all needed to work together for maximum understanding and support.

When the opening day arrived, we were all well prepared and ready for whatever might happen. The participants entered eagerly into each exercise, openly sharing whatever thoughts and feelings they had. They made suggestions for how they could take what they had learned back to their communities. Evidence of their enthusiasm and satisfaction was manifest when they asked me to travel to five different areas of the province, from the Northwest to New Mexico, and offer a short version of the workshop to the Franciscans in each locality.

I was pleased yet pained by their invitation. While I truly loved these men, I was still drawn to a life of greater autonomy and intimacy than was permitted to us as ecclesiastics living in celibacy. But I thought it untimely to share my struggle with anyone in the community.

One particularly poignant workshop session had to do with the matter of celibacy. Not one person in the room had ever been presented with a healthy, thorough understanding of his body, much less of sexuality—not by family, not by schools, not by theological trainers, not by any ecclesiastical figure. The traditional approach to sexuality was dualistic.

Body, though God's creation, is burden to soul, needing to be regarded with utmost care. As confessors-to-be, we newly ordained priests had been taught to measure the gravity, kind, and number of sinful sexual acts. Marriage, the only clear venue for the expression of sex, was, though a sacrament, a lesser state than vowed celibacy. Jesus, we were told, was celibate.

I remember how unworthy I felt for so many tortured years. I wondered whether Jesus had passed through the confusion and excitement of pubescence, achieved puberty, experienced erections, had nocturnal emissions, had sexual fantasies—as had I. He was the Son of God. We were left with the implication that these mundane, physical impulses of our lower nature were beneath His dignity.

The discussion about sex in our workshop was so intense, informative, and supportive that everyone voted to abandon our carefully laid out schedule, start up immediately after lunch and continue as long as we found it fruitful.

The pain in the room was palpable. Tears flowed quietly, partly for the suffering brought on by our ignorance and partly from the comfort of brotherly sharing. At the end of the first session, an eighty-year-old priest, a former provincial, said quietly and tenderly, "When I was the head of the province, I had no idea that this sort of suffering was going on in so many of you. I ask your pardon for my insensitivity."

By the spring of 1974 I knew that I had left the Franciscan community. Michael Novak, ex-seminarian now a professor and well-known author, once told me that the last hurdle to leaving the priesthood was often the fear of disappointing others: family, fellow members of a religious community, priest friends, parishioners, students, etc. This was true for me as well.

I had already carefully weighed the pros and cons of leaving the cocoon of community. In religious life, loving care into old age is assured. Facing old age alone with neither the warmth of friends nor the security of money terrified me. I saw myself marching out into the world where I could find no job, or a menial one at best. I was a year-and-a-half shy of my fiftieth birthday. I had not paid a dime into Social Security or into any sort of pension plan. In a sense I was stripping myself as did Saint Francis when he left his father's home and marched out into the world to live in Gospel poverty. But there was an optimistic, daring side of me.

I had confidence that I would be able to hook on somewhere, as a teacher, perhaps a counselor. There was a chance that the Catholic parishes in the Oakland archdiocese would continue to refer troubled marriages to me. Or a non-profit organization serving the poor might hire someone like me, bilingual in Spanish with a strong background in community service.

I still had to confront the haunting fear of letting people down. In many ways, particularly in personal matters, I had provided significant help to many Friars. Would they lose respect for me? On the other hand, I thought, there were other Franciscans who had left, and despite my sadness at seeing them go, I had not been judgmental about their decision. They had to follow their conscience wherever it led.

Slowly I saw that I could safely share my decision with any person—except my mother. She was now seventy-four years old. How could I lay the heavy burden of my leaving the priesthood and Franciscan life on her aging shoulders? How would she respond? She was so proud of her son, the priest. What would other families say to her at Sunday Mass? Would this be an overwhelming public embarrassment for her?

I had seen Franciscans leave the priesthood and community without informing their parents. The result was often that word of their severance would first reach members of their parish. These parishioners, assuming that mother and father had already received the news, would approach them to express their condolences. The parents would be blind-sided, shocked. I resolved that when I left, my mother would be the first to know.

One Saturday, just before making my final decision to leave, I attended an ordination ceremony at the Oakland cathedral. A few Franciscans were being ordained as part of a large group of young men from the diocese and from other religious communities. I felt alienated from the all-male, heavily clerical ambiance of the occasion. I wore ordinary street dress; I wanted to sit with the lay persons in attendance, among those living the mysteries and challenges of human love, marriage, bearing and raising children, laboring in the world, dealing with financial insecurity, providing for retirement, coming to terms with losses.

My reverie was interrupted by a rustling throughout the cathedral. Heads were turning toward the vestibule where a huge assembly of clergy had gathered: priests, ordinands, episcopal assistants, and the bishop. Then to the martial strains of a trumpeting organ, the vast clerical body entered the cathedral and started their solemn march down the main aisle.

I thanked God I had chosen not to take my place among them. They seemed so set apart from their origins, so complacent with their separation from the ordinary people they were meant to serve. In that moment it was graphically clear to me. I could no longer be a part of this antiquated, irrelevant system.

Then, just as the clergy positioned themselves in the proper places in the sanctuary and turned toward the body of the faithful in the nave, a dog came running down the main aisle toward them with an embarrassed, out-of-breath usher in pursuit. There were discreet titters at first, then a ripple of laughter as the entire congregation became aware of what was happening. The usher and others vainly lunged to catch the animal. It was such a welcome relief from the ceremony's stiff formality. When the dog was finally caught and removed from the cathedral, I felt gratitude for the little beast's innocent gift of levity.

Just a few weeks later I asked Father Alan McCoy, the provincial, for a six-month leave of absence. I told him I was seriously considering leaving the community and the practice of the priesthood but I needed time to test my decision. His manner was gracious and he granted my request. Within the week I knew unequivocally that I wanted to leave the community and make my life as a lay person. I returned to ask him to petition Rome for a release from my solemn vows and from the obligations of the priesthood. Again he was receptive and understanding and said that he would immediately proceed with the paperwork. "But I can't predict how long this will take," he said. I thanked him and left.

In 1974 the Holy See established a Commission for Religious Relations with the Jews.

It was critical to prepare how to tell my mother about my decision, to think through what I wanted to say and how best to say it. At the time she was in Chula Vista vacationing with my oldest brother, Joe. I called her there, grateful that she would be with other family members when she heard my news. I knew what I had to say would hit her in the stomach; the presence of family might soften the blow. After a few pleasantries, I told her that I had important personal news. I wanted her to hear it first. "After serious, lengthy reflection, years of it, I've decided to leave the Franciscans and the priesthood. It was important to do this with the approval of Church authorities. I've already taken care of all the necessary Church permissions and dispensations. I know I'm doing the right thing, mother. My heart is at peace."

"This is a shock, of course," she responded quietly, "but I've always trusted you to do what is best. I want you to know that I'm not blaming you for anything."

I thanked her for understanding, chatted a bit further, and hung up.

Now I turned my attention to declaring my decision to all the Franciscan communities on the West Coast. To avert the birth and circulation of inaccurate rumors, I drafted this letter:

Dear Brothers in St. Francis:

I am writing this letter to every house in the Province to forestall any rumors that lack of information might trigger. After a good deal of struggle and with professional help from within and outside our fraternity, I have decided to leave the Order and the practice of my priesthood. I do so with peace of mind but with a heavy heart.

My sadness of course comes from my love for you born of thirty years of life spent together in prayer, ministry and fraternity. My serenity is grounded in the conviction that my decision is the correct one for me.

I intend to continue my work in the field of therapy. Many of you know that I have been doing this work since 1967 and that I received a master's degree in counseling psychology two years ago. I am working toward licensing as a marriage, family and child therapist so that I can either establish a private practice or work for a non-profit agency.

Most of all I want you to know that I consider your loving support throughout the years a priceless gift. Indeed it was the loss of this aspect of my life that most delayed my decision and caused me the most pain.

Please remember me in your prayers.

Lovingly,

Armando Quiros

Now that all the significant players were informed of my decision, I considered myself a layman committed to make my life in the world.

Part VII
Life as a Layman

AT SOME LEVEL MY choice to leave the Franciscan community was life-changing, yet my day-to-day life continued much as before. I had already been wearing ordinary street attire for some time; I continued to live in the apartment on East Ninth Street, though now alone. My roommate had gone to a Franciscan community nearby. I continued my work as a therapist and consultant. For the moment this would be enough to sustain my few financial needs. My rent was cheap; I prepared all my own meals. It was as if I had been a piece of fruit ripening on a tree and had finally fallen of my own natural weight.

Responses to my leaving came almost immediately by phone and by mail. For the most part they were loving and touching. Some commended me for my courage, especially considering my age (just shy of fifty); some asked me not to be a stranger but to visit on occasion; some thanked me and said that I had taught them how to live in community; some wished me courage and strength along the way. There were two exceptions.

One letter was from a classmate who felt hurt by my leaving. He felt disrespected, complaining that I had never given him a clue about my decision to leave. Of course he was right. For all my emphasis on openness, I had not let it be generally known that I was growing deeply disaffected from both life in community and in priestly service.

The other letter was from a former student that roundly blistered me for abandoning him.

"I had been wasting away in an emotional wheelchair," he wrote, "and you convinced me that I could stand up and make my own way. And now you blithely walk away from me—you're the cripple!" As I read his letter, I recalled an article by the writer John Cogley, in which he strongly questioned Sister Corita Kent's decision to leave the Immaculate Heart Sisters Community. His reasoning was that leaders need to think about something broader than their own personal needs. The position of importance which they have assumed requires that they defer to the needs of their community.

I didn't agree with him, not then and not now. It seemed plainly wrong to maintain a way of life that had lost its meaning for me.

Important papers concerning my dispensation from the obligations of the priesthood arrived from the Vatican through the Cardinal's office in Los Angeles. I found them insulting and duplicitous especially in one important regard: they wanted me to confess that I had a Herculean sex drive that could at any moment overwhelm me and bring great disrepute to the Church in general and the priesthood in particular. It was this consideration, they suggested that I confess, that was leading me to petition a dispensation from my obligation of celibacy. From their perspective, marriage would provide an appropriate outlet for my sex drive, delivering me from its domination.

I refused to say this and wrote back that I wanted to leave because the celibate state in the Church precluded the autonomy and intimacy I had awakened to.

It was just about that time that I received a call from a woman who had participated in a training I had done at the Berkeley Center for Human Interaction some two years before. Her name was Lois. She was phoning from a local hospital where she was having some tests done and thought she would like to say hello. Thus began a casual relationship which later turned serious. She was beautiful. Her eyes sparkled. I loved her sense of humor. Her familiarity with the world of therapy attracted me. She worked as a receptionist in the mental health unit of the county hospital in Martinez.

A Presbyterian, she was interested in spirituality but was not a frequent church-goer. Increasingly she remarked that she was emerging from a lifetime of hiding and was letting me get to know her like no one ever had. Our exposure to therapy gave us both a perspective and a set of experiences that we enjoyed talking about. She was easy to be with. When over the months we fell in love, a psychiatrist friend of hers instructed her that in the light of my monastic background she should be gentle and patient with me in the matter of lovemaking.

In January 1975, the Vatican issued "Guidelines and Suggestions for Implementing the Conciliar Declaration Nostra Aetate, *its Declaration on the Relationship of the Church to Non-Christian Religions."*

Rome swiftly released me from the priestly obligation of celibacy, though with a cautionary note which I found medieval: since lay people were incapable of handling scandal I was not to live within 200 miles of any city where Catholics had known me as a priest.

One evening I proposed marriage to Lois at the most romantic place I knew, Fisherman's Wharf in San Francisco. She accepted. Fortunately for us, Lois' previous marriage was a civil one to a baptized Catholic; as such it was declared null and void for lack of proper form. Four months later Lois and I were married. Since ours was a mixed marriage we exchanged vows in a private ceremony presided over by my classmate, Father Robert Pfisterer.

From the start we got along well and with the months I grew to love her dearly. Shortly before we had gotten reacquainted, she had attended two weekends of the newly popular Erhard Seminars Training (EST). By this time the EST style had become less apocalyptic, less visionary, and seemed to have served her well in many regards. The ninth of ten children raised on a farm where men took the primary roles, she grew up thinking of women as secondary, subservient, and entitled to few rights. EST restored a sense of personal dignity to her precisely as a woman.

That pleased me. But there was one major problem: she had a long history of recurrent depression. I became aware of her illness early in our courtship and at times this made me doubt the wisdom of making our life together. Her illness had once grown to such severity, she confided, that early on she had undergone Electro-Convulsive Therapy (ECT), in those days massively invasive. In response to the electric shock, her body had lurched, injuring several vertebrae. But when I met her, she seemed in relatively good health and was depression-free.

Looking back, I wonder why I didn't flee from a relationship with a depressed person. In my ignorance, I psychologized the illness, believing it to be due to the severe stress and constriction of her life with the alcoholic to whom she had been married. I was certain our life together would be quite different. Neither of us abused substances. We cared deeply for one another. We were both adept at negotiating our differences. She was an experienced, responsible manager of the practical affairs of living, an area where I had little or no expertise. I would help her expand the narrow circle of her life by introducing her to my numerous supportive friends and to the world of spirituality, education, music, and the arts.

My ignorance of the etiology of her illness was understandable; I had never been taught anything about the biological roots of some kinds of depression. The Center for Studies of the Person, the Berkeley Center for Human Interaction, the University of Santa Clara all ignored the issue. Only in the work of Albert Ellis, founder of Rational-Emotive Therapy, had I found a reference to emotions of physiological origin as opposed to those issuing from irrational beliefs.

Out of a combination of ignorance and the wish to believe, I placed Lois' depression in the latter category of feelings. The sadness, helplessness, hopelessness came from irrational beliefs which we could certainly handle if we worked hard enough. I was confident that both beliefs and feelings would heal in an environment of a healthy relationship. I chose to ignore the information given me by a psychologist friend who said prophetically, "Depression only gets worse with age."

Somehow I managed to consign this distressing information to my scrap heap of inconvenient considerations. Surely we could make it work. We both wanted to. Our first major decision was to move to Santa Barbara where I was well known in the Catholic community. I was sure I could build a private counseling practice there. Meanwhile I would get a job, any job, to finance the basics of living; Lois would supplement this with a small pension from her former hospital position in Contra Costa County.

In 1975, the American bishops issued a statement acnowledging that most of the essential concepts in the Christian creed had roots in Judaic soil.

We moved to Santa Barbara and found a lovely apartment on De La Vina Street directly across from Pinecrest Hospital; its medical services included a residential alcohol and drug treatment program. Lois and I had driven down two weeks before our move so that I could seek employment. A non-profit agency called Community Free Employment Service seemed happy to hire me as a job placement specialist since I could speak Spanish and was accustomed to meeting the public. Maria Elena York was my boss; she proved pivotal in launching me into the field of addiction and recovery. This was an area of therapy that most explicitly tied in with my dedication to Carl Rogers' research and the theology of Maurice Blondel and Gregory Baum.

While I enjoyed working with the people who came into the agency looking for work, I disliked having to beg employers when they were hiring to offer our clients special consideration. On occasion I was treated very rudely. One potential employer said in a sarcastic tone, his face inches from mine, "'Free employment service,' you say! My ass! Those are my taxes that are going to provide derelicts your so-called free service."

No one had ever spoken to me this way. But back at the office the other two employment counselors were gracious and understanding. Mrs. York was kind, constantly looking for ways to promote me in the community. She considered me over-qualified for the job and sought opportunities for me to serve the community more appropriately. She showcased me whenever and wherever she could.

To this end she told me to attend meetings of El Concilio de la Raza, a community-based group interested in promoting Latino causes in Santa Barbara. This led me to an engrossing chapter of my life—political participation in a variety of Latino causes. A humble beginning, this was my first contact with the work-world. But it led me directly to a job that fit my talents and my psycho-spiritual orientation.

One of the people I met at El Concilio was Gabriel, the clinical director of Zona Seca, a Latino alcohol and drug treatment program. A recent graduate of the University of California, Santa Barbara, he didn't feel he had enough experience to do justice to his job. First he asked me to lead groups in Spanish at his agency. Then a short time later he invited me to apply for his job. I had serious questions about my qualifications as a specialist in the field of addiction and recovery so I consulted a therapist friend, coincidentally another former priest, David Richo. David was clinical director of counseling services at the Santa Barbara County Alcohol and Drug Office. He and I had first met one another at a gathering of former priests hosted by the Casa de Maria Retreat House in Montecito, the site of my early training in person-centered groups. Thanks to his confidence in me and the reading he recommended, I was hired as the clinical director of Zona Seca where my new salary, minuscule though it was, nearly doubled what I had been earning. The counseling staff was small and responsive and I was back in the spiritual world which I loved most, the facilitation of growth in others through dialogue grounded in supportive, acceptant love.

From the beginning I received nothing but appreciation for what I brought the agency, both in terms of its staff and of the people served. That is, for the most part. There was the occasional person who filed an unfounded complaint with the county. Once I was falsely accused of promoting controlled drinking by alcoholics, a point of view diametrically opposed to my approach. I had learned from Alcoholics Anonymous that at the center of recovery or sobriety is total abstinence, one day at a time.

I had no inkling of how personally important and rewarding my work with alcoholics was to be. The psychological and spiritual depths of twelve-step work as practiced in Alcoholics Anonymous and Alanon were not yet part and parcel of my way of viewing recovery.

With the alcoholics who came to Zona Seca I was as supportive, understanding and accepting as I had been with other clients. But the narrow way in which I had been interpreting Rogerian non-directiveness in my previous therapeutic work did not allow me room to confront the alcoholic's denial. It had not yet occurred to me that it was important to set conditions for clients to continue in therapy with me. The most basic condition was that the alcoholic attend Alcoholics Anonymous meetings and find a sponsor with whom to work.

I made many referrals to these meetings, but never having attended one myself, I had not yet developed an experiential appreciation of what occurred there. Without this information I could not relate my therapeutic work to the principles of the Twelve Steps of recovery. Little by little clients who had achieved sobriety in AA helped me understand the program.

Eventually I saw that participation was critical for one to stop drinking and stay stopped. This insight made me aware of a serious problem. What were our monolingual Spanish-speaking clients to do? The number of Latinos referred to our agency was growing and there was not a single AA meeting for them in South County. I decided to take steps to change the situation.

I approached a bilingual man in the community who had fifteen years of sobriety, David D., and prevailed on him to start an AA meeting in Spanish. He wouldn't want for participants; my staff and I would be funneling every Spanish-speaking alcoholic in our drinking-driver program to the group.

The move proved fruitful. For the first time the area's Spanish speakers were finding sorely needed help. Those early, tenuous meetings in Spanish marked the birth of a growing program of sobriety that recently celebrated its second decade of life.

My increasing absorption in my work was providing precious refuge from my life at home which, after a brief respite, was growing tumultuous. Lois' episodes of depression increased in number and intensity. Depression lurched in and out of our home like some insensitive, mindless brute. Each random and severe interruption of our life together left me feeling increasingly helpless and hopeless. It was a daunting challenge to keep my heart open when at any moment, even in the very midst of dinner, her depression might suddenly appear.

Her jaw would begin to clench, her eyes glaze over, her whole body gently rock back and forth, her throat emit an eerie, high-pitched keening, like a mother who had just lost her child. I became the words of the haunting, melancholic '60s Simon and Garfunkel song, "Hello, darkness, my old friend; I've come to talk to you again."

"How many times can I open the door to this heaviness?" I would ask myself. Come morning, the depression might lessen and I would go off to work where I could be useful to those who were willing to walk the path to recovery.

Addiction in my office and depression at home sent me to lectures, to the library, to bookstores seeking information. I read avidly about metabolism, about the brain and about the physiological consequences of stress. I was searching for ways to enhance medical and psychological treatments, whether of addiction or of depression. For Lois antidepressants alone were clearly no longer effective. We had come to the end of all available medications. Feelings of hopelessness and helplessness pressed in on both of us. There must be alternative ways to alleviate the severity of her crippling illness. For the next sixteen years we would seek remedies in holistic medicine: special diets, intravenous amino acids, megavitamin supplements, acupuncture—anything that might work.

Meanwhile, my growing sophistication in the field of addiction began to make me suspicious about the behavior of Lois' son, Rick. The increasing unpredictability of his life challenged any attempts to make sense of it. The hypothesis that he might be drinking alcoholically helped to explain his strange behavior. We faced him with our suspicions. Amazingly he readily acknowledged that indeed he had a problem. But he assured us that his problem was not severe; he could resolve it himself.

The problem, however, turned out to be far more severe than I had imagined. I knew that without a program of recovery he would continue to deteriorate. Despite this certitude I kept "helping" him with money and a receptive ear. To put it baldly, I was part of the controlling system that he had co-opted to keep himself drunk. I was hurting him, not helping.

And then, for a time, Lois seemed to have significantly improved. She got well enough to participate in a couples' group that dealt with the special issues faced by alcoholics and their families. I had grown weary of Rick's nocturnal phone calls, resentful of his interminable pleas for financial help. I firmly refused to participate any further in his intrusions into our life.

Lois reacted angrily. Our exchanges grew heated. I was no longer her hero and savior. I had abandoned her son. At the peak of just such an alienation from one another, we arrived for our evening couples' group. Our rigidity and distance from one another was observed by the people already there.

As we settled into our seats one of them observed, "You guys are in trouble with one another, aren't you? I spotted it almost the minute you walked in. Do you want to talk about it?"

The group gave us time. They listened, then they gave us some advice: "Go to Alanon, alone and to separate meetings."

Alanon was a program that almost immediately sprang up alongside Alcoholics Anonymous. Its particular focus, however, was on the family and friends of alcoholics rather than on the alcoholic himself. From very early on, it had become clear that the inner circle of the drinker's intimates were severely impacted by the alcoholic addiction; they developed a self-destructive preoccupation with prevailing upon the alcoholic to stop drinking. Utilizing the traditional twelve steps, the relatives or friends admitted their powerlessness to let go of this co-dependency and turned their lives and will over to a Higher Power as they understood it.

Going to Alanon was a difficult challenge for me. I would be openly sharing my problems with an alcoholic. There might be clients of mine present who did not know this vulnerable side of me as stepfather of a son addicted to substances.

Despite all the pain in my relationship with Lois, I was able to maintain a spirit of hope and optimism at the meeting. The twelve steps written by the early members of Alcoholics Anonymous fell on the fertile soil of my soul, previously plowed, enriched, tilled and seeded by years of spiritual training. The luminous courage of those who shared filtered through the cloud cover of my own dark fears and I found myself able to open up with a great sense of relief.

In the group I confessed what had become too obvious to

deny any longer. I was powerless to control Rick or his mother and my life had become unmanageable. It had become obvious to me that at the level of this hand-to-hand combat with my co-dependence, my psychological and substance-abuse education and training availed me little. I, like everyone else, needed the trans-forming touch of the Higher Power present when I honestly shared in the supportive environment of other co-alcoholics.

Carl Rogers had talked about this phenomenon as healing through being genuine, through being heard empathically and accepted unconditionally. Baum theologized about it from the perspective of the insider God, immanent in the human condition in his mode of transcendence, enabling us to move beyond blind-ness and rigidity.

In 1977, the California Commission on Alcoholism for the Span-ish Speaking (CCASS) issued a paper urging the non-profit agen-cies under its supervision to search out, hire, and train bilingual Latino lay counselors. I considered the policy highly reasonable. Our experience had already shown that lay persons in true recov-ery from substance abuse through a twelve step program could counsel very effectively. With some intense training, they could do the work of inspiring and guiding alcoholics and other addicts toward living a clean and sober life.

In truth the state's policy delighted me. Its point of view fit well with my Rogerian training, which had become an intimate part of my outlook. I could set up trainings, experiential as well as theoretical, to develop in my lay staff the qualities that make for a healthy therapeutic relationship. These skills were definitely teachable.

Fortunately the management of Zona Seca was not only open to this approach, they enthusiastically encouraged it. So we ac-tively sought out from within the recovering community those Latinos who were bilingual in Spanish. Training in the intensive group experience would lay the foundation for basic counseling skills. Presentations from experts inside and outside the agency would build on this, introducing the lay staff to personality theory and alcoholic family systems. Active participation in twelve step groups of one sort or another was encouraged for all.

*On March 12, 1979, Pope John Paul II said at an audience for
Representatives of Jewish Organizations: "I am, moreover,
happy to evoke in your presence today the dedicated and effective
work of my predecessor, Pius XII, on behalf of the Jewish
people."*

*On November 17, 1980, in an address to the Jewish com-
munity of Mainz, West Germany, Pope John Paul II acknowledged that "the Old Testament has its own permanent
value...since this value is not wiped out by the later interpretation of the New Testament, which on the contrary gave the Old
Testament its full meaning."*

On the day after Christmas in 1980 my brother Henry called to
tell me that our mother had died. I was expecting the news; she
had been critically ill for some time. I immediately started to prepare for the trip to Phoenix. The Zona Seca staff was on vacation
but needed to know that I would be taking a week off. I drove over
to the agency and drafted an explanatory note to the agency director and the office manager. As I left the building I met Felipe, the
custodian. When I explained that I was leaving for Phoenix to
bury my mother, he took off his cap, placed it over his heart, and
gave me a tender homily on the uniqueness of a mother's love.

On my trip home I recollected the last time I saw my mother
alive. I was on vacation and before I left I asked her for a few minutes alone. As I closed the door and pulled a chair up close to hers,
my heart was pounding so hard that I imagined she could hear it.
I told her how much she meant to me, how grateful I was for her
acceptance of my sometimes confusing journey, and how much I
admired her.

"With your gifts," I said, "you could have done anything you
set your mind to."

"I know I could have," she said simply. "Before I reached my
teens I was already keeping the books for Uncle Gus's little gro-
cery store. Three years later a bigger store wanted me to work for
them. I wanted to be a wife and mother; I chose to be a wife and
mother. And I have no regrets."

The rosary spoke volumes about how much my mother meant
to large numbers of people. Family and friends thronged the

mortuary chapel, visiting loudly with one another before entering, reminiscing with tears and laughter, celebrating the strong, loving presence she was in their world. The officiating priest had to be very patient that evening because the crowd would not budge until it was ready. After the Mass and burial we went to the home of Henry and Terry, with whom my mother had lived until she entered the hospital. A cadre of parishioners had prepared the space to receive us and placed food on the dining room table for all the mourners.

Soon my wife's depression was accelerating again. The diet, the vitamin and mineral supplements, the intravenous amino acids were no longer effective. For a year or so acupuncture and Chinese herbs had provided some help and hope. Their effect however gradually diminished, leaving her needier than ever. She was withdrawing from everyone around her; all the household chores were falling to me. My creative interventions in her behalf had taken much of my energy and time but to no avail. I was exhausted. It was at this time that George walked back into my life.

A few years before I had presided at George's marriage. He was a veteran member of Alcoholics Anonymous; like many there he suffered depression. In times past we had discussed how intimidating it was for alcoholics to admit at meetings that they were taking antidepressants. Often some misinformed recovering person would comment that antidepressants were mood-altering drugs. Since drugs were incompatible with sobriety, they reasoned that taking them was a form of relapse. The solution was to stop antidepressant treatment immediately and count this as the first day of recovery.

George and I both disagreed sharply with this attitude. We knew that in its official declarations AA defers to medical experts who might wish to prescribe non-addictive medicines for their recovering patients, especially when they judged this to be medically necessary.

George wanted to discuss the idea of starting an anonymous group for depressives, whether complicated by addiction or not. It would utilize the traditional twelve steps of AA. He understood first hand that those suffering from this malady tended to isolate themselves, and with their isolation came catastrophizing thoughts. What did I think about his suggestion, he wanted to know.

I could see a fundamental difference between alcoholism and depression that militated against his proposal. So my initial reaction was negative. My reasoning was that first of all, some depressions seem to be biologically or physiologically caused. Therefore, even when these depressives are doing everything in their power ("working their program") to deal with their helplessness and hopelessness, their incapacity for joy, their agitation, their sleep and eating disturbances, there is no assurance that the heaviness will lift and the mood return to normal. It might even deepen, whereas in the case of some who are doing nothing at all for themselves ("working no program") the depression may sometimes mysteriously go into remission on its own. In sharp contrast with depressives, if alcoholics regularly attend meetings and diligently work the steps, the strength to continue in sobriety is usually assured. Research did indicate, however, that in the case of depression, therapy combined with antidepressants, good nutrition, and exercise could significantly increase the chances of its remission. So perhaps we could adapt the steps to the differing profile of the depressive.

As in the case of AA's first step, these men and women could acknowledge that their own illness was more powerful than they, that without some kind of help their lives were unmanageable, that therefore they needed the help of a Higher Power to restore them to sanity. Turning their lives and will over to this Power (as they understood it) would lead to a program of recovery: consulting their doctors faithfully, carrying out the prescribed regimen of medication, eating properly, exercising, planning and carrying out tasks they found manageable, fighting the inclination to isolate by connecting face-to-face with others at least in the group, leveling with other members at the meeting about their progress toward recovery, and reaching out to group members for help by telephone in moments of special need.

George asked me to attend a planning meeting with him and three other AA men who also suffered depression. We would consider starting a weekly twelve-step group. The five of us met in his living room, seated around a large, old venerable coffee table. We brainstormed the pluses and minuses of our proposal. Ultimately the potential benefits led us to decide it was worth the effort. The word needed to go out that in the next month Depressives Anonymous would be meeting every Monday in this very room on Mission Street from 7:00 to 8:30 P.M. If this were the *kairos*, the right moment, these meetings would take root and hold. If not, the effort would still have been in the service of a noble cause.

I reminded them that though I myself did not suffer depression, I wanted to attend the meetings. Family members, too, needed the help of the twelve steps and should be invited to join us. The steps could help us maintain our focus on accepting what we could not change, courage to change the things that we could, and the wisdom to know the difference. My thought was that other family members and I might spin off an Alanon-like group which we would call "Families of Depressives Anonymous." With renewed hope I returned home to tell my wife about this new resource.

Over all, she seemed to receive the news favorably. My intention to attend the meetings with her was a source of comfort. Her only concern was for the future when my family group would split off. I would be leaving her alone in the depressives' group to fend for herself. I assured her that as a veteran depressive she could be a resource for newcomers to the group and that this feeling of giving to others would enhance her own life.

In 1985, President Ronald Reagan and the Chancellor of Germany, both Christians, met together over the graves of Nazi SS troops in Bitburg to forgive each other for acts of war. In 1986 Pope John Paul II visited a Jewish Synagogue, the first Pontiff in history to do so. In 1987 and 1988 Pope John Paul II had a friendly meeting with Kurt Waldheim of Austria, who had concealed his anti-Semitic activities during World War II.

There were about two dozen people at the first meeting. It was touching to be with all of them. A feeling of mutual recognition and acceptance filled the room. Sharing was frank. Almost from the start we realized that cross talk was necessary because persons with depression needed reassurance, sometimes even loving confrontation. I was the sole family member of a depressive; soon others would come.

My work at Zona Seca with alcoholics and addicts was enhanced by this new referral resource of Depressives Anonymous. Many of our alcoholic clients suffered an accompanying depression. Indeed, they may have been self-medicating with alcohol or drugs to deal with the heavy burden of this pernicious mood disorder. Whenever possible, I referred the family members of depressives to the Monday night meetings, hoping eventually to get enough of them to start our own group.

Meanwhile, at Zona Seca I began to take notice of the number of Jewish counselors who were moving into my life. In my first year there was only one, a young Jewish woman. We worked together professionally but never discussed religion. Suddenly in the mid-'80s, three other women therapists with a connection to Judaism came to the agency. Two were Jews married to Christians; the third was a Catholic married to a Jew.

This sudden and unusual influx of Jews into my life piqued my interest. For some reason I felt impelled to talk to them about their interfaith marriages. They were more than happy to oblige. This event marked the birth of my sensitivity to the faith of those whom Catholics called our "elder brothers."

In the fall of 1988 I received a phone call from a therapist in the community who was inquiring about a position at Zona Seca. From the very first moments of our telephone conversation we felt a special kinship. We met for an informal interview at Little Audrey's, a popular down-home restaurant on State Street. There in the midst of the swiftly moving waitresses, shouted orders, and the clatter of dishes, I met one of the warmest, most gifted men I have ever met. His name was Max Lan. He was to be an extraordinary resource for the agency and an invaluable support to me.

Born in Mexico City, he had grown up as an avid student, completing his doctorate in psychology at the Universidad de Mexico. In addition to our connection as Latinos and therapists, we were both admirers of Carl Rogers, the man and the psychologist. Max had known Rogers intimately. While still in Mexico he had arranged for Carl to provide person-centered group training for psychiatrists and psychologists in Mexico City. Max had co-led these groups with him. After years of teaching in the university and doing therapy, he had gone through a painful divorce from the mother of his three daughters. When his sabbatical came up he decided to come to the United States and do some research at the University of California at Santa Barbara, but just before he was to depart from Mexico he suffered a heart attack. Following his recovery he came to Santa Barbara and, ever the student, pursued a second doctorate at UCSB, this time in confluent education.

Having completed this, he had worked part-time in several non-profit agencies. Now he was looking for a full-time position. It was Zona Seca's good fortune that someone had told him good things about me and that he and I would work well together. I was delighted with the prospect of a bilingual veteran therapist on our staff, not only knowledgeable in the field of substance abuse but also schooled in the discipline of Rogerian respect for the client. I hired him on the spot.

Months later when we got to know one another well, he shared with me the most personally important piece of information about himself. I knew he had been born in Mexico and he was at ease with my having been a priest. Putting these two things together, I had simplistically assumed that he was a Catholic. Weren't all Mexicans?

With a smile, he told me that he was Jewish. He had three siblings. His mother and father had fled persecution in Eastern Europe, settled in Mexico and raised their family there. At times he had found it painful growing up in a predominantly Catholic country. Often the figure of a crucified Jesus was used to shame him for his Jewish "stiff-necked unbelief."

As we grew to know one another better, I learned more and more from him about his struggle. In a moment of great vulnerability we both wept as he read aloud a piece he had written several years before. It was an anguished address to Jesus, his fellow countryman, pleading for an understanding of how a Jew had become such a sign of contradiction, an implacable, punishing, insatiable and mortal enemy.

Despite what I had read about the Holocaust, this was my first personal grasp of the blasphemy of Christian anti-Semitism. I was sixty-three! Together we wept. How could I have been so dead to this reality? Why had I never heard a word about the Holocaust in my theological studies, especially Christology? Through Max I would get a first-hand understanding of how my old doctrinal beliefs were intrinsically connected to cruelty and hatred.

> *In August 1989, despite protests from the Jewish Anti-Defamation League, Pope John Paul II sounded the traditional supersessionist theme: the Chosen People broke their covenant with God; Jesus came to establish a new covenant with the world through the Church. At the same time the conflict over the Auschwitz convent of the Carmelite contemplative nuns erupted again. The Archbishop of Cracow, Cardinal Franciszek Macharski, repudiated a six-month-old agreement in which it was stipulated that the convent would be removed from the site, so sacred to the Jews. Cardinal Jozef Glemp, the Primate of Poland, vociferously defended Macharski and insulted the Jews, accusing them of arrogance and abuse of their power as controllers of the mass media throughout the world. Two weeks later the Vatican, through Cardinal Willebrands, called for the implementation of the original agreement and offered the nuns financial help to construct an ecumenical center where they could reside away from Auschwitz.*

The agency continued to be blessed; another veteran therapist began to work with us part-time as a clinical supervisor. He was born and raised in Majorca, the largest of the Balearic islands off the coast of Spain. Since he had done his undergraduate and graduate studies in a university in England he spoke English fluently. He and I spent a lot of time together away from the office sharing our family backgrounds and education. Again, I had assumed that as a Spaniard he was a Catholic. In actuality Clive Cazés was a Sephardic Jew.

By the spring of 1990 my fifteen-year-old marriage was drawing to a painful end. Except for the prescribed antidepressants, Lois had withdrawn from all other assistance, even from the support of her friends. She turned her back on the depression groups that had once been helpful to her. Despite my reluctance to admit it, I was carrying an impossible burden. Either I left the marriage or I would perish in the impossible task of holding it together. She did virtually nothing at home and pushed me away emotionally.

With a pained heart and a sense of failure Lois and I sought out a divorce lawyer to negotiate a settlement and a therapist to help us say goodbye. I assured her that I would be as supportive of her as my emotional and financial resources would allow. These counseling sessions were the most difficult hours of my entire life. Had it not been for the assurance of friends who confirmed that my decision was appropriate I might never have left the marriage. One of the CFM couples, Joanne and Burt Miller, let me stay with them until I could get on my feet.

> *On November 8, 1990, in an address to the New Ambassador of the Federal Republic of Germany to the Holy See, Pope John Paul II said: "For Christians the heavy burden of guilt for the murder of the Jewish people must be an enduring call to repentance."*

Part VIII
Suddenly—Jews and Judaism

IN NOVEMBER 1991 I left Zona Seca and took the position of co-clinical director of a large non-profit agency working with adolescents and their families. The management of Klein Bottle Youth Programs was in the capable hands of its director, David Edelman, yet another Jew. In times past I would not have paid any attention to this matter; I certainly would not have interrogated him about what his Jewishness meant to him. But with my new sensitivity to the Jews that were entering my life I asked him about his religious background.

He told me a story that I have heard many times since. In preparation for his *bar mitzvah* ceremony, one task was to learn to read and chant from the Torah in Hebrew. This seemed a boring task to which he could bring little enthusiasm. Disheartened by the rote nature of what he had to do, he kept asking his teachers for help. He wanted desperately to understand what he was reading and how this related to his coming of age.

His instructor dismissed every expression of concern and interest and simply ordered him to train his tongue to wrap around the words of the text smoothly. The instructor's failure to take him seriously hurt and angered him. In his training and preparation for the ceremony he kept promising himself that while others might think he was committing himself to an adult Jewish faith, he was not. His *bar mitzvah* would be his last participation in Jewish worship. And so it had been.

I continued to go to the Families of Depressives Anonymous meetings. Attendance there rose and fell, mostly fell. Finally there were only two of us left, Ruth Glater and I. At the time she came to the meetings she was sharing her home with her daughter, Selina, who suffered bipolar disorder. Under these intimate conditions Ruth was finding it impossible to attain any sort of emotional separation from her. The groups helped Ruth solidify her resolve to establish separate residences for the two of them. I supported her arduous efforts to find a place her daughter could afford. Finally, with the help of the Veterans Administration (Ruth was a disabled WWII Navy veteran), she found a place through Section VIII of the City Housing Authority.

Ruth needed ongoing support for the more difficult step of becoming less and less available to a bipolar daughter who constantly and insistently turned to her mother for financial and emotional support. At my urging Ruth attended Alanon meetings. As expected, the groups helped her be more proactive in her interactions with Selina. After our Families of Depressives group terminated, Ruth and I began to spend more and more time together. We discovered that in our roles as caretakers we were remarkably similar.

It was interesting to discover that on the very day I was ordained a Catholic priest, June 29, 1951, Ruth had received her doctorate from UCLA in botany with a specialty in medical mycology. She was the daughter of two Jews who had fled Russia because of religious persecution and settled in the Bronx in 1904. Though in a totally different direction from mine, she too had a sense of calling. Her dream was to earn a doctorate, then teach and do research in a university setting. While UCLA had permitted her to achieve a Ph.D., not a single university was willing to hire her. In the days and years that followed her academic achievements she discovered that there was no room for her at the inn of science where men ruled. To deal with this shocking rejection she sought therapy from a Freudian psychiatrist whose sexism undermined the help he could have otherwise offered. The loss of her dream had disastrous effects on her not only as an academic, but as a person, a wife, and a mother.

She later chronicled this story as a wake-up call in a book,

Slam The Door Gently: The Making and Unmaking of a Female Scientist. Ruth was Jewish to her core; in many ways I still identified with the Catholic faith. The closer we felt to one another, the more incredible it seemed that we who had come from such polar extremes could meet in love.

For we did draw closer. And as we did I felt stirred to understand her tradition. The best way to understand Judaism, I thought, was to attend Friday night services with her at Congregation B'nai B'rith. I had never once in my entire life attended anything specifically Jewish, whether religious or cultural. As a Catholic I had once believed that participating in one of their religious services was absolutely forbidden me.

This left me clueless about what to expect. What would I hear there? Would the congregants see me as an interloper and treat me with suspicion? Should I disclose that I was formerly a Catholic priest? Should I ask forgiveness for my blind acceptance of Christian anti-Semitism in the past?

Each time I considered going to the temple, a colorful image from Catholic Good Friday services would push into my mind. I was standing at the high altar of the Old Mission, my back to the congregation. Clad in the purple vestments of the Lenten season, I was chanting a prayer "for the perfidious Jews." My plaintive cry, ostensibly in their behalf, reached out to a merciful God: "Remove the veil that covers their hearts, so that they might acknowledge Jesus Christ as their Lord and Savior," I sang.

The course of action driven by this Jewish perfidy had been described earlier in the Good Friday ceremony. In Saint John's Passion of our Lord Jesus Christ I had read to the congregation about the machinations of the Chief Priests and Pharisees. Bent on forever stilling the voice of God's prophet, Jesus, they sent a cohort to the garden of olives in the Kedron valley to apprehend him. When he disclosed that he was indeed "Jesus the Nazarene," they fell to the ground in awe. Then obdurately discounting this clear evidence of his divine power, they apprehended him. Then they pressured the Roman authorities to judge, condemn, and execute him by crucifixion.

One lovely Friday fall evening I picked up Ruth at her home on the East Side. We drove to Congregation B'nai B'rith, a Reform Temple nestled in the foothills of Santa Barbara. All that I knew was that we were going to an Erev Shabbat service. I had no idea of the shape of the service or where this experience would take me. We arrived in good time and were warmly greeted in the lobby by Ruth's friends. To prepare for entering the Temple itself she led me to a wooden bin to the left of the entrance. I reached in and selected a satiny white *yarmulke*.

As I placed it on my head I wondered whether my baldness could provide secure anchorage for it. On the way down to our front row seat next to the center aisle, congregants smiled at me, wishing me *Shabbat shalom* or a *gut Shabbes*. We were no sooner seated than members of her *chavurah* group came over to our pew to greet her and meet me.

In the midst of the excitement we heard the voices of the cantor and the rabbi from the rear of the Temple. As they entered, the cantor intoned the *L'cha dodi*, the joyful song greeting the Sabbath, the feminine, creative *Shechinah* or Presence of God. The words were touching; the melody danced. When the celebrants arrived at the *bima*, I was warmed by the fact that the cantor and rabbi were vested in garments familiar to me. They wore a *kittel*, a white floor-length linen garment (alb), as well as a *tallit* (stole) that I had worn as a priest. In addition, each wore an embroidered *yarmulke* on his head, similar to the *soli Deo* of my Franciscan days.

The rabbi turned to face us. I saw a tall man with piercing, laughing eyes. He wore a neatly trimmed beard and mustache. His name was Arthur Gross-Schaefer. At his side stood the cantor, Sam Cohen, a much younger man who sang without accompaniment that evening. My eyes scanned the sanctuary, noting especially what was already familiar to me: there was a pulpit, a sanctuary lamp that burned eternally, a tabernacle in a place of prominence cradling the Torah—the very heart of Judaism, the Sabbath candles, and a chalice of wine.

I could not follow the Hebrew prayers, of course, but in my Siddur I followed the loose translation of the Hebrew prayers as they were chanted. Many of the prayers were from the Hebrew Bible, the same ones that had fed me spiritually since childhood and lay at the heart of my thirty years of celebrating the Catholic liturgy and reading the Divine Office.

At a central place in the night's service, the *amidah*, we sang a
verse from the psalms in Hebrew and in English. It greeted me
like an old friend. It had been on my Franciscan lips thousands of
times both before and after my ordination to the priesthood:
"Adonai, sefatai tiftach ufi yaggid tehilatecha," "Lord, open my lips
that my mouth may declare your praise."

On one level the entire evening felt like a homecoming after
years of absence. On the other, I knew that most of my Catholic
life was still out on the porch in pieces of luggage too numerous to
count, each containing significant items incompatible with this
Jewish household.

The service was followed by an *oneg Shabbat*, or celebration of the
Sabbath, at which congregants shared food, drink, and conversation. My shyness was no match for the warm outreach of Ruth's
friends, who wanted to greet me, to accept me, to know more
about me. All the while my heart was telling me that this night
was just a first step on a journey of who-knew-how-many thousand miles.

Weeks later, Arthur Gross-Schaefer was formally installed as
the rabbi of the congregation. At the *oneg* afterward, congregants
seated him and his wife in separate chairs and hoisted each aloft.
In wonder I watched the group boisterously parade around the
social hall to a jubilant melody I had never before heard but somehow seemed familiar. My heart joined them in their tuneful recognition and celebration of the married state of the rabbi and his
wife. How sharply this contrasted with the traditional Catholic
decorum and reverence for exclusively celibate priestly service.

I began to study Hebrew through the Temple's adult education program. Our teacher, Devorah Sprecher, was a lively Israeli
now a transplant to America. Hebrew words danced on her lips,
like notes of a lilting melody. In these basic Hebrew classes we
chose to focus on modern Hebrew. Occasionally we would dip
into the liturgical Hebrew of the Siddur, which in turn would
expose us to Scriptural Hebrew.

At the start the mere letters themselves were a challenge, not
to mention the practice of reading Hebrew from right to left. My
love of solving puzzles and my background in languages served

me well as I rose to the task with playful enthusiasm. To learn the Hebrew alphabet I adapted it to the ABCs song of my childhood and practiced it when driving alone to and from work: *alef, beth, ghimel, dalet, heh, vav.* Ever so slowly I began to recognize the letters and configure words. Eventually I bought audio-tapes that supported our classroom text and listened to these in the car to and from work in Lompoc and Santa Maria. By year's end I had moved a bit toward my goal of tracking the prayers as they were recited and even understanding a few of them.

As Ruth and I grew more serious about our relationship, we made a point of carefully examining our differences. Intellectually I had moved a light year from my seminary days. There was, however, no denying that a substantial part of the old paradigm was still in my bones. We needed to ferret out and process any religious differences that could prove a stumbling block in our relationship. To this end we signed up for a six-week interfaith group at B'nai B'rith. In that brief time we happily came to agree that in terms of our beliefs, very little if anything stood in the way of making our life together.

I was already quite content with, even excited about, the Jewish faith. I especially liked its disaffection with doctrinal pronouncements. Ruth had told me, and I had heard with amusement from many others, that where there are twelve Jews you have thirteen opinions. At the time I hadn't really appreciated the stress Jews place on intellectual freedom. In my first temple celebration of Yom Kippur I read with amazement, "I am a Jew because it requires of me no abdication of the mind."

As a Catholic I had increasingly resented the demand that I conform doctrinally not only to truth infallibly defined but to views taught by the "ordinary magisterium" of the Church. My own small attempts at intellectual freedom as a priest had been frowned upon, sometimes judged to be deviant and divisive.

Here at the Temple I could move at my own pace; my participation was welcomed without a hint of proselytism, without negative judgment. Not once did I hear an anti-Christian or anti-Catholic sentiment—not even when we celebrated Yom Hashoah, the commemoration of the Holocaust.

*On October 15, 1991 Pope John Paul II said in an address to
Jewish leaders of Brazil: "As the Bible says, 'The Lord has
loved Israel forever....' He has made a covenant with it, which
has never been broken, placing in it the messianic hope of the
whole human race."*

I joined Ruth's Temple *chavurah* or fellowship group. We met
monthly. Starting in the '60s, these groups were made up of like-
minded *chaverim*, or friends, who would meet to worship, most of
the time in a home of one of the members. They were a
countercultural alternative for Jews disaffected from their synagogue.

At that time in the Catholic Church a parallel movement was
flourishing. I myself regularly took part in small group worship in
homes. The intimate environment provided us support for life's
challenges, especially those issuing from our involvement in social
change.

This was three decades later, however, and Ruth's *chavurah*
group was quite different. There was little focus. Our monthly
gatherings were not about praying together but were mainly
friendly visits that centered around a pot luck meal. I did, however, meet some pleasant people there. One couple especially
moved me in a rare and unique way.

In all of my life I had never before had personal contact with
Holocaust survivors. I had read and been touched by Elie Wiesel's
Trilogy as well as some of his essays. I had struggled through Emil
L. Fackenheim's *The Jewish Bible after the Holocaust: a Re-reading*.
But here at my first *chavurah* meeting the Holocaust took on flesh
and blood.

I met Tito and Erica Gold, two Holocaust survivors (this status alone was enough to earn them my respect and reverence).
Both had lost all of their family in that disaster, had met during
their internment in Dachau and at war's end had married. By now
they knew I was a Catholic priest. I expected from them if not
stiffness toward me at least some wariness until they got to know
me better. But remarkably, they reached out to me with a smiling
acceptance that confounded me.

It disturbed me that in the succeeding months I wasn't getting to know them at a deeper level. There was so much in my heart that I wanted to say to them. I wanted to learn from them the secret of their survival. I wanted to ask how they had coped with this devastating blow to their Jewish faith. In order to facilitate this, Ruth and I invited them over for coffee and dessert one Sunday afternoon. I was delighted when they accepted.

The visit began with a few pleasantries. Before long our conversation had grown intense. I told them of my feeling privileged in their presence. The mere fact of their survival was more than I could absorb emotionally. I told them how touched I was by Elie Wiesel's reflections on the Holocaust. They probed me about my interest in Judaism. Was I intending to convert to Judaism? Why would anyone not born a Jew embrace this most difficult of all religious callings?

They confessed that their faith in God had been severely shaken—for them the pre-*shoah* God no longer existed and they could offer nothing more real than their anguish. Simple, holy honesty. It was all I needed. We decided to keep in touch outside the *chavurah* meetings.

By the spring of 1992 Ruth and I had grown so close that we wanted to declare our love at a public gathering of close friends, both Jew and non-Jew. Ruth thought that perhaps we could do this at a *tannaim*, an ancient solemn betrothal ceremony once commonplace in Europe, very rarely celebrated in this country. With this in mind we approached Rabbi Gross-Schaefer. He agreed to design and preside over this ritual at the end of the Havdalah service.

Because I was not a Jew it would take place not in the Temple sanctuary but in the patio outside the social hall. The Havdalah is a brief ceremony that celebrates the end of the sacred Sabbath and divides it from the rest of the profane week. He explained that the traditional braided candles would be the symbol of our growth together in love; the wine in which the candles would later be extinguished would remind us of the sacredness of our commitment; the spices would stand for the sweetness of the friends that surrounded us. The celebration would take place on June 20, 1992.

Louie Zandalasini, Ruth's unofficial godson who teaches culinary science at Mission College in Sylmar, graciously took over all the food arrangements. With confidence that this important task was in good hands, we began our preparation for the ceremony. Each of us was to select someone to speak in our behalf that evening. Ruth chose Helen Matelson, a close friend from her days at the Pritikin Clinic. I chose my old friend, Max Lan. Then we wrote statements to one another to be read at the ceremony.

Mine flowed easily from a full heart. Ruth was a beautiful woman with impish eyes and an enchanting smile. Her artistic soul was manifest in her flair for color in her clothing and tasteful adornments. She had become a loving friend, accompanying me ever so deftly and gently in the delicate enterprise of looking into Judaism. She was validating. She was enthusiastic. She was enchanted by the beauty of creation. She was prayerful. She was challenging. She was real. She was a doer. She had emotionally survived what could have been mortal blows both in marriage and in academia. Without a doubt I loved her and would love her until the day I died.

The day of the *tannaim* itself was everything that I had hoped for. Seated before us as we stood at the social hall steps were our friends, Jewish and Christian, persons who had played central roles in our lives. I would have loved to have my family present, but time and circumstance didn't allow for this. Against the backdrop of the Havdalah service our friends spoke; Ruth and I offered our statements to each other; the rabbi as usual spoke substantively and warmly. Pointing to the braided candles, he invited us to offer one another our solemn commitment to pursue the path of marriage. We did. We drank from the cup of our mutual love and delighted ourselves with the aromatic spice of our friendships. When finally he extinguished the flame of the candle the Sabbath was at an end and we were united in an ancient Jewish commitment to marry. From that moment on we thought of ourselves as married.

My search to understand what it is to be Jewish pushed me to read voluminously. Catholic faith formulations no longer expressed the mystery of life as I experienced it. I had not lost the sense of sin, for example, but I no longer thought of sin as creating the need for the redemptive death of Jesus. My failures and moral lapses were simply one aspect of being human that needed attention and change. Consequently I could not relate to the Mass as the re-presentation of that Sacrifice.

I found an understanding of this personal religious shift in the work of Carl Jung. He noted, as did Blondel and Baum, that a substantial number of Christian westerners today are witnessing the death of their centuries-old religious paradigm, the outsider God, that used to pull together their experiences and give them meaning. The current move was to the myth of the insider God, intrinsic to the human condition.

There had been a time when for me to entertain these "doubts" would have been shocking. Not now. I knew that many, perhaps most, Catholics would dismiss this shift in me as heresy, even a loss of faith. They continued to believe that their Christian faith alone perceived reality as it truly is, its essence captured over the centuries in carefully elaborated theological concepts and words. Of this they were solemnly assured by an infallible Church.

But from my emerging awareness their vision, like mine, was necessarily limited, only one way of seeing and expressing religious experience. I had arrived at a place in my life where the ultimate sin would be to discount what I believed to be reality or truth. My current faith was based on an honest, painstaking search; it was based on my own personal experience and growth. For me this crisis was a *kairos*, a time out of time, a sacred moment. I had to be sensitive to God's call. Was He requiring of me the same sort of trust He had asked of Abram when He said, "Leave your country, your family and your father's house for the land I will show you"?

Not that this invalidated the spiritually rich aspects of my Catholic tradition. I would always hold dear my early and intense introduction to prayer, to silence, to the "preferential option toward the poor," to simplicity, to humility, to ritual, to mindfulness. My parents, my brothers, my extended family and later, my religious community were by and large exemplary people with high values. Judaism, however, as the community of "our elder brothers" was becoming not only a familiar biblical place to be, but invited the kind of responsible freedom to investigate that I now yearned for and respected.

Within this ancient religion there was no official institution of oversight (by whatever name) over all of Judaism. There was no Inquisition, Holy Office, Congregation for the Doctrine of the Faith, Vatican to police professors, especially in *yeshivot*, to punish those proposing points of view differing from the official line or to prohibit publishing houses from disseminating books lacking official approval. With this kind of breathing room there was un- derstandably a wide range of beliefs and practices within Judaism. Sometimes the strain between its practitioners was critical, espe- cially between the Orthodox and Reform movements, especially in Israel.

On my sixty-ninth birthday, my curiosity about and participa- tion in Judaism unexpectedly shifted direction. The change was launched when Ruth's cousin, Dr. Benjamin "Jerry" Cohen, pro- fessor of international political economy at the University of Santa Barbara, California, gave me a birthday present. Since his arrival in Santa Barbara three years before in July of 1991, he had often expressed his interest in my fascination with Judaism. He himself was in a mixed marriage; his wife was raised in the Presby- terian Church.

When he once asked me whether I considered myself a Catholic or a Jew I answered, "I'm a Jew with a twist."

We both laughed. But I really meant it. His birthday gift to me was *The Satanizing of the Jews: Origin and Development of Mys- tical Anti-Semitism* by Joel Carmichael. This volume was to open my eyes, stun me, shame me, and fire me up to pursue the issue of anti-Semitism in greater depth. In all of this Ruth did not push me. On the contrary she continued to practice her Judaism and gave me wide berth to pursue my own path.

The Christian world that I was born into was unquestionably anti-Semitic. That world believed that Jesus, God's Son, had come to redeem each and every person from their sins. The Jews not only rejected Him as the Messiah but had Him killed. Deicide was the formal charge lodged against them. Terrible sins, both. Carmichael reminded me that early Christians projected yet an- other layer of evil into this dire situation. These sins were com- mitted by the Jews out of pure malevolence: that is, with full knowledge of where Jesus came from, who He was.

With tragic effects the early Christians folded these alleged reasons for Jewish "hardness of heart" into the very center of their theology. The Jesus that the Jews malevolently crucified ultimately triumphed and was now glorified in the kingdom of heaven, seated at the right hand of God. While the Jews, by their deliberate and malicious rejection of Jesus, chose to be subjects of another kingdom, that of God's ancient enemy, Satan.

For the first time in my life I understood how this stance moved the relationship between Christians and Jews far beyond history to an ontological order in which the hostility of these combatants is owing to something much deeper than entrenched egos. At this metaphysical level the face-off is between two mighty powers, good and evil, pitted against one another in eternal enmity. The grinding, metallic clash of their combat is accessible only to the ear of faith.

This attitude of Christian toward Jew is a far cry from the mere xenophobia of that era. We know that non-Jews early on regarded Jews as odd, and that this attitude worsened as Hellenism spread and dominated the Middle East. Central to this distrust was the Jewish belief that Israel was the Chosen People of the Universal God. We can see the serious problem precipitated by Jewish separateness in the book of Esther (3:8): "There is a certain people scattered abroad and dispersed in all the provinces…their laws are different from those of all other people…therefore the king should not spare them." But this observation merely notes a difference between this people and all others. It does not characterize the Jews as evil. Surely not evil to the very core of their being.

The more I read Carmichael and others, the more uncomfortable I became about Christian anti-Semitism and its destructive reach across the centuries. On the positive side there was no discounting recent Church efforts to undo some of this damage. There were a number of important admissions: the charge of deicide could not be laid at the feet of the Jews as a whole; Jews are the "elder brothers," the vine onto which Christians have been grafted; the Torah has the power to sanctify those who study it and live by its instruction.

On the other hand, I was still concerned that in all this Christian outreach to the Jews, the core of the problem was left virtually untouched. What about the ancient charge of satanic malevolence to be found in the New Testament itself? Saint John (8:44) calls the Jews "children of the devil." Would the Church take her courage in hand and specifically refute this scriptural charge? Would the Church have the courage to admit that her scriptures contain serious error, error which contributed to countless pogroms and persecutions?

What of the Jews' refusal to accept Jesus as the Messiah? Is their stance reasonable and in the truth? Is their faith complete? In his public utterances, Pope John Paul II was giving with one hand and taking away with the other. First he conceded that Israel's chosenness, her covenant with God, is still in place and is an instrument of sanctification. Then he insisted that the Jews accept Jesus as the only way to God.

My "going to school" around the issue of Christian anti-Semitism was personally illuminating. But I found myself asking: is there anything that I can personally do to contribute to the righting of this wrong? Hand-wringing and *mea culpa*s as I struck my breast were simply manifestations of sorrow and regret. Without action they would remain meaningless. I felt I needed to do something concrete to make amends.

In the twelve step program of AA, the eighth step urges persons in recovery to make "a list of all persons we had harmed" and to become "willing to make amends to them all." Step nine directs them to make "direct amends to such people wherever possible, except when to do so would injure them or others." I decided to make formal amends for my anti-Semitic attitudes and behavior despite my lack of awareness at the time.

The appropriate venue soon came to me: I would do this in our home when we hosted the *chavurah* group on the following Sabbath. I prepared what I wanted to say carefully. First I would ask them as representatives of their people to accept my amends. Then I would detail the sources of Catholic anti-Semitism. I would confess the sins of my mindlessness and uncritical acceptance of what was imposed on me as authentic Catholic teaching. Last I would ask them to respond to my Confession from the depths of their hearts, whatever those sentiments might be, and to forgive me.

In a letter of April 9, 1993 to the Carmelite Nuns at Auschwitz Pope John Paul II said: "Now, according to the will of the Church, you should move to another place in the same Oswiecim."

On the day of the meeting I waited patiently for the meal to be over and for the ten couples to crowd into our living room. I got their attention and began. As I spoke, their silence and demeanor spoke to me of their acceptance and appreciation. When I finished there was a brief and welcome silence. Then they began to respond. Without exception they were understanding and forgiving.

One woman added, "I've been wondering how long it would take you to say this."

A man explained, "We don't need you to be a Jew; we just want you on our side."

This was a good start. I knew that I wanted to do much more. I wanted to examine and express where I was on my spiritual journey from Christianity toward Judaism.

Ruth and I had prepared diligently to conclude our gathering with the Havdalah service, the ceremony utilized by Rabbi Gross-Schaefer for our engagement ceremony. Oscar, fluent in Hebrew, offered to read the prayers for me.

"Thanks," I said, "I want to do the reading myself; it's part of my healing."

With Ruth by my side I co-led the prayers and the special music. That evening I felt totally accepted by this band of Jews and by the people they represented.

In his1994 best-selling book Crossing the Threshold of Hope, *Pope John Paul II said that Church history is "full of protests against all those who attempted to force faith, 'making conversions by the sword.' In this regard," he added, "it must be remembered that the Spanish theologians in Salamanca took a clear stance in opposition to violence committed against the native peoples of America, the Indios, under the pretext of converting them to Christianity."*

However, I still needed to learn more and more from scholars about the origins of Christianity. Studies published by The Jesus Seminar, particularly the work of John Dominic Crossan, helped to move me along the path. I knew that many Christian scholars scorned the work of this group, but I needed to read it for myself. Especially because it could be argued that *a priori* loyalty to Church doctrines probably contaminates objectivity.

Increasingly I accepted that the Gospel Passion Narratives, the accounts of Jesus' arrest, trial, scourging, crowning with thorns, and crucifixion, had been written with an anti-Semitic pen. As such, whatever the level of awareness of those who read them, they were still serving to fuel this virulent hatred throughout the modern world. *Dateline: World Jewry*, a monthly publication of the Institute of the World Jewish Congress, kept me informed of anti-Semitic outbreaks, especially in parts of Eastern Europe, as well as in Spain and in South America, violence perpetrated by ordinary people in response to resurgent nationalism, failing economies, racism, and panic in the face of helplessness and hopelessness. Until recently I had never thought of these passon narratives as anything but historical truth. But now Crossan was pointedly asking me, were these stories "history remembered or prophecy historicized?"

> *On April 7, 1994, as part of a ceremony in the Paul VI auditorium commemorating the fiftieth anniversary of the Warsaw Ghetto uprising, a ten-year-old daughter of a Holocaust survivor lit six of the seven candles of the menorah.*

There were some encouraging signs. Some Christian and Jewish leaders were acknowledging that anti-Semitism in Christian story and religious imagery prepares the way for victimizing the Jew in times of national stress. Cardinal Joseph Bernardin of Chicago, held in high esteem by many in the United States, was the boldest and clearest of all Catholic critics. In a blunt speech on anti-Semitism at Hebrew University in Jerusalem he pointed out that among the factors responsible for the rise of Nazi Germany was the impact of the Gospel accounts of Jesus' death. This cannot be ignored.

"There is little doubt," he observed, "that classical Christian presentations of Jews and Judaism were a central factor in generating popular support for the Nazi endeavor."

There were other positive steps that various Christian churches had taken to set the record straight. In 1965, at the Second Vatican Council the Catholic Church issued a formal statement in its document, *Nostra Aetate*, declaring that Jews as a people are not collectively responsible for the death of Jesus, and that they should not be seen as accursed or rejected by God.

The Lutherans later repudiated the anti-Semitic statements of its founder, Martin Luther. He had begun by pillorying the Catholic Church for its anti-Semitism, but ended in exasperation over the Jews' unwillingness to convert. Like other anti-Semites, he too called for the burning of their synagogues, the destruction of Jewish homes, and the confiscation of their sacred writings. Then the Alliance of Baptists urged its members to turn away from proselytizing Jews and toward mutually enhancing dialogue. In 1993, Pope John Paul II established diplomatic relations with the State of Israel, a dramatic reversal of the Church's teaching that the Jews, for their sinful rejection of Jesus as Messiah, were condemned forever to wander homeless and outlawed.

In 1997 on one June morning I awoke and knew it was time to consult with the rabbi at B'nai B'rith. Rabbi Gross-Schaefer had left to teach ethics at Loyola Marymount College in Los Angeles and Rabbi Richard Shapiro had replaced him. What precisely did I want to say? I wanted to tell him of my interest in Judaism. I had been reading voraciously, though randomly, about the topic from a variety of aspects. I had moved far away from the Christian Fall/Redemption paradigm. The Christian presentation of Jesus as hypostatically united to the Son of God, and as humankind's Savior rejected by the Jews (though not crucified by them), led to the demonizing of the Jews. Jesus had lost the meaning He once held for me. I still believed, however, that in some preeminent way He was a carrier of God's love and power. And I was not yet at the point of conversion.

Rabbi Shapiro welcomed me into his office at the Temple. The book-lined walls comforted me. I was feeling strangely at peace and was looking forward to naming my current spiritual stage in the presence of a rabbi. I had not thought beyond this point. Something had become critically important to me: to declare myself in a formal way in this place where for several years I had been worshipping with a community of my elder sisters and brothers. Whatever might come from my statement and the rabbi's response I knew I would have accomplished a great deal.

I began. His posture was attentive. As I expressed what I had prepared his smiling face was receptive and encouraging.

When I finished I said: "I really don't know what I want from you except to hear me. It has become important for me at this stage of my journey to tell you, especially you as rabbi of this Temple, where I find myself on the path toward Judaism."

"I don't need you to be anywhere but where you are at this moment," he replied. "I know that with other Christians who contemplate conversion the issue of Jesus is significant, even momentous. I can say this: you are most welcome to worship with us regardless of where you stand with Judaism. Even if you were to become a Jew, the issue of Jesus might remain with you for some time, perhaps forever. All that I would ask is that if you do convert you do not discuss with other members of the congregation the Christian belief that He is the Messiah, the Savior of the world. We cannot accept that notion."

"One last thing," I said. "Can you recommend some books that might help me? I'm finding a lot of confusion about the question: exactly what is Judaism?"

"We use several books in our basic Judaism course; they might prove helpful in answering your question."

On my way home I weighed the step I had just taken. I could see that I still needed to work through my relationship with Jesus. My head said one thing; my nervous system quite another. *Head*: "We can accept Him as a carrier of divinity as we do the Buddha, as we do Moses. We can even consider Jesus the preeminent vessel for God's presence in the world. We can say He was the fully awakened one." *Nervous system*: "Jesus was uniquely united to God the Father. He died for our sins and transformed the world in its root. Billions of Christians throughout the world have accepted this. Weigh the mountain of testimony to this Christian reality: holy people, worship, music, art, architecture, literature, courageous agents of social change." However persuasive they had once been, the signals from my nervous system were growing weaker and weaker.

> *In October, 1997 the French Bishops begged forgiveness for the Catholic Church's tacit support of the Vichy regime and wartime silence in the face of official policies of anti-Semitism. In turn the French Premier, Lionel Jospin, promised to lift a sixty-year embargo on accessing the national archives. He wanted to facilitate research into the actions of the wartime Vichy regime.*

Tito and Erica Gold, the Holocaust survivors, invited Ruth and me to attend a Shabbat service at Congregation Young Israel. This Orthodox group met in a small storefront on the Mesa, an elevated area at the southwest corner of the city overlooking the sea. The two of them were to be honored guests and wanted us to share in their joy. I had never attended an Orthodox service. I had been attending services at B'nai B'rith, a reform temple, all these years. I was unprepared for what I saw. The men and women were separated from one another by a hip-high wooden divider, women with heads covered seated in the back half of the synagogue, men crowding around the pulpit in the *bima*. After the rabbi welcomed the Golds, Tito responded for them both, taking care to mention us, his guests, and referring to me as a former Catholic priest. One of the men, a visitor from Israel, then approached me, selected a *tallit* from the table, and, with affection, placed it around my shoulders. The service began. The men prayed aloud in Hebrew with the speed of light; I was the tortoise to their hare, inching along through a paragraph as they read whole pages. Most of the time the only intelligible words were the first two or three words at the beginning of each prayer; the rest was a guttural mumbling. I smiled as the scene took me back to my childhood when I sat in church mesmerized by the half-shout and mumble of the rosary recited in Spanish by priest and congregation. Here at Young Israel no one else but me seemed ill at ease with this style of worship.

The comfort of these Orthodox Jews with old ways didn't surprise me. I had lived through the '60s, when after Vatican II many Catholics, shocked and offended by the removal of the familiar in worship, rebelled against any liturgical innovations. They too strongly preferred the old ways and suddenly they faced: altar abruptly turned around, priest facing the congregation, liturgy in English, traditional hymns scrapped, silent focus disturbed. From the perspective of this experience of mine I could understand the attachment of Young Israel to their traditional form of worship: the extensive use of Hebrew, the mantra-like recital of prayers, the separation of men and women, the absence of musical instruments. But I was convinced that I could not worship with them, especially on a regular basis. During the lengthy service the issue of relevance kept surfacing for me as it had with Catholic theology. Perhaps most importantly the separation of men and women, while still meaningful to them, jarred me. In my world this arrangement was now symbolic of anti-feminism, of discrimination against women, whereas the need of our age was to enhance our openness toward women, our welcoming of them to parity, our acknowledgment of their capacity for leadership in every regard including the rabbinate, Christian ministry and the priesthood. Secondly the rapid droning of prayers reminded me of the old Catholic distinction of *ex opere operato, ex opere operantis*, meaning that the essence of a religious act by which God is glorified is its correct physical performance, while the disposition or attitude of the actor heightens or enhances but is not essential to the act. Last I was shocked when the rabbi, referring in his sermon to the Torah portion which included Leviticus' condemnation of homosexuality, slammed his fist down on the pulpit and shouted out his anger at the countervailing attitude of the rabbi at Congregation B'nai B'rith, where a gay rabbi had recently been invited to address the congregation at an Erev Shabbat service about the issue of homosexuality. Ruth and I were present at that moving sermon.

After the final hymn the Israeli who had draped me in the *tallit* came over to introduce himself. He was a Holocaust survivor. I said I was honored to meet him. Alluding to my unconscionable ignorance in those days of horror, I offered my regret and my respect. He took my hand in both of his and thanked me.

"Every single night since the Holocaust" he said, "the most painful memory comes to haunt me; I see the face of a little girl whose pained eyes stare at me as they kill her." His eyes brimmed with tears. *"Gut Shabbes,"* he said and walked away.

Something in Judaism was still missing for me at the synagogue, something vital, namely spirituality, including an in-depth treatment of Jewish prayer. Now and then spirituality was referred to, at times disparagingly, as if it were a New Age excess in contrast with the practical, hard-hitting *tikkun olam*, or repair of the world. I needed this information to help me get a fuller picture of Judaism.

I decided to ask the former rabbi of the congregation, Arthur Gross-Schaefer, whether he had any suggestions for me. A rare opportunity for this soon presented itself after a Friday night service. "I would like a moment of your time, Rabbi," I said. He nodded to me to continue. "I have been reading and reading about what it is to be a Jew but the picture isn't getting any fuller or clearer."

"I highly recommend Michael Lerner's book, *Jewish Renewal*," he responded with typical directness and brevity. "This rabbi spells out clearly the issues that Jews need to address in order to revivify Judaism."

I thanked him and he added: "If we don't pursue the direction he points to, we Jews could become irrelevant."

I thanked him again and turned to leave. "Hold it," he said, "now you have to recommend a book to me that you think important."

After a moment I replied, "I liked *The Condition of Jewish Belief: A Symposium Compiled by the Editors of Commentary Magazine.* This represents the answers of thirty-eight prominent rabbis, theologians and religious leaders to six basic questions."

He expressed his gratitude for the suggestion and promised to read it. I gathered that by this gesture of equality he was acknowledging my capacity for finding my own way.

Lerner's book reinforced my path and my attitude toward life. His was a message full of hope: in the depths of reality there lies a Transcendent Presence that, given an opening, can transform the hardest heart. As my favorite poet, Gerard Manley Hopkins, put it, "There lies the dearest freshness deep down things." Everything in Lerner's book spoke to my own beliefs, rooting them solidly and explicitly in the Hebrew Bible. It isolated five themes

already dear to my own heart: (1) the self as the image of God
from which flows the obligation to respect oneself and fully develop one's particular gifts, as the psalmist indicates (ps 139): "O
God, I thank you for the wonder of myself, the wonder of your
works"; (2) the other person as God's image and therefore the
need to respect him or her as the incarnation of God's beauty; (3)
the right of all human beings to live in a society that respects what
is necessary for all to realize themselves fully; (4) the environment
as God's creation, calling for grateful respect rather than exploita-
tion; and (5) the reincorporation of women as equal partners in
societal structures and practices. This last task Lerner referred to
as "the new Sinai."

When I finished the book I was so moved and grateful that I
wrote a letter to Rabbi Gross-Schaefer expressing my thanks and
noting that I resonated to everything that Lerner had to say.

The book helped me understand how religious practices must
remain connected to the Judaic dedication to repair the world.
But I was still needing more input on Jewish prayer. Then I remembered that in a recent telephone conversation Max Lan, my
Jewish friend from long ago at Zona Seca, rather insistently recommended that I read *The Jew in the Lotus* by Rodger Kamenetz,
a poet and professor of English at Louisiana State University. I
had bought the book and put it on my to-read list. The volume's
jacket pointed to the timeliness of Max's recommendation. Referred to by its reviewers as "Rodger Kamenetz's discovery of...a
more nourishing Judaism," and "A highly entertaining personal
account of one man's surprising journey into the mystical heart of
Judaism," the work was exactly the introduction to Jewish prayer
I had been missing and sorely needed. In 1989 the Dalai Lama,
himself in exile in Dharamsala, India, turned to the Jewish people
to learn their "secret of Jewish spiritual survival in exile." He also
professed interest in Jewish teaching about kabbalah and meditation. Kamenetz went along not as a primary consultant but as a
chronicler of the Dalai Lama's meeting with the group of nine
Jews, four of them rabbis, four professors and one a physician.
The group represented a wide range of Judaic allegiances, "a quilt
of the Jewish Diaspora," as one of the team put it, "a microcosm
of the wanderings of the Jewish people."

The gathering and unifying of the team in Europe and their arduous trip to India already impressed me for many reasons, especially their courage to face their own Jewish differences and to achieve some measure of agreement among themselves. Without this effort they could not respond coherently and authentically to the Dalai Lama's request for information. They asked one another truly hard questions and sometimes had to wince at the answers they received. What was the secret of the Jews' spiritual survival in the face of all manner of terrible repression and hatred in the world? How could they express this to him? What concrete suggestions or recommendations could they offer him that were adaptable to the Buddhist culture? Were they here as mere consultants or could they themselves learn from what inspired Buddhist survival?

Rabbi Omer-Man was one of the rabbis that travelled to India. "It is my opinion," he said, "that true dialogue must change the speakers from you and me to we and us all."

The openness of these Jews as Jews impressed me. Grounded as they were in their own tradition, they were confident that they could safely and profitably dialogue openly with their non-Jewish host. This kind of unauthorized risk was not permitted in my centralized Catholic tradition.

In the '60s, the Catholic writer John Dunne had daringly proposed that we "pass over" into the religious point of view of the other. Thus enriched, he maintained, one could return to one's own tradition but now seen in a new light.

Harvey Cox, the Baptist theologian and writer, had done this in the '80s. Curious over the popularity of Eastern spirituality among young Americans, he decided to pass over into the Hare Krishna movement in the United States, the better to understand and profit from it. He even went so far as to spend an entire year in an ashram.

Rabbi Irving "Yitz" Greenberg admitted to his fellow delegates to India that most Orthodox Jews considered religious dialogue to be impossible; few would allow themselves to attempt it. On the other hand, he confessed, he himself had engaged in it and found it less and less a problem. The only condition he set himself was to draw a clear line about how much to share and in what

arena. Under this rubric he, as an Orthodox rabbi, held that sharing in the liturgy of another religion would be wrong because this
would send the message that you are a part of their faith system.
These limitations aside, Yitz was convinced that, despite the dan-
gers of relativism, pluralism in the matter of beliefs was the challenge of today's world. He said touchingly, "God's will is for us to
learn how to affirm our full truth doing full justice to the other,
not partial justice or twisted justice or a secondhand treatment."

As I read I developed a deep affection for Kamenetz himself
and for the music of his writing; both his lyrics and his melodies
were superb. In his book the deeply spiritual, authentically human
Dalai Lama took form. So did two Jews whose work has since nurtured me, the charismatic Rabbi Zalman Schacter-Shalomi, whose
background is Lubavitch Hasidism, and Rabbi Jonathan Omer-
Man, both thoroughly versed in Jewish mystical tradition. Thanks
to Max Lan, another charismatic Jew who long ago had by his example drawn me to look into Judaism, my prayer to discover Jewish prayer was being answered.

All the participants in the Dharamsala dialogue were deeply
affected. Kamenetz himself, with very little Jewish education, had
gone along as a scribe to record what transpired in Dharamsala.
When the visit was over, Kamenetz wrote, "I realized that the religion of my birth is not just an ethnicity or an identity, but a way
of life, and a spiritual path, as profound as any other. That path
has three parts: prayer, study, and acts of loving-kindness." The
familiarity and simplicity of this kind of path drew me as did the
paucity if not absence of metaphysical speculation, all against the
background of the Torah's rich imagery, the texts of which had
formed me from my youth.

One day Ruth and I received a flyer in the mail announcing
that Rodger Kamenetz and Rabbi Omer-Man were to speak at
Brandeis-Bardin Institute in Simi Valley, an hour's drive southeast
of Santa Barbara. She and I had been totally unaware of this precious resource and decided on the spot that we must go.

On a lovely Sabbath day in the early afternoon we began our
drive south, strangely excited about the prospect of finding our
way into the depths of Jewish prayer. On the way we listened to
tapes of Professor William Scott Green of the University of

Rochester lecturing on *God and God's People: The Religion of Juda-ism*. The grandeur of this ancient faith was reflected in the Chan-nel Islands visible to our right, thirty miles out into the vastness of the Pacific Ocean. Despite the supersonic speeds of the traffic on Highway 101, our hearts were content. We made the transition to Highway 118 East and soon began to notice the eerie stony to-pography of earthquake country, a reminder of the awesome power of nature. We exited at the small town of Brandeis and made our way into the Institute. "The lecture is at the House of the Book about a mile and a half up into the hills," a young man at the gate told us, "you can't miss it." Minutes later we were in an already busy parking lot. There towering above us was a steep hill crowned by a massive, round, concrete, high-domed structure, the House of the Book.

A crowd of about 300 people was gathering in the temple, whose concrete walls reminded me of the high-ceilinged seminary chapel in Santa Barbara. We learned that the people gathering here were not just interested individuals from all around Los An-geles, but a community of Jews who had come here many times before for similar presentations, for concerts and for worship. They were part of a community built by a variety of shared expe-riences.

The speakers arrived. I had seen the bearded Kamenetz in pictures and recognized him immediately. He was trailed by a middle-aged man on crutches, legs in metal braces. He wore a braided *yarmulke* and wore no beard. It was Rabbi Omer-Man who, since the visit to the Dalai Lama, had become one of Kamenetz' principal mentors.

Dr. Alvin Mars, the director of the Institute, introduced the speakers and alluded to a new book by Roger Kamenetz. It would soon be in bookstores all around the country; its title, *Stalking Elijah: Adventures with Today's Jewish Mystical Masters*, refers to an account of Kamenetz' pursuit of Jewish spirituality which had been triggered by the visit to the Dalai Lama detailed in his first book. The dialogue between the two presenters began, at first a bit stiffly, then spontaneously, about their personal reactions to their historic trip to Dharamsala. Rabbi Omer-Man shared that when he had first come into the holy man's presence he was immobilized until the Dalai Lama stood up, came over, and positioned his face uncomfortably close to his own. This antic caused both men to burst out laughing, breaking the tension and allowing for a comfortable discourse. Omer-Man expanded on what Kamenetz had written about him in the *Jew in the Lotus*. He found it still difficult to speak of Jewish spirituality to mainstream Jews, though he knew it to be grounded in authentic Jewish tradition. I realized that I had been picking up this negative attitude at Temple B'nai B'rith and had naively concluded that Judaism simply lacked a strong tradition of mysticism. This gap or deficiency disturbed me. Interiority was an essential part of my personality and spiritual training. Though I had great respect for Jewish dedication to the repair of the world and to Jewish respect for the individual conscience, I couldn't imagine fully embracing a faith not formally and enthusiastically dedicated to a deeply prayerful heart. My personal meeting with these two men broadened my vision beyond what I had learned in the book. If I wanted to know still more about Jewish prayer there were modern spiritual guides, both men and women, available to me through books and lectures. With my background I could take what they taught me and incorporate it into what I already knew. The vocabulary and the images might be different, but the experience was the same. This crossover was what helped me fasten on one of the most beautiful prayers said during the High Holy Days, "Teach me to stand in awe before the mystery of being. Praise be to the One who is present in the miracle of prayer."

This being the Sabbath, we concluded the day with the Havdalah, the service separating this holy day from the profane week. It was by now dark outside. When the Temple lights were extinguished, we were left in semi-darkness, comforted by the spiritual light and warmth of candles lit by the rabbi at the *bima*. In their flickering I could see the faces of three men, the two presenters and the Cantor. Arms around one another they began to lead us in chanting a haunting melody, *Hine el yeshuati*: "Behold here is the God of my salvation. I will have faith and not be afraid; for the Lord is my strength and song." I felt the arm of a man to my left reach out and envelop me. I reciprocated his gesture and then put my right arm around Ruth. We began to sway gently and rhythmically. Carried by the wings of an ancient melody, we blessed the wine, the spices and the candlelight. Finally we sang our praise of the One who endlessly educes unique individual shapes from a formless universe. The moment was special. At that moment the ritual felt like *my* tradition, this temple *my* home.

I continued to read widely from the works of The Jesus Seminar scholars, from the most recent research on the Dead Sea Scrolls, and from specialists in Jewish prayer. Each book loosened a finger in the tight grip with which I had been holding the conflicting images of Catholicism and Judaism. As old absolutes softened, I discovered old familiar concepts beneath their Jewish garb. And the less defensive and more trusting I grew, the more I discovered that the best of the old was present and could still be pursued in Jewish spirituality. Judaism was suiting me better than Catholicism. Jewish faith offered freedom from authorities neurotic about doctrinal conformity and uniformity. It trusted in a reality which precisely as human is full of God, *immanuel* ("God with us"). It prayed, "May we show forth your image within us, the divine spark that makes us human." It possessed a treasuretrove of archetypal biblical images which we could understand in contemporary ways. Finally it manifested respect for the particular gift that I brought to the enterprise ("Your God is a true God," Rabbi Schachter-Shalomi had said to the novice Kamenetz in Dharamsala).

Finally *Stalking Elijah* appeared in Santa Barbara bookstores and I could read not only about his spiritual journey, but about the teaching of the various Jewish mystical masters that were referred to in the subtitle, *Adventures with Today's Jewish Mystical Masters*. There was a great advantage in personally having heard Kamenetz lecture. As I began to read, the memory of this searching poet, writer, and professor of literature was in my eyes and bathed the pages before me with a holy light. I felt a powerful kinship with this Jew. For a long time both he and I had been on a similar spiritual journey. I too had been trying to put what I had learned from mysticism together with my daily experience and that of my contemporaries. For me, too, triumphalism was repugnant in its assumption that one religion possesses the truth. The statement of the Christian Brother, Gabriel Moran, came to mind, "Revelation is a happening and a happening isn't a happening unless it's happening." Since Vatican II in the mid '60s I had increasingly allowed myself to be in process, to be discreetly receptive to the new. This attitude sharpened my hearing and opened my heart. There was a clear difference between Kamenetz and me. He was deepening his understanding of and commitment to his own tradition under the tutelage of Jewish mystical masters. I was taking the best of my Christian tradition and finding it in Judaism where I was no longer paralyzed by the constraints of Fall/Redemption theology. While in the thrall of that system there seemed to be no way for me to enter deeply into the tradition that had birthed and sustained the Jew, Jesus. I smiled when I read how Kamenetz describes himself denominationally as an "under-constructionist" Jew wearing "a yellow hard-hat *yarmulke*."

The book deepened my appreciation of the two rabbis, Zalman Schachter-Shalomi and Jonathan Omer-Man. As I read, I developed a surprising kinship with Zalman, the Jewish mystical master. All that he was, all that he said, all that he did landed on fertile soil within me. Zalman is just a year older than I. He studied psychology as did I. He specialized in the psychology of religion. I did too. We probably share a similar profile in the Jungian Myers-Briggs Inventory. He is considered by some to be a "loose cannon," a reputation Zalman earned by his "forays into the America of the '60s, into psychedelics and non-Jewish mysticism." My own '60s' testing of ecclesiastical limits had disturbed many Franciscans, as well as the Cardinal of Los Angeles. Zalman was a powerful force in the *chavurah* movement. I was a small player in a Christian Family Movement group which later grew into a community of couples committed to the best of Catholic renewal. Kamenetz presents Zalman, warts and all. I was drawn to the whole man, both the imperfect container and the marvelous unfolding mystery within it.

It was Rabbi Omer-Man who became the *mashpi'a* (influencer) or constant guide previously lacking in Kamenetz' search. I had sensed their strong relationship at Brandeis-Bardin Institute and now I could see why. Jonathan too lived on the edge of the Jewish community. Privately ordained, without a synagogue to support him, he was a non-denominational Jew. More importantly, he was concerned with teaching Kabbalistic spirituality, and was keenly aware of the coolness, the wariness of mainline Jews. Jonathan shows himself to be a man of prayerful leadership who can, for those receptive and committed enough, provide an opening to reality.

There were at least a dozen other masters mentioned in *Stalking Elijah*. Each pointed out an avenue for me to pursue, each shone a light on the path I had been walking, each helped to liberate my heart for the final and full embrace of Judaism. At a purely rational level I could see that the stakes were high. I was closer to leaving a tradition that had formed me for decades. This could revolutionize the way my family and friends related to me. But for the first time in quite a while, I was at peace. I was almost home.

Almost—I must confess I had some misgivings. I noticed that at Friday night services, when the rabbi received converts into the Jewish faith, I could not yet put myself in their place. I felt this particularly at the moment they were given the Torah Scrolls and asked whether they would accept it as the centerpiece of their lives. What did this mean? The Tanach or Hebrew Bible was certainly a rich source of revelation to humankind. But there were portions of its teaching I didn't accept because they were time- and culture-bound. Could I say I accepted the Torah and mean "I accept the Torah in part?" But as I read and reflected further I realized that the Reform tradition allows a great deal of latitude in this regard. Torah as instruction, as ongoing revelation was a central truth in my developing faith.

One of the most touching moments in all my years at the Temple centered around the invitation made to a gay rabbi from Los Angeles to address the B'nai B'rith congregation at an Erev Shabbat service. The courage displayed by Rabbi Shapiro in setting this up impressed me; his decision risked strong resistance from some in the congregation where there were bound to be homophobic attitudes. Then came the moment of the gay rabbi's presentation. A slightly built man with a confident manner, he addressed himself directly to the well-known, often-cited passage in the Book of Leviticus. The biblical verse pronounces an abomination upon the man who lies together with another man. The rabbi didn't get fancy. He didn't skirt the issue of homosexuality. He didn't say that the focus of the scriptural passage concerned only promiscuous love. The plain truth, he maintained, is that the biblical condemnation of homosexuality is a reflection of the understanding of a particular culture at a particular time, long past. Therefore it was off the mark. In our time and culture we have come to see that gay/lesbian love can be as mature and reflective of God's love for us as any other.

My mind drifted away from the speaker for a moment. I found myself thinking about my own unofficial godson, Louie. We have grown very close over an eight-year period. He has shared with me his experience with a condemning Catholic Church. Early in his puberty Louie had been told by a priest in Confession that if he was intending to act out as a homosexual he might as well take his life and spare others the contamination. However distorted this message, it carried power for a teenager. The judgment was that of a trained representative of a world-wide religion holding itself out as the custodian of the divine truth. Louie had no way of rebutting it. How he got to be the responsible, upright caring man that he is today says something for the indomitability of the human spirit. When we were first getting to know one another, he was newly in love. I was upset over how difficult we make it for gay people to celebrate this holy event. Because they trusted Ruth and me, we were privileged to witness the growth of the mutual love of Louie and Chris, to see how like our own it was—at times noble and generous, and at others perhaps less than that. When after several years Chris died Louie's tears of grief were as salty and bitter as any I had ever shed.

I interrupted my reverie and refocused my attention on the rabbi, who was now making the point that believers, both Jew and Christian, ignore other condemnations and abominations in the Book of Leviticus. With an impish smile he turned our attention to Mike McCafferty, former Colorado State University football coach and now founder of Promise Keepers, the Christian men's movement. "How is it," the rabbi asked, "that football coach McCafferty stops with the verse in Leviticus condemning a man who lies with another man, and will not consider that in a later passage God pronounces the same abomination on those who touch the skin of a dead pig?"

Later at the *oneg Shabbat* following the service I thanked both Rabbi Shapiro and the visiting rabbi for their willingness to risk and for their courage and clarity.

In 1997, Georges Passelecq, a Belgian monk, and Bernard Suchecky, a Jewish historian, published The Hidden Encyclical of Pius XI, *despite formidable barriers placed in the path of their investigatory research by the Vatican. In this work they recounted the story of their quest for the encyclical* Humani Generis Unitas, (The Unity of the Human Race), *written by the Jesuit Father John LaFarge and several of his confreres. The document was to have condemned anti-Semitism.*

Conversion to Judaism was becoming more and more clearly a focus in my mind. Unlike an obsession, which torments and narrows our vision, my interest was a fascination which opened me up to a fuller life. One after another I let go of my barriers. For a long time it bothered me that, unlike Ruth and my Jewish intimates, I could not resonate with Jewish feasts and customs. "For you they just aren't evocative," a friend had helped me phrase it. But now I could accept this. I had simply not grown up in the Jewish tradition, so there weren't familial memories to evoke. But I could by study and prayer discover Judaism's message for a *ba'al teshuvah*, that is, someone coming to it from outside. And in Judaism there was room for a variety of nomadic paths; the dwelling places of Israel were the lovely tents of Jacob. A new book by Gabriele Boccaccini helped me to understand this. Its title is *Beyond the Essene Hypothesis: The Parting of the Ways Between Qumran and Enochic Judaism.*

In this scholarly work on "middle Judaism" (the period of the second temple, 300 b.c.e. to 200 c.e.), Boccaccini helped me understand, more than ever before, the close connection between Judaism and early Christianity. In my theological training, the Catholic stress, however scant the treatment, was on the gradual degeneration of Judaism during this time. Jews, on the other hand, considered this to be the "early stage in the evolution of Rabbinic Judaism between the Tanach and the Mishnah." The book's theme is that both sides "failed to recognize its fundamental character as the transitional age…when both Christianity and Rabbinic Judaism emerged from their common 'biblical' roots." His conclusion: "Our walks of life are different and will remain such, but our genetic code is largely the same: whether we like it or not, we are children of the same parents." The forebears of Rabbinic Judaism was Zadokite Judaism; the forebears of Christianity was Enochic Judaism, blood brothers, who for a long time were in dialogue and worshipped at the same altar. If I were to become a Jew, would I not be coming home after long years away?

In the late summer of 1998, Ruth and I received an invitation from Metivta (an Aramaic word in the Zohar, meaning *yeshivah*, a school for spiritual training) to attend an event in Los Angeles. "Spend an entire day with Rabbi Omer-Man," it announced, "to prepare yourself for the High Holy Days." The offer was irresistible; we both enjoyed sharpening our receptivity for these spiritual times, and looked forward to doing this with an acknowledged master.

Metivta is presently quartered in a nondescript, uninviting business building in a largely commercial area of West Los Angeles. Other attendees at the workshop made up for the lack of architectural warmth, however, guiding us with welcoming smiles to the appropriate building, floor, and room. We were curious about how many people would participate. We found there were chairs for about fifty people in the room. Our early arrival enabled us to position ourselves in the front row where we could easily hear and absorb all that was said.

Rabbi Omer-Man spoke in a measured way, but with intensity. Because of my background in mysticism, I found his lyricism attractive. And because of my burgeoning interest in Judaism, I found myself hearing all of his plaintive melodies against the pedal point of conversion. One cannot be reborn, he told us, without first dying to oneself. What I heard was that I needed to let go of the easy comfort of old spiritual categories, and of those people who might not understand my bold direction. Only then could I open myself confidently to whatever lay ahead. I heard further that Hasidism started not with beliefs, but with where the person was at the moment. At times, the early Hasidic rabbis would even provoke spiritual crises in a complacent Hasid in order to stimulate movement.

"Own your doubts," Jonathan said to us, "not so much in the spirit of self-forgiveness but of self-acceptance."

These words too gave me comfort. They fit with the notion I had learned long ago: look inside with a sense of discovery rather than with disparaging judgment, and accept what you see there as truly yours. This is not a self-satisfied self-complacency, but rather the beginning of change.

Jonathan then posed a provocative way of getting at the meaning of an event. He suggested, "Ask what is the question for which Rosh Hashanah, the New Year, is the answer?" Or, "What is the question for which our life is the answer?"

In this spirit I was moved to ask myself, "What is the question for which my conversion to Judaism is the answer?"

As I sat patiently with this challenge my thoughts crystallized slowly. I came up with several such questions: "What can I do to ground my spirituality in the biblical tradition without doctrinal baggage?" And, "How can I pursue life's meaning trusting my innate sense of responsibility rather than authoritative dicta?" And, "How can I prayerfully adapt my spiritual beliefs to the modern paradigm without threats of heresy?" And, "How can I dedicate myself to one form of divine revelation while holding myself open to the utter truthfulness of others?" Framed this way, conversion, a form of *teshuvah*, seemed more and more to be my path.

"Spirituality," said Jonathan, "is the ongoing battle to open the human heart."

My psychological training had taught me that this implied two processes.

The first was to be discriminatingly receptive to whatever was being said to me by people, by life events, both joyous and painful, by books, etc. I had recently been trying to practice this in terms of the word spoken to me by Judaism.

The second process was appropriately to share with others the direction of my growth. I could see that talking about my conversion with significant others might take some courage. My cowardly ego might try to dissuade me by conjuring up any number of catastrophic consequences: ridicule, loss of friendships, isolation. I felt I could deal with those. I trusted being real because God is in the truth. One of my favorite prayers and melodies from the Siddur had become: "Purify our hearts so that we may serve you in truth." Whatever the consequences of sharing my process I needed to open my heart and keep it open.

"One way to keep our hearts open," said Rabbi Omer-Man, "is to go voluntarily into the place of heart-breaking."

This is what the liturgy of Yom Kippur does when it ponders the mystery of who shall die and who shall live in the coming year, and when it lists all manners of dying. Ruth and I looked at one another, faces softened with the sadness of the recent loss of several friends in death. We had learned to prize the preciousness of each moment together.

The workshop passed swiftly for Ruth and me. Toward the end of the day, Jonathan spoke for a half-hour on the nature of the High Holy Days. I remember particularly his remarks on the blowing of the *shofar*, or ram's horn.

"The *shofar* is the subject of much sentimental nothingness. What is it then? It is not the wail of the congregation reaching for God. It is not the cry of the soul to God. It is nothing more than this: it's a wake-up call! We must continually fight sleep."

Had I been asleep? Was I waking up? Was I willing to accept whatever greeted my mind's eyes? Psychological and spiritual health called for waking up and entering into the world that greeted me. I resolved that I would consciously carry this focus with me during the sacred time before us.

In 1998, Erev Rosh Hashanah, the eve of the Jewish New Year, took place Sunday evening, September 20. In the sanctuary on the *bima* sat our two good friends, Tito and Erica Gold, survivors of the Holocaust. Their prominent presence served to open my heart to the awesome days before us. Rabbi Omer-Man had pointed out that Rosh Hashanah celebrates the rebirth of the world. It hails God as the Creator who draws new life from death. It is the start of a ten-day period ending with Yom Kippur, a time out of time and space where our busy, planning, practical ego moves and has its being. It is a hallowed time of no-thingness. It is a quiet time to discover ourselves and invite into consciousness our slumbering potential.

It was from this place of honed receptiveness that I read and heard the prayers and melodies of this wondrous evening and the days that followed.

Cantor Mark Childs, a magnificent baritone with a prayerful heart, brought out the feelings of this sacred time: he sang pleadingly, remorsefully, tenderly, gratefully, grandly. Thanks to him the vivid images of the Tanach rolled over me and delighted me: God spreading out the skies, giving breath to his people, taking us by the hand, tenderly keeping our foot from slipping as we try to scale the insurmountable mountain, kindling the bush in the desert air, dazzling us with stabs of lightning and rolls of thunder.

For the first time it wasn't I who sang the ancient prayer, but the prayer that sang me, *Shema, Israel*, "Hear, O Israel: the Lord, our God, the Lord is One!"

The melody urged me to recommit myself "in the face of the many, to stand for the one; in the presence of fragments, to make them whole."

This year the focus of my concern was the mostly wary and sometimes violent relationship between world religions. I prayed that they, like couples in love, could respectfully be different from one another and unite their uniqueness at the place of their deepest connection, which is God.

We prayed for the dead. We blessed and blessed and blessed. We asked for awakening, for strength. We thanked for the gift of freedom in every sense of the word. We prayed to be delivered from our ego run amok. We welcomed the obligations issuing from our departure from our Edenic innocence into the world of responsibility. We pledged a return to honoring father and mother, performing acts of loving kindness, attending to the meaning of revelation by every means available, welcoming the stranger, visiting the sick, rejoicing in the new love of bride and groom, consoling the bereaved, praying with sincerity, making peace where there is only strife.

When on the holy day of Rosh Hashanah we came to the prayer, *Unetaneh tokef*, "Let us proclaim the sacred power of this day; it is awesome and full of dread," my mind turned to Omer-Man's theme: the broken heart is the open heart.

The powerful metaphor in the prayer is that "On Rosh Hashanah it is written, and on Yom Kippur it is sealed, how many shall pass on, how many shall come to be; who shall live and who shall die; who shall see ripe age and who shall not...."

As we intoned the mournful melody my mind reviewed the year gone by.

There were significant absences from my friends here at the Temple, including the very recent death from cancer of the sweet, smiling Rose Chansky, spouse of the equally thoughtful and generous survivor, Hesch. Together they were friends to everyone, mindful of everybody else's needs.

My own Ruth had also just lost a long-time friend and neighbor, a person of extraordinary kindness.

Other intimates in our life were presently battling cancer. Odds were we would not be together next year at this time. Ruth's favorite prayer sung at every joyous occasion and celebration was, "Blessed are You, Lord our God, who has given us life, sustained us and brought us to this day."

This morning tears were in our eyes as we opened our hearts to whatever came our way. Again we resolved to be mindful of the gift of each moment of our lives together. And we would share our respect for life with others. These qualities, the prayerbook said, "temper judgment's severe decree." I took this to mean that our openness, our mindfulness and consideration would dispose us to be more acceptant of our destiny in the coming year, whatever it might bring either to ourselves or to our loved ones.

Even the ceremony surrounding the readings from the Torah and the Haftarah meant more this year, especially on Yom Kippur. The twenty-four hour fast begun the night before heightened our awareness to all things. I was more aware of the survivors of the Holocaust who rotated the places of honor in the sanctuary. I appreciated more the blessings of the scrolls before and after the readings. These were sung now by teenagers, now by elders prominent for their service to the community, now by a host of persons who had converted during the past year, now by recent *bar* and *bat mitzvah* congregants.

Little children always open my heart. So I was delighted when for one of the readings all the little children who had gathered in the adjoining social hall were now herded into the sanctuary and up to the *bima*. Like a cloud of butterflies they entered, a hundred

or so of them, tended by skilled *Beit Hayeladim* school staff. It took
ten minutes for them to flutter to a landing at the feet of those in
the carpeted *bima*, where they perched with remarkable patience.

It was inspiring to see a succession of young men and women
position themselves confidently at the *bima*, look out over the
hundreds of congregants before them and sing the unvocalized
Hebrew words of the Torah. Their fluency told us of the hours of
patient tutoring by Temple staff. The rabbi and cantor were
beaming.

Physically exhausted but spiritually refreshed, we arrived at
the end of the day. There was only a little way yet to go in the
machzor.

In the concluding *Neilah* service, we prepared ourselves to
pray for our deceased loved ones, the *Yizkor* prayer.

Then we prayed for them by praising God who had created
our loved ones, now departed, and put them in our lives.

We addressed God in the haunting melody of *Avinu
Malkeinu*, asking one more time that we might be forgiven, have a
good year, be on the side of those who promote wholeness, be receptively aware of the transience of all things.

We concluded by singing the full *Kaddish* for the deceased.
The cantor sang the *Yizkor*, set this holy day to a new melody. It
danced playfully, joyfully. Despite the weariness in my worshipping bones, my body moved to the notes and was carried by their
pulsating rhythm to the end of the service.

Yom Kippur had come to an end. Only the blowing of the *shofar* remained.

Cantor Childs and Rabbi Shapiro turned toward one another.
The cantor joyfully trumpeted our invitation to the rabbi to sound
the *shofar*, "*Tekiah!*"

I could see the rabbi's mouth struggle for moisture. He took a
deep breath as he lifted the ram's horn. His "wake up!" call started
softly, built in volume, leaped upwards, sustained for what seemed
an eternity, and ended with a downward flourish. In the first moment of silence afterwards, I knew that something dramatic had
happened within me in response to this ancient rallying call of the
Jews—some palpable movement beyond intellect and will. I still
couldn't give it a name. It had the flavor of arrival, of completion,

of total response to a call. I turned to Ruth, the loving woman who for me had been the gate we had just prayed about. I kissed her with special tenderness and wished her a Good New Year. She responded warmly and we exited.

Tonight the Jews all around me seemed more my brothers and sisters than ever before. The relationship had somehow grown unconditional. My heart was joyful.

Pope John Paul II beatified Cardinal Alojzije Stepinac on October 3, 1998 during Mass at a Croatian national shrine, despite strong evidence that the Cardinal may have been a Nazi collaborator. The Simon Wiesenthal Center had previously asked that the beatification be postponed until his wartime record could be cleared through an examination based on full access to Vatican Archives.

We arrived home moments ahead of Ruth's cousin, Jerry, and his wife, Jane. Awaiting us were fresh bagels and bialis, cream cheese, lox, a traditional honey cake and coffee. I passed on the lox. I would never be that Jewish.

For some reason I couldn't yet share with the three of them what had just happened to me. But I was near tears of happiness the whole evening, for me always a symptom of significant personal change.

After two days this oceanic, organismic feeling finally began to permit verbal descriptors. I realized with joy but also with shock: I had somehow, without a conscious, formal act of the will, become a Jew.

No longer a seeker. Nor one deeply interested in Judaism from outside. I was a Jew. Their God was my God. Their Torah was my Torah. Their chosenness to carry this revelation in their lives was my chosenness. Their Holy Land was my Holy Land.

All of this was inside me, defined me. It was my essence. I would have to say out loud who I had become. I must declare it to others. I must make a date with Rabbi Shapiro to see what needed to be done to formalize my conversion.

First of all, of course, I told Ruth. I knew that she would welcome my announcement. Ever a person of fairness, she wanted to be reassured that my intentions were in no way a response to pressure from her.

"Of course not," I said. "You have never hinted at this directly or indirectly. You have always given me wide berth in all my decisions, especially in matters of faith."

The next day at a wedding reception of a couple in the congregation, I asked the rabbi for some time for us to talk. He was warm and inviting. "I would love to chat with you again. It's been a while."

"The High Holy Days deeply affected me this year," I explained, "and I want to share with you where this is taking me."

I waited a few days before calling. I needed a little time to ponder what I wanted to say and how I should say it.

My intention was to make a formal conversion. I would ask what would be required of me by way of preparation. Over how long a period of time?

I would bring along a partial but substantial list of Judaic books that had educated me, moved me in this new direction. He already knew the extent of my eight-year participation at the Synagogue. With Ruth I had once attended the course on basic Judaism offered by the temple. I had studied the Hebrew of the liturgy and the Bible. I would share what had brought me to this moment: my movement away from the powerful Catholicism I came from (he already knew that I had been a priest) and my movement toward the Jewish faith. I would talk about my joyful discovery of the mystical aspects of Judaism. I would say that thinking through and writing about my spiritual journey had crystallized my movement in an amazing way. Finally, I would take whatever steps he would require before receiving me into the Jewish community.

On October 13, two weeks before my seventy-third birthday, I met with Rabbi Shapiro in his office at the Temple. An amazing clarity, confidence and peace held my heart. He let me express all that I had prepared to say.

When he responded, it was with gentleness and uncommon understanding. The burden of his message was that my case, for all the reasons that I had outlined, was exceptional. For me there would be only two requirements: I would have to undergo a ritual *michveh* or bath and appear before a *beit din*, a three-member panel to whom I would explain the motivation behind what I was seeking. It was not a panel of professors administering an oral exam, but a group of learned Jews interested in my wish to join them in Judaism.

"Since you've been trained to read theological literature I would like you to read two books: *To Life* by Harold Kushner and *Judaism* by Arthur Hertzberg. When you've finished, we'll talk again and set up a time table for receiving you at a Friday night service."

"Thanks," I said, "I'll get to the books immediately."

"Do you have any preference for how soon you want this to happen?" he asked.

"I prefer sooner than later," I answered. "Let's first see how quickly I get through the two books." He gave me a copy of Hertzberg's book (I had the other one at home), shook my hand vigorously and bade me goodbye.

Outside there was a stillness that mirrored the quiet in my heart. From the parking lot I looked up at the beautiful mountains, the symbol of what had seemed most enduring and unchangeable in my life. As I gazed at them I recalled the words of Psalm 97: "The mountains melt like wax at the coming of the Master of the world." Then I got into my car and drove home. Not even the heavy traffic could spoil my inner peace.

When I arrived at the house I shared the story of my morning with Ruth. We held one another closely, united now more than ever before. I had indeed come home.

Epilogue

ON FRIDAY MORNING, DECEMBER 18, I went to the Temple to appear before the *beit din*, the panel that would interview me about my desire to embrace Judaism. Sensing my need for emotional support Ruth offered to accompany me. I gratefully accepted. With her nearby I could more easily give myself permission not to get lost in performing, but simply to be myself.

Rabbi Shapiro and Cantor Mark Childs were joined by Rabbi Steve Cohen from Hillel at UCSB. Their faces and manner could not have been more encouraging as I entered the rabbi's office. There, surrounded by four walls of floor-to-ceiling books, I gave them a brief account of my long and intense journey from Catholicism to Judaism.

At the end Cantor Childs asked, "Why did you choose the Reform branch of Judaism?" I provided two reasons for my choice. First, I answered, Reform Judaism remains linked to the centrality of the oral and written Torah as well as to ancient Jewish symbols, language, prayers and music. And second it is open to a carefully considered adaptation to the modern experience, thus maintaining a critical relevance to the lives of today's Jews.

Rabbi Cohen asked, "How do you understand the notion of the Jews as God's Chosen People?" My response was that this is a way of expressing our commitment to model a fully human life through our sensitivity to God's ongoing revelation and through our profound respect for his creation.

Rabbi Shapiro was curious about the reaction of friends and family to the news of my conversion. I had to admit that in large part the jury was still out, especially on my family. Only days before I had sent a long letter to my three brothers and their thirteen adult children. In it I described the years of studying, praying and pondering that led me to become a Jew. There had not yet been time for any of my family to respond. Ultimately my conversion was a matter of such moment to me, that, regardless of their feelings, no one could divert me from my chosen path.

The hour we sat and talked together (mostly it was I who spoke) seemed like moments. At the end we were obviously linked to one another by a common faith. I left the *beit din* to its assessment of me and returned alone to Ruth in the Temple lobby. As I approached her I felt paradoxically excited and serene as if I were bounding in a verdant field in slow motion.

"I can tell from your face that things went well," she said with a smile.

I was overcome and could only nod.

Minutes later Rabbi Shapiro came out and approached us. He put his arm around me and said, "Understand that you can say 'no' to what I am going to ask of you. But the three of us have decided that we would like you to address the congregation on January 8 for about fifteen or twenty minutes. This will be the sermon for the evening. The three of us think that it is important for the congregation to hear some of what you told us in the last hour. Would you do that?"

"I would love to," I answered spontaneously. "My only concern is that I am a very emotional person about these matters and I worry that I'll break down and be unable to speak."

In response he just smiled.

"I'll risk it," I said.

The following week Ruth and I spent at an Elderhostel program on the Pentateuch offered by the University of Judaism. The setting for the occasion was Camp Ramah in Ojai, an hour's drive to the south of us. Forty-eight other Jews from all over the country attended.

The weather was unusually cold. Even at midday shards of ice stabbed the soil beneath the orange trees. As cold and forbidding as it was outside, the community of Jews that had gathered in the Camp was warm and inviting. At our introductions I revealed that I had been a Catholic priest, and that I was converting to Judaism on January 8, just two-and-a-half weeks away. Their supportive response moved me and made me realize how comfortable I now was among Jews. In the course of the next six days, Rabbi Jack Schechter and his wife, Leah, provided us with well-prepared, provocative lectures. With my new Jewish ears, I could hear more clearly their classroom commentary on stories in Genesis. I could see and appreciate the prominent figures as magnificent archetypes mirroring my own insides. As broken men and women, they revealed themselves in this sacred document in their wholeness— weak and strong, blind and profoundly insightful, selfish and loving.

After dinner on Friday evening most of us quietly gathered at one end of the huge, high-ceilinged, dimly-lit mess hall around a long, bare table. In the stillness I could imagine the sounds of hundreds of youthful voices and clattering dishes reverberating in the cavernous space, for this was a summer camp serving thousands of Jewish children.

On the mess hall table there were perhaps three dozen candles awaiting their chance to light up the darkness of the departing day, and greet the Sabbath. Leah Schechter, the *rebbitzen*, reminded us that the candle-lighting ceremony was the domain of the women, although the men were welcome to attend. Some of the women wore make-shift head-coverings. Ruth did not. Each of them lit at least one candle. Ruth lit two, one for each of us. Then all of us chanted the traditional prayer blessing God who sanctifies us by all of his bidding, especially by his command to light Shabbat candles.

Finally Leah led us in a prayer of her own composition. In it she stressed the Sabbath as a time of leaving behind the turmoil and agitation of the previous six days, and entering a time out of time, a time of simple presence rather than action. The soft, penetrating light of the Sabbath presence was to light up the depths of our being and invite us to see our true selves with clarity and acceptance. As all the lights flickered in the semi-darkness we thanked God for the gift of light and for the beginning of this special day dedicated to its shining.

At the last gathering of the Elderhostel one of the participants invited me to join two Jews by choice, both young women from a special conversion program offered by the University of Judaism.

Though our paths were significantly different, the three of us felt and shared an immediate bonding in the few minutes that we had before starting. When I finally rose to speak, I was full of sentiment but unusually calm. Only when I alluded to my witless participation as a Catholic priest in ecclesiastical anti-Semitism, did I momentarily lose control and cry. The faces of the attentive audience grew soft. And I saw some tears fall. Ruth wiped her nose.

Afterwards their remarks and their questions manifested their warm welcome of me into their Jewish community. Having been told that I do not like cream cheese and lox, Rabbi Jack Schechter assured me with an impish smile that there was no *halachic* obligation to eat these items. He and Leah promised to invite us to a Shabbat dinner at their Thousand Oaks home.

On January 8, 1999, I was received into Judaism at the Erev Shabbat services.

The simple ceremony was powerful because it formalized the inner, quiet conviction that had crystallized within me on Yom Kippur, 5759.

Rabbi Shapiro summoned me to the ark, opened it carefully, took out the Torah and placed it in my welcoming arms.

In a tone as firm as I could muster I said, "I accept the Torah as if I were standing this day at the foot of Mount Sinai. In this sanctuary, in the presence of God and before this congregation, which represents the household of Israel, I affirm as did the Jewish people then, *Na'aseh v'nishma*—We will do and we will obey. *Sh'ma Yisrael: Adonai Eloheynu, Adonai echad.* Hear O Israel: The Eternal is our God, the Eternal One alone."

The rabbi then bestowed upon me my spiritual name. At Ruth's request I had chosen Jacob, the name of her beloved father and the name of the biblical patriarch who had strenuously wrestled with an angel until he wrested spiritual meaning from their mystical encounter.

With a full heart, I approached the lectern to speak. For the first few moments I allowed myself to look over and savor the faces of the congregants. I saw smiles and encouragement. Then I briefly outlined the most significant persons and events of my journey to the faith that in many ways had long been so familiar to me, yet was now in truth my new spiritual home.

Some time has passed since my conversion ceremony. What strikes me most about my new home is that there is room here, room to flex spiritual muscles, room to flesh out my faith.

When I first began to go to Temple B'nai B'rith, the lack of a clear answer to "What is a Jew?" puzzled me.

I was accustomed to a tradition where the question, "What is a Catholic?" could receive a quick, terse, clear response. The Church had a defined creed, a Western way of understanding the concepts within those beliefs, a code of moral behavior, a single way of worshipping, a massive canonical structure to contain it all and a potent authority to hold everything in place.

In Reform Judaism I have now come to delight in the absence of all this control. More positively I revel in the open-ended, holy challenge to develop my own spiritual understanding. Obviously I can only identify with Judaism from a faith perspective because I lack the historical, ethnic, and cultural aspects of what it means to be a Jew. But about these matters Ruth can teach me some of what I lack.

And perhaps I can contribute something to my Jewish brethren's vision of our common faith. In some small way I already have. As someone interested in Jungian psychology, for example, I can, from that perspective, listen to the oral and written Torah, and derive contemporary applications from them.

I find myself responding with enthusiasm to the Ten Principles for Reform Judaism, a fourth draft of which is currently being discussed and commented on in Reform Temples throughout the country.

These principles center around three things: God, Torah and Israel, both as a people and as a land. While Reform Jews may conceive of God in diverse ways, my own experience, prayer and study have led me to believe in an Insider God whose breath is mine from birth, and Who meets me in the challenges common to each of us regardless of the shape of our beliefs. When on those very human occasions I yield to God's presence I am transformed. When in any way the Holy One confronts the ungodliness of my isolation, my narrowness, my stinginess, my sloth, I know I am being challenged to transcend these elements of my inhumanity. Whenever satanic evil erupts in the world I will remind myself that the capacity for hatred and violence lies slumbering in each of us as human beings, and that I must make this reality an increasingly conscious part of my identity. I take responsibility for engaging in quiet, wordless prayer when alone, and for the quality of my community worship in the synagogue.

I embrace Reform Judaism's call to be sensitive to ongoing divine revelation. Perhaps the most defining example of this is the emergence of feminism, in the light of which deep-cutting changes in Judaism are taking place. This serves to remind me that, as a member of the Jewish community, I am to "hear," "see," "feel" God in individuals, communities and events, especially when these challenge old familiarities and open me to a more human way of being. In addition I know that I am failing the essence of Jewishness if I don't respond to calls for social justice and for sharing both material and personal resources with the oppressed and needy.

As a *ger*, or convert, I am aware that I am just beginning to shape a life of recognizable *mitzvot*. But, as a meaningful start, I long to develop a prayerful, restful celebration of the Sabbath that will interrupt the ego-driven activities of the rest of the week and make me mindful of the glory of God's creation. Among other activities on that day, I want to develop my facility with Hebrew so that I can worship with greater understanding and compassion, and appreciate the richness of the Tanach even more.

After I spoke in the Synagogue on that remarkable night of my conversion, Rabbi Shapiro remarked that Reform Jews prize humanity above all religions because all of us are created *b'tzelem Elohim*, in the image of God. My ultimate dream is to engage in a respectful dialogue with all religions in which we can all come to admire the numerous ways in which God is present in the world.

Long ago I left behind the Fall/Redemption paradigm which postulates that the death of Jesus, the Son of God, was necessary to placate a Father God whom we had offended. It was because the Mass was the re-presentation of this atoning death that I stopped celebrating Mass long before I left the practice of the priesthood.

Now, I have even more reason for abandoning the notion of a universal Messiah who redeems by His death. I firmly hold that this belief contributes significantly to anti-Semitism—even today. Though the Vatican no longer charges Jews with deicide, it still maintains that they must accept Jesus as their Lord and Savior. I find this offensive because it still sounds the contemptuous theme of supersessionism, which is that Judaism is an important, but merely preparatory, stage in God's plan for the world. The final, full dispensation is to be found in Christianity.

On the other hand I firmly believe that throughout history epochal human beings have appeared and continue to appear. Their contribution is to effect profound changes in the way we perceive reality. Jesus was one of these. Many Christians would claim that He was the paramount shaper of human consciousness. But there were also the patriarchs and matriarchs, Moses, Job, the prophets, Maimonides, countless mystics, and others through the ages. Their gift is that they perceive a reality beyond narrow reason and are able to enunciate this transforming vision to a world sorely in need of it. These are the revelatory moments found in human history which if heeded by all would usher in a messianic age of peace and dignity and good will. This perspective in addition views *every* person as a potential co-creator of humanity and of the better world which one day we can hopefully inhabit. *Ken y'hi ratson.* May this be God's will.

Ten years ago at a Jungian dream therapy workshop which I attended, our assignment was to bring a recent dream to share with the group. I brought one that seemed archetypal and ominous. When my turn arrived I read it rapidly in the foolish hope that I could skate past the something fearsome within it that I did not understand. The workshop presenter felt my fright and asked me to re-read the entire dream—slowly. As I walked through the dream, the coiled presence of the unconscious, personal and collective, struck quickly. I dissolved into tears, sobbing for God knows what. Terror? Aloneness? Awe?

In my dream I enter a massive structure which seems to be a church reconfigured as a theater. The building is carved from one gigantic piece of white marble, not a seam or a joint anywhere. The stage plunges down-

ward from the level of the entryway. From there tiers of seats soar steeply almost to the ceiling. There are no supportive rails anywhere. On the stage stands Bojangles, bathed in a soft spotlight. He is about to sing the sad song that bears his name, "I knew a man, Bojangles, and he'd dance for you in worn out shoes." Somehow I know this is Jesus. He beckons me to join him. I don't respond. I hear an awesome voice. It is the voice of God the Father ordering Jesus to sing about his pain. He begins, plaintively. I will not hear. I leave the building. Outside all is dark. In the dim light everything seems threatening. I am frightened and get down on my hands and knees and begin to feel my way. I know I can never go back to the ghostlike building which grows more and more indistinct behind me. After what seems a long time I come to a cliff. There is no place to go but into the darkness below. I cry out for help.

I have never forgotten this dream, nor have I had any satisfactory interpretation of it—until now. Since my decision to convert to Judaism, I am convinced that I understand what the unconscious was telling me. I was leaving the perfect edifice which reflected the white seamless garment of Christ and his Church. I could no longer sing from that stage. God the Father had ordered Bojangles to sing but had sent *me* out into the night—a nomad seeking a new home. The cliff that once threatened me is no longer deadly. It leads steeply into a valley below that is lovely, ancient and verdant. Its thousands of years of history have known countless encounters with God. The villagers are not strangers to me. They are my new/old Jewish brothers and sisters. I am honored to be a part of their history.